Daily Life in Ancient Rome

B

Daily Life in Ancient Rome

Florence Dupont

Translated by Christopher Woodall

BLACKWELL
Oxford UK & Cambridge USA

First published 1989 as *La vie quotidienne du citoyen romain sous la République*
by Hachette, France
English translation first published 1992
Reprinted 1993 (twice)
First published in USA 1993

Blackwell Publishers
108 Cowley Road
Oxford OX4 1JF
UK

238 Main Street
Cambridge, Massachusetts 02142
USA

British Library Cataloguing in Publication Data
A CIP catalogue record for this book is available from the British Library.

Library of Congress Cataloging-in-Publication Data
Dupont, Florence.
  [Vie quotidienne du citoyen romain sous la République, English]
  Daily life in ancient Rome/Florence Dupont, translated by
Christopher Woodall.
    p.   cm.
  Translation of: La vie quotidienne du citoyen romain sous la
République.
  Includes bibliographical references and index.
  ISBN 0–631–17877–5
  I. Rome—Social life and customs.   I. Title.
DG78.D8713   1993
937′.02—dc20   92–11082

Typeset in 10½ on 12pt Sabon
by Hope Services
Printed in Great Britain by T. J. Press (Padstow) Ltd., Padstow, Cornwall.
This book is printed on acid-free paper.

Contents

Illustrations

Figures

Plates

Preface

The Roman republic can be viewed either as a chain of events – a history – or as a web of institutions – a culture. Adopting the latter approach, this book describes the daily life that Roman citizens led between the downfall of the kings in 509 BC and the seizure of royal power by Augustus in 27 BC. Within this timespan, no distinction is made between different periods.

The Roman republic was a specific culture, a way of life organized around one kind of individual: the Roman citizen. Each citizen played many roles, however: soldier, voter, estate-owner, householder and slave-master, *paterfamilias*, priest, party-goer, farmer and city-dweller. It was citizenship that shaped Roman notions of space, time, human nature and the human body.

The events that punctuated the history of the Roman republic left Roman perceptions largely intact. Roman culture, forced to grapple with the ups and downs of history, incorporated new developments within a traditional framework, and adapted old ideas to fit new circumstances. The rise of the monarchy put an end to this: monarchy could never be 'reinterpreted' in republican terms. Everything came unravelled: the calendar changed and with it the Roman's understanding of time; physical space was rearranged as were its symbolic meanings; and war, the founding-stone of liberty, vanished. Under *Pax Romana*, citizens mutated into subjects.

The way in which this Roman culture of citizenship responded to change may be seen in alterations to the qualifications demanded for noble status. Until the middle of the fourth century BC, nobility in

Rome was purely hereditary. Thereafter, to be noble one had only to be wealthy and to have occupied at least one superior magistracy. But this social revolution had no cultural consequence whatever. There was nothing either in the mindset or the conduct of a fifth-century hereditary patrician to distinguish him from a second-century patrician of plebeian birth. The term used to designate them was the same, as was the role they played.

Only one watershed divided the Roman republic into separate periods and it remains historically inexplicable. In the fourth century BC the Roman view of war underwent a profound change. Until then, Rome was just another town in Latium waging traditional wars on its neighbours. None of the warring towns ever dreamt of destroying or annexing their enemies. Then, in 368 BC, Rome conquered and subjected all the other Latin towns, overran their land and drafted their peoples into its armies, while granting them Roman citizenship. Rome then set out to conquer the world.

At first, this sudden break with the past had no cultural repercussions. The day-to-day life of Roman citizens went on as before, except that wars were now more distant and public feasts somewhat more frequent and lavish. Yet this first break eventually led to the disintegration of republican culture. In the preface to his monumental *History of Rome*, Livy, writing at the very beginning of the empire, described the downfall of the republic in the following terms:

> no state was ever greater, none purer or richer in good examples, none into which avarice and luxury came into the social order so late, or where humble means and thrift were so highly esteemed and so long held in honour. Indeed the less riches men possessed, the less was their greed. Of late, wealth has made us greedy, and excessive pleasures produce a general desire to carry wantonness and licence to the point of personal ruin and universal destruction.

We should not dismiss the Romans' own view that they had lost their liberty as a result of Rome's conquests and their morally undermining consequences. For as long as it could the republic steered a course through the stormwaves unleashed by the sudden influx of plundered riches. One expedient was to organize enormous parties at which the gold seized in conquest could be expended – even systematically squandered. Streets flowed with precious wines and the blood of exotic wild animals and innumerable oxen. Makeshift theatres were thrown up and bedecked with gold and ivory. In a hopeless attempt to empty both its own coffers and those of the nobility, the republic endowed the city with temples, basilicas and colonnades. But the world was too rich, too vast, and Rome, at its centre, choked on all its wealth.

Part I

The City and its People

I

Naming and honour

The year was 46 BC. In Africa the sun was about to rise for the last time on the last free Roman. Caesar would soon reign supreme and Romans would be subjects. Cato had therefore chosen to die. Caesar's army was drawing near and the republican army was defeated. Marcus Porcius Cato still held Utica but its townspeople were ready to surrender. Cato had lived for the only thing that had ever counted in Roman eyes – glory. Now that liberty itself was about to be lost, life held no further meaning for him. Honour would become the monopoly of a single man, and Cato could never live like a docile slave, attendant on his master's favours. He would rather die than cease to be a free citizen in a free city. In dying, he would bring distinction to the name that his great-grandfather, Cato the Censor, had first dignified. By his death, Cato might wrench from Caesar the honours he had refused him throughout his life. And by sacrificing his life, Cato would seize immortality: he would forever be known as Marcus Porcius Cato of Utica. Just as others had assumed the names of the countries they had conquered, so Cato would take on that of the town where he died, turning his defeat into victory.

Plutarch described Cato the Younger's last hours as follows:

> the birds were already beginning to sing when he fell asleep again for a little while. And when Butas came and told him that the harbours were very quiet, he ordered him to close the door, throwing himself down upon his couch as if he were going to rest there for what still remained of the night. But when Butas had gone out, Cato drew his sword from

its sheath and stabbed himself below the breast. His thrust, however, was somewhat feeble, owing to the inflammation in his hand, and so he did not at once dispatch himself, but in his death struggle fell from the couch and made a loud noise by overturning a geometrical abacus that stood near. His servants heard the noise and cried out, and his son at once ran in, together with his friends. Shocked and horrified, they saw that he was smeared with blood, and had disembowelled himself, but his eyes were open and he was still alive. The physician was summoned, and, seeing that the entrails were uninjured, he tried to replace them and sew up the wound. However, when Cato became aware of what was happening, he pushed the physician away, tore at his entrails, widening the wound further, and so died . . . Almost at once the Three Hundred [the Senate of Utica] were at the door and a little later the people of Utica had assembled. With one voice they called Cato their saviour and benefactor, the only man who was free, the only one unvanquished. And this they continued to do even when word was brought that Caesar was approaching. But neither fear of the conqueror, nor a desire to flatter him, nor their mutual strife and dissension, could blunt their desire to honour Cato. They decked his body in splendid fashion, gave it an illustrious escort, and buried it near the sea, where a statue of him now stands, sword in hand . . . When Caesar, however, learnt of his death, he said only this, we are told: 'O Cato, I begrudge thee thy death; for thou didst begrudge me the sparing of thy life.' For if Cato could have consented to have his life spared by Caesar, he would not be thought to have defiled his own fair fame, but rather to have adorned that of Caesar.[1]

With its blood-spattered theatricality, sophisticated appeal to glory, crowd manipulation and image fabrication, Cato of Utica's exemplary death provided a gaudy yet faithful portrait of Roman man. Every Roman adolescent was a potential Cato. His *ingenium*, or character, was revealed in the course of the life he led. Wherever he might go, whatever he might do, he had but one duty: to be a citizen. Tyrants were monstrous, and slaves vile.

The population of Rome was divided into citizens and others – non-citizens. These 'others' existed only by virtue of their relationship to a citizen. Surviving funeral inscriptions refer to them as, say, the son or daughter, wife, slave, freedman or freedwoman of Gaius, Titus, Lucius, Marcus, Quintus, Tiberius or Gnaeus. One essential trapping of citizenship was the name by which you were entitled to be known. Each person had a forename, a *praenomen*, or personal name, of which there were relatively few, as well as a family name, *nomen*, which was that of the group of families or clan to which the person belonged. In addition, they usually had a personal name, or

Plate 1   Cato the Younger, opponent of Caesar
Reproduced by kind permission of the Ancient Art and Architecture Collection
(Ronald Sheridan)

surname, *cognomen*. Freedmen took their original owner's forename
and name, adding their own *cognomen* at the end. Women were
usually known by the feminine form of their *nomen*. Slaves, however,
were usually called by their own single *cognomen*. Roman citizens

addressed each other by their forenames as a mark not of familiarity but of honour. Magistrates, though, were hailed using their titles of office – 'Hail! Praetor' rather than 'Hail! Gaius'.* This practice was rooted in the nature of Roman identity: the name was the man. No distinction could be made between a man's name and his renown. If you were a citizen, the city acknowledged it by giving you a title – your name.

GEOMETRICAL EQUALITY

In the beginning was the census. Every fifth year, each male Roman citizen had to register in Rome for the census. He had to declare his family, wife, children, slaves and riches. Should he fail to do this, his possessions would be confiscated and he himself would be sold into slavery. Registration meant freedom. An employer wishing to free his slave needed only to enter him in the census register. Throughout the entire republican era, census registration was the only way that a Roman could ensure that his identity and status as a citizen were recognized. Fathers registered their sons, employers their freedmen.

The census served to count the number of citizens and to assess potential military strength and future tax revenue. Most important, the census transformed the city into a political and military community. No longer were Romans a featureless crowd, a barbarian rabble liable to slip through one's fingers: they became a *populus*, a people, capable of collective action in unconstrained obedience to their elected magistrates. The job of compiling the census was not simply abandoned to an army of zealous scribes, well-versed in writing and arithmetic: it was overseen by two incorruptible and high-born men of substance appointed for their proven integrity and authority. These two elected censors – their office was the highest Roman magistracy – were accounted so upright that even the allocation of public markets was entrusted to them.

They scrutinized each man, carefully evaluating his riches and his rank in order to locate him in his rightful niche within the civic hierarchy, in the position that was best both for him and for others. In assessing the humblest, little was taken into account but their possessions; however, the higher a citizen's position in the hierarchy,

---

* In a body of superior magistrates, elected for one year, was concentrated the essence of political power. The two consuls were presidents of the republic and heads of the armies, the praetors administered justice, the aediles bore responsibility for public entertainments and town planning, and the quaestors managed the republic's finances.

the more penetrating became the gaze of the censor. On looking into a man's public and private lives, the magistrate might decide to move a citizen a few rungs down the social ladder if he had, say, turned a blind eye to his wife's adulteries, fathered no children, committed perjury, appeared on the stage or failed to cultivate his land properly.

Everyone below the ranks of the very highest magistracies was therefore assigned to a class, or to an order, and, within this class or order, to a division known as a century. At the summit of this hierarchy stood two orders which bore the main military and tax burdens: the senatorial order, which constituted the nobility and was regularly referred to as the *optimates*, the best class; and the equestrian order. These two orders were followed by the five classes of those often referred to as plebeians. At the bottom of the ladder were those who, owning neither house nor land, were disqualified from military service.

This system was justified by a theory known as 'geometrical equality', which contrasted with 'arithmetical equality'. The obligations incumbent upon each citizen were in direct proportion to his rights. These rights were essentially political. Senators alone could become superior magistrates, and in elections a rich man's vote carried more weight than that of a poor man. 'The knights [that is, those of the equestrian order] were called upon to vote first, then the eighty centuries of the first class. If there were any disagreement, which rarely happened, the centuries of the second class were called. The voting almost never continued until it reached the lowest class.'[2]

FREEDOM OR DEATH

The Roman citizen, the free son of a free man, was said to be *ingenuus* – free-born. Citizenship and freedom went hand in hand, but freedom was no mere matter of legal status; it was a human ideal that governed one's entire life. Every free-born Roman would, at the appropriate time, play his allotted role as soldier, elector, father of a family, manager of an estate and master of a household. He would officiate at household sacrifices, hear law-suits and take part in public games. He would travel regularly to Rome, unless he already lived there, which, if he were a member of either the senatorial or the equestrian order, he would be obliged to do. At his first census registration, having assumed the *toga virilis*, the toga of manhood, the light-coloured cloak that set free men apart from humble folk clad in brownish clothing, the Roman citizen would be officially attributed a name, a forename, a tribe and a century. For the rest of his life, it was as a member of his tribe and century that he might be called upon to go to war or to vote. The sole duty of the citizen was to bring honour to his name. If, thanks to his noble stock and wealthy family, he was enrolled in an equestrian century, he could aspire one day to become a magistrate. For with freedom went the right of the richest and most talented nobles to take a part in public life, to have a say in the affairs of the people, to rise to positions of power and to accede to those magistracies that Romans referred to as *honores*, or 'honours'.

But whatever position he occupied in society – that of peasant, senator, centurion or general – the Roman citizen had only one aim: to glorify his name in the eyes of the people. At every level in society, liberty brought with it a right to glory, binding the citizen to the people by a web of gratitude and admiration, linking him to all those he had helped or protected. In their turn, they would, if called upon, stand by him before the law. But they would also expect him to help or protect them again if need be.

Roman citizens aspired to nothing more than to be free men. The only choice was between freedom and death. Any citizen who fell into the hands of enemies, or was enslaved within his own country, would abandon his hold on life. Survival at any price was unthinkable. If a tyrant seized power in Rome, a Roman had only two alternatives: to murder the tyrant or to commit suicide. Tarquinius Superbus, by raping Lucretia, the wife of a patrician, and Appius Claudius the decemvir, by scheming to abduct a plebeian's daughter, had treated the Romans as slaves whose wives and daughters lacked any legitimacy. These acts filled the people of Rome with horror and nobles and plebeians abandoned the culprits, casting them out as monsters. Barred from the city, Tarquinius, the king, went into exile to escape death. Appius was forced to take his own life. Several centuries later, the senate could find no better way to bring about Caesar's downfall than to heap honours on his head, while passing over the rest of the political class. Caesar the consul, Caesar the life censor, Caesar the triumphator, Caesar the president of the senate: for the avengers of liberty, Caesar was a marked man.

Liberty and hierarchy were inextricable. If liberty entailed the right to honour, it also entailed the right to the *honores* – positions of power. An attack on the political privileges of any social group was an attack on freedom, for Roman society, although based on divisions of class, was not a caste-based one. The civic ideal was the same for all and, in theory at least, there was nothing to prevent the son of a prosperous freedman from working his way up to the supreme magistracies. Cato the Elder and Cicero were the best known of these ancestorless men – or 'new men' as the Romans called them. Not only did they both rise to the highest offices in the state, but in the eyes of everyone they were exemplary men, and not just parvenus.

THE CITY OR DEATH

While life without liberty was unthinkable, liberty itself was inconceivable outside the only framework within which it could be exercised: the city. Romans were social beings: they did not consider themselves human unless they belonged to some form of society, however rudimentary. In Roman epics and stories, one never encounters a solitary roaming hero. Robinson Crusoe could never have been a Roman. In the ancient world, any hapless sailor abandoned to solitude and a diet of wild fruit on a desert island would soon have turned into a monster, if he had not first died of mental and physical distress. To remain human, people needed both bread and free – that is, regulated – commerce with their fellows. For the Romans, civilization was more than a ragbag of survival techniques and ethical precepts. At the very least a civilized man required a family or a group of companions. Anything less was tolerable only for the briefest of periods, a time of crisis in which, like Aeneas searching for a place to found his city, a man might find himself forced into solitary wanderings. To stand between himself and the world, a Roman needed some form of community, whether this was called a city, a culture or a civilization.

Civis, civitas, civilis – Latin vocabulary has left in English traces of words that in Roman minds linked city and civilization. The Roman city was no mere political regime; it was a whole culture. As far as the ancients, both Greeks and Romans, were concerned, the only civilized people were those who dwelt in cities. Roman man was not Daniel Defoe's *homo faber*, he was a citizen, and nothing but a citizen. Man's mental and moral being could not be dissociated from his political nature: he could realize his potential only through and in civic institutions, by the exercise of his freedom. The ultimate fountainhead of all that was good was honour. And honour demanded a free city.

Every Roman belonged simultaneously to several communities: family, village or district, administrative tribe, *collegium*, or professional guild, religious body, or the provincial town of his birth, which Cicero referred to as one's 'little fatherland'. In each of these communities, the Roman citizen had to prove his humanity. He must demonstrate that he was a benevolent father, a just master, a careful land-owner, a respectful son, a steadfast friend, a generous employer, a loyal client. But the best men, those whom Romans acknowledged as possessing 'great souls', nourished more high-flown ambitions. The great soul, to fulfil its potential, required the backcloth of the city and the gaze of the entire populace. Great souls demanded great challenges if they were to achieve great feats. The city alone was of a scale that befitted great men. And the greater the men, the greater the city had to be. Indeed, it might be confidently predicted that a city fit for heroes would one day stretch to the ends of the earth. Unlike the barbarian, the Roman lived in the city, for the citizen, the civilized man, possessed a greater and more stalwart soul. After all, if Rome had conquered the world, it was surely because the Roman soul had attained universal dimensions.

Viewed from another angle, the Roman *animus*, or soul, was a conglomeration of mental and spiritual drives. It was a Roman's *animus* that caused him to act instinctively as a man, urging him towards that which was good, endowing him with the necessary strength to endure pain and exertion, bracing his body to withstand doubt or adversity. A Roman's soul was a tissue of cultural values that, internalized, gave the Roman personality its psychological and ethical structure. The term *animus* also covered intelligence and imagination. Citizens alone were possessed of souls. Children, slaves and women were soulless bodies: their father, master or husband provided their *animus*.

Social hierarchy was, in effect, constructed according to size of soul.

THE GAZE OF OTHERS

From his first census onwards, it was to the city that a Roman must look for any endorsement of his identity. For confirmation of his own existence and an assessment of his worth, the Roman turned to other people: comrades-at-arms on the battlefield; district or village neighbours; members of his order; or even the entire *populus* when they were canvassed for their votes. No man could be his own judge. Romans could see themselves only through others' eyes. They knew nothing of psychological inwardness or introspection; for them only the outward man existed. The mirror in which each Roman could survey his own honour – or his shame – was held up to him by his fellow men. The gaze of others lay in wait for him wherever he went, and whatever he did he would be aware of others sitting in judgement over him. Romans were never alone; there was always a witness to a man's good or wicked actions, even if it were only a neighbour strolling across a terrace, a servant gossiping at the fountain or his wife confiding in her aunt.

'Who is the "good man"? "He who observes the senate's decrees, the statutes and laws; whose judgement settles many grave suits; whose surety means safety for property; whose testimony wins suits at law." Yet this very man all his household and all his neighbours see to be foul within, though fair without, under his comely skin.'[3]

In more general terms, the vocabulary of glory and honour was that of brilliance and clamour. To belong to the nobility was to be well known, even famous, and fame was won by doing brilliant deeds and making sure they were bruited about in Rome. People would recount the feats they had witnessed, the tales would be inflated by gossip, and flattering rumours would do the rest. At the other extreme, dishonour spelled disgrace. There was no stopping a vicious rumour: the crowd would turn away, and downfall and voluntary exile would ensue. Rehabilitated in 57 BC, Cicero returned to Rome to the rapturous welcome of a cheering crowd. Yet Cicero himself related how his adversary, Piso, the consul in 58 BC, had returned incognito from the province he governed, for fear of encountering hatred or, worse still, indifference on his entry into the city.

Any exercise of power, *honos*, was at once a reward for previous actions and a new test for the people's appointee. News spread rapidly in a society that spent at least half the day cultivating the art of gossip. Graffiti covered the walls of the city and songs flitted from shop to street-stall, from bar to banquet. At the theatre, in front of the assembled populace, actors would interrupt the action to linger over a line heavy with innuendo, using it to denounce or to heap praise upon a particular public figure.

In Rome only that which was honourable – that is, honoured – was considered good. And the only evil was that which was dishonourable – that which brought dishonour. Whereas the Greek language confused beauty and morality, using the same word, *kakon*, to mean ugly and evil, and, *kalon*, to mean beautiful and good, Latin confused morality and honour (*honestum*), evil and shame (*turpe*).

Like many ancient societies, including Greek and Celtic ones, Rome was a society of blame and praise. Collective approbation and reproof regulated everything that law and institutions overlooked – in other words, the whole of moral life. This had been the role of

Aristophanes' theatre in Athens and was that of comedy in the Dorian cities of southern Italy, funeral orations in Athens, the poems of Simonides, the iambic verse of Archilochus. In Rome, however, praise and blame did not give rise to works of art. The only benefit to be derived from honour was access to superior responsibilities. Anyone who won renown in a civilian or military capacity had immediately to reinvest this accrued glory by applying for a new post. From one honour to the next, he would pursue his career as far as he might, in the hope of eventually entering the senatorial order. In the beginning (and at the end too) was the census. The life of every Roman citizen was an obstacle race; if he did well, his son would then have to rerun the same race in order to uphold his family rank and retain, at the very least, the position accorded him by his birth. A son would commemorate the glory of his father by becoming a living monument to him.

THE OBLIGATIONS OF NOBILITY

'The strife of wits, the fight for precedence, the endless toiling, night and day, to mount the pinnacle of riches and to lay hold on power.'[4] In Lucretius' estimation, such was the gruelling life reserved for men who belonged to the political class.

The civic ideal imposed on every Roman citizen a life of constraint and effort. He was weighed down by a mass of duties, the price of his rights and ambition. His life was circumscribed by the obligation to live up to the image of himself projected by the revered men of his family, his father and paternal uncles. Whether he was a member of the nobility or a simple peasant from Latium, from his earliest youth he would have to prove his *virtus*, his worth as a man. Regardless of rank, Romans had to do their duty as citizens to gain recognition as men.

It was no accident that the political definition of the citizen, as provided by census registration, was a military one. Political life demanded of the citizen the same virtues as did war: courage, intelligence, constancy, discipline. To make quite sure that the humble peasant did not go short of virtues in civilian life, Cato the Elder extolled ploughing as a civic activity, the virtues of the ploughman being those of the combatant. For members of the nobility everyday life was indeed an uphill struggle.

Political activity consumed the energies of every high-born Roman. Public life was a series of career moves; private life was a pause in which to restore one's strength, rest one's spirit, rebuild one's fortune and win new friends at sumptuous banquets. The more illustrious were a man's ancestors, the harder was the task, for he had to prove himself at least their equal. To do so he must combine the qualities of the orator, soldier, jurist and financier.

At Rome the only way to acquire nobility was by participating in public affairs and by rising to those superior magistracies known as *honores*. A high-born Roman had to live up to his noble birth. Those known as noblemen belonged to the hundred or so families who possessed the necessary wealth to have their sons enrolled in the equestrian class. Thereafter it was up to the sons to reach positions that would enable them to become senators. The senate was an assembly of former magistrates, all men of at least middle age, whose task was to advise the serving magistrates and to make sure that the laws enacted by the people conformed with the traditions of the city. The power of the senators was primarily of a moral nature, referred to as *auctoritas*, authority, which meant that their views, although they had some weight, were not in principle binding. Their moral authority and place in the city elite were acknowledged. The senators formed an aristocracy of merit and not of birth, even if most of them were sons of former senators and few were 'new men'.

Generally, therefore, noblemen would come from a senatorial family and were expected to become senators in their turn. If, owing to idleness or inability, a nobleman failed to rise to the *honores*, disgrace would fall not only on him but on his family, which would be seen as having lost one of its members. So from early childhood, the sons of the most distinguished families were schooled for a life of competition in which they had ceaselessly to prove that they were the best, the *optimates*.

In late adolescence, the son of a senator would serve in the staff headquarters either of a close family relative or one of his father's friends. There he would be under the eye of the soldiers and also the general. Everyone would observe his capacity for obedience, his ability to withstand not only fatigue, cold, fear, hunger and thirst, but also the seductions of luxury and foreign women, and the inebriation of victory. Above all, everyone would be watching to see if this young man would fall prey to the temptation besetting all triumphant warriors: to bury their fear of death and the enemy in an orgy of pillage and gratuitous cruelty. Succumbing to this temptation was the mark of mediocrity.

In civilian life, during the lull between two military campaigns, the young nobleman would have to engage in another sort of warfare. On

Plate 2   *Roman senators*
Reproduced by kind permission of the Ancient Art and Architecture Collection (Ronald Sheridan)

reaching manhood, he was duty bound to revive old family vendettas and to avenge any humiliations suffered by his father that had remained unpunished. The field of combat was the law court and words were the weapons used. The young nobleman would bring his father's foes to justice for their political crimes: electoral intrigue, bribery, embezzlement, assault on a citizen. Much was at stake, for the young man would be bent on achieving no less than the political destruction of his adversary. If he succeeded, he would win everyone's high regard and might even be rewarded with the rank of the man whose downfall he had secured and the seat in the senate that he had vacated.

> We are told that a certain young man, who had got a verdict of civil outlawry against an enemy of his dead father, was passing through the forum on the conclusion of the case, and met Cato, who greeted him and said: 'These are the sacrifices one must bring to the spirits of our parents; not lambs and kids, but the condemnations and tears of their enemies.'[5]

Not to be avenged was the worst misfortune that could befall a father and the deepest shame that could sully a son's name. It happened to Metellus Macedonicus for, although he had four adult sons to carry him to his grave, not one of them purged the offence that their father had suffered at the hands of a tribune of the people.

At about the age of thirty, a Roman nobleman would set out to scale the superior magistracies. This was the hardest time of his life. He would accept all sorts of duties in an effort to establish a support network of political friends, backers and electors. He would bankrupt himself and wear himself out, from early morning, when he would receive his clients, to late evening, when he would drag himself from banquet to banquet – not to mention the long mornings he had to spend at the forum defending some client or other in the law courts. He would travel to the country districts where his electors lived, shake their hands, and commit to memory their names and family histories. He had to be on permanent call, always ready to donate time and money, lend out his houses, horses, carriages, and write letters of recommendation. Above all, he had to put on the right face and voice, be affable with the humble, courteous with his peers and deferential towards the honour-laden aged.

If elected, his responsibilities would change and multiply, with all the attendant worries and obligations, until the day when his sons took over from him, enabling him to retire to the country. There he would await death and the solemn funeral that would crown both himself and his family with fame and honour.

VERTICAL SOCIETY

If census registration gave society a horizontal structure, political realities created a vertical dimension. Nobles and would-be nobles required the broadest possible support network staffed by influential men from every echelon of society. This network would consist of relatives, friends and clients.

Romans sought to multiply their family ties because such alliances entailed obligations between relatives who could then rely on one another for mutual assistance. These bonds of kinship resulted from marriages – increasingly frequent due to divorce – and from adoptions. Neither divorce nor adoption cut children off from their original family, or the family of the wife from that of her former husband. The son of Aemilius Paullus, adopted by a Scipio and thereafter known as Scipio Aemilianus, spoke of both his fathers in equally affectionate terms. Cicero, whose daughter married several times, no doubt in order to further her father's interests, remained on excellent terms with both his former sons-in-law.

FRIENDSHIP

Like relatives, friends belonged to the same social environment. In Rome friendship was a complex relationship between two people, based on affection and self-interest. First and foremost, friendship was a set of reciprocal obligations of assistance and non-aggression. If, owing perhaps to bonds of kinship, one had to bring an action against a friend, it was best first to disown the friendship, in the same way that a city would renege on a treaty of alliance with another city before declaring war on it. But Roman friendship was also a strong emotional tie, involving friends in all the torments of jealousy and betrayal, or the raptures of devotion and admiration. Like comrades-at-arms, noblemen who led dangerous lives were bound by passionate friendships: the loyalty of friends was a Roman's salvation but, equally, their desertion spelled his downfall.

When Camillus, after taking the Etruscan town of Veii, was accused of keeping part of the plunder for himself, and in particular of fitting his house with bronze doors, he appealed to his friends for support:

He assembled his friends and comrades-in-arms, who were many in number, and begged them not to suffer him to be convicted on base charges and to be made a laughing-stock by his foes. When his friends had laid their heads together and discussed the case, they answered that, as regards his trial, they thought they could be of no help to him; but if he were punished with a fine, they would help him pay it. This he could not endure, and in his wrath determined to depart the city and go into exile. Accordingly, after he had kissed his wife and son goodbye, he went from his house in silence as far as the gate of the city.[6]

The reaction of Camillus' friends and peers was eloquent. These nobles, these former magistrates, were willing to help Camillus in his misfortune, as duty dictated, but not to oppose a sentence that they in fact approved. It was this tacit approval that dishonoured Camillus. An unjust conviction was distressing, but not ignominious. More than any decision taken by a court of law, the desertion of Camillus by his friends, which all Rome would have witnessed on the day of the trial, condemned him in the eyes of the city. Unable to come to terms with his civic demise, Camillus left Rome for another city in Latium.

Friendship often went hand in hand with kinship, and marriage might place the seal on a friendship. To share children was for the Romans a means of strengthening bonds of friendship. The best, wisest, most energetic and most courageous men seemed to act as magnets for groups of admirers. Envy, *invidia*, was not an honourable sentiment: either one felt oneself the equal of the person in question and so competed with him to determine who was in fact the better man, or, deeming oneself from the outset an unequal match, one bowed before the other man's superiority and became his friend.

This is how Cato the Younger, the future Cato of Utica, gathered around him his many admirers.

Among the many lovers and admirers of Cato there were some who were more conspicuous and illustrious than others. One of these was Quintus Hortensius [the great orator of the aristocratic party, ten years Cato's senior], a man of splendid reputation and excellent character. This man, then, desiring to be more than a mere associate and companion of Cato, but in some way or other to bring his whole family and line into community of kinship with him, attempted to persuade Cato, whose daughter Porcia was the wife of Bibulus and had borne him two sons, to give her in turn to him as noble soil for the production of children.

Hortensius even suggested that if Bibulus was really loath to part with his wife, she might be returned to him once she had given him (Hortensius) a child. Cato politely turned down Hortensius' strange request.

> Then Hortensius changed his tactics, threw off the mask, and boldly asked for the wife of Cato himself, since she was still young enough to bear children, and Cato had heirs enough. And it cannot be said that he did this because he knew that Cato neglected Marcia, for she was at that time with child by him, as we are told. However, seeing the earnestness and eager desire of Hortensius, Cato would not refuse, but said that Philippus also, Marcia's father, must approve of this step. Accordingly, Philippus was consulted and expressed his consent.[7]

Hortensius thus married Marcia, who returned to Cato after the death of Hortensius. The old orator was very wealthy and Cato gained considerably from this game of musical beds.

CLIENTS

A citizen's clients were of lower rank than his friends. Clients supported one particular patron, *patronus* – which later gave rise to the Italian word *padrino*, the term used for a godfather in the Mafia. Clients provided the social basis and grassroots support for their patron's political career and were linked to him by an exchange of services. The patron would protect his clients' interests and take their part in any brushes with the law; in their turn, clients gave their patron their backing by escorting him on public occasions.

> Men of small means are only able to earn favours from our order or pay us back in one way and that is by helping us and following us about when we are candidates for office. It is not possible and it cannot be asked of us senators or of the Roman knights that they should attend for days on end their friends that are candidates. If they come in large numbers to our houses and on occasion accompany us down to the forum, if they condescend to walk with us the length of a public hall, we consider that we have received great attention and respect. It is the poorer men, who have more free time, who provide the constant attention that is habitually given to men of standing and to those who confer benefits. Do not, then, Cato, take from the lower class this fruit of their attention. Allow those who hope for everything from us to have something to give us in return.[8]

This link between patron and client was guaranteed by a moral and legal pact founded on reciprocal loyalty, *fides*, which for the Romans, along with justice, constituted the basis for social life. 'For both patrons and clients alike it was impious and unlawful to accuse each other in law-suits or to bear witness or to give their votes against each other or to be found in the number of each other's enemies; and whoever was convicted of doing any of these things was guilty of treason.'[9]

Client–patron relations united families more than they united particular men, and they therefore survived from one generation to the next. Such links might also bind larger groups of people to a particular noble family. Entire professions, grouped together for funerary purposes in religious associations known as colleges, might share a single patron; so might town districts whose solid backing could be guaranteed by solemn feasts, such as the Compitalia, or crossroads games; so too might colonies established through the intervention of their future patron. Even kingdoms could become the clients of the general who had conquered them. The fact that Pompey was the patron of the whole of Picenum obliged Titus Labienus, Caesar's loyal lieutenant throughout the Gallic War, to switch to Pompey's side at the outbreak of the civil war since, as a native of Picenum, Titus owed Pompey his loyalty as a client.

This example, relating to the civil wars, shows that it was but a short step from moral support to armed assistance. Even in peacetime, the patron could, if he so desired, levy troops from among his clients or form his own personal guard or even army. There was nothing shocking about this. The force embodied by the client system was essential in Rome, where there were no police and where every judicial decision had to be implemented by those involved.

Some kind of vertical solidarity or cohesion was absolutely essential. The state did not take care of individuals, particularly humble ones. Every Roman had to belong to a group – a family, a professional guild, a village, a district – and via such a group to a clientele, otherwise he stood no chance of survival. He would be subject to assault and robbery. If he went away, his land would be occupied, his goods pillaged, his wife abducted. Group solidarity, on the other hand, provided him not only with security but also with help should misfortune befall him. He would be lent money, his daughter would be provided with a dowry, there would be a collection to pay for his funeral.

Such groups also served to bring miscarriages of justice to the attention of those in authority. Demonstrations in the town square were almost an institution, a way of bringing an individual grievance to the notice of officialdom. A ragged procession might suddenly appear, the victim in its midst yelling his protest at injustice. A gang armed with sticks would surround a man, shove his companions out of the way and threaten him, shouting that he was a criminal, a swindler, a bloodthirsty brute.

THE TWO TRADITIONAL PARTIES

The existence of these vertical structures meant that people voted at elections in accordance with personal connections rather than ideology. In the later republic there were, it is true, two main parties in Rome, the *populares* ('on the side of the people') and the *optimates*, or senatorials. The *populares* demanded land, the cancellation of debts, and the extension of citizenship rights. They unswervingly denounced the economic and political privileges of the nobility. The senatorials opposed any form of innovation, praised tradition and celebrated the austerity of the good old days, the glory of bygone nobles, and the respectful discipline of the people. Each party accused the other of cowardice, cupidity and of harbouring tyrannical ambitions.

The leaders of the popular party, however, were just as high-born as those of the senatorial party, and party allegiance was hereditary. Some families were traditionally *populares*, others traditionally senatorial. It was a matter of clienteles. Campaigning for land reform and the establishment of colonies in territory that Rome had conquered was a way of creating for oneself a clientele among the future colonists. Likewise, to urge that citizenship rights be granted to Rome's allies was a sure way of winning Gallic or Samnite votes. One should not therefore be taken in by the rabble-rousing speeches delivered by the Gracchi or by Cato. They were merely playing a part, even if they did it with passion, breathing astonishing life and vigour into wooden party blather. No one was prepared to die for their ideas, but for power – that was another matter.

Perhaps the division of the city into so-called plebeians and patricians was after all a purely functional matter. It is a matter of debate whether Rome was really the theatre of social conflicts fought out as political struggles or whether the city's political duels, essential to its smooth functioning, were rather 'dressed up' as social conflicts.

RULERS OF THE CITY

Such passion for power, given that to belong to the nobility entailed a long stretch of service to the state, remains inexplicable unless one grasps what power really involved in Rome. Magistrates were not simply ministers, or servants of the state. The power, albeit temporary, that they possessed, even under conditions of collegial responsibility, was regal in scope. Political power, *potestas*, which Romans distinguished explicitly from personal power, *potentia*, conferred on those who exercised it such rewards that they were prepared to sacrifice everything – peace and quiet, wealth, their own lives, and even, paradoxically, their honour.

Magistrates were not instruments of executive government, for under the Roman republic there was no separation of powers between the judiciary, the legislature and the executive. And all three forms of power were concentrated in the hands of the consuls, the highest magistrates of the city, in peacetime as well as in time of war. More than anyone else, they embodied the regal power of the magistrates:

> The consuls, previous to leading out their legions, exercise authority in Rome over all public affairs, since all the other magistrates except the tribunes are under them . . . As for preparations for war and the general conduct of operations in the field, here their power is almost uncontrolled. They are authorized to spend any sum they decide upon from the public funds, being accompanied by a questor who faithfully executes their instructions. So one may reasonably pronounce the constitution to be a pure monarchy or kingship.[10]

Consuls, like praetors, had inherited the trappings and pomp of the Etruscan kings: the purple-hemmed toga, the purple-striped tunic, the 'curule' chair, or 'chair of state', and the twelve lictors. When the consuls were out and about, their lictors would form a human rampart around them; when they called at a particular house, the lictors stood guard at the door; and whomsoever the consuls pointed out, the lictors would immediately arrest. The splendour that surrounded consuls inspired a tremendous sense of awe and their appearance dazzled any humble folk who came near them.

Even less elevated magistrates acted as kings within their own realms, whether as praetor responsible for justice, aedile in charge of games or quaestor in control of finance. Each had his own *provincia*, a domain in which he could legislate, see that his laws were enforced and punish any who contravened them.

This notion of *provincia* provided an institutional framework when, from 227 BC onwards, former magistrates were appointed to govern the territories that Rome had conquered. Provincial governors, proconsuls or propraetors lorded it over huge territories: Spain, Greece, southern France (Gallia Narbonensis), the valley of the Po. They exercised full civil and military powers over people of whom most were not Roman citizens. The only limit to this power was the specific law governing the towns and kingdoms of the province. It was the custom of many of the subject peoples to worship their sovereigns as gods; the man they saw as succeeding their vanquished king was therefore treated in the same way. This of course only heightened the regal delusions of the governors. Roman proconsuls would see clouds of incense rising towards them and hear the echoing prayers of the prostrate faithful. Many allowed themselves to be worshipped, and even began to doubt that they were mere humans. They sometimes became capricious and cruel tyrants. But on their return to Rome they had to beware. There was no shortage of young ambitious men to drag them through the courts. This is precisely what happened to Lucius Quinctius Flamininus, the governor of Gaul (see pp. 284–5), who was expelled from the senate in 185 BC, eternally dishonoured.[11]

Rome was full of pretend-kings: magistrates and senators. The senate, entirely composed of former magistrates arrayed in purple-hemmed togas and royal tunics, created an impressive show. Foreigners who witnessed the senate in session might have thought that they had stumbled upon an assembly of kings. Yet the political philosophy that underpinned this republic was utterly hostile to monarchic power. To the Roman mind, no mere mortal could possibly be the ideal person, in every place and at every time, to assess a situation, reach a decision and take the correct action. But one might reasonably hope that the right man to deal with any given eventuality could be found among the best men of the city: the shrewdest man if the situation demanded astuteness; the bravest if it demanded resolve; the calmest if it demanded moderation. Choosing the right man for the situation was the essential role of the people in electoral assemblies, and of the senate when confronted with difficult circumstances. Laws were enacted or thrown out on the basis not of their provisions but of the man proposing them. This is why a politician desperately needed to build a good image for himself and nurture his fame.

Each noble family had its own forte, which it took care to cultivate, and senatorial families taken together covered the whole range of political virtues, including such contradictory ones as patience and audacity.

FUNERALS AND THE RIGHT TO AN IMAGE

Because nobility was ephemeral and attached more to an individual than to a particular lineage, duties weighed heavily on Roman noblemen. Nobility could only be achieved by becoming a magistrate, for magistrates alone enjoyed what was known as the 'right to an image' – that is, they were entitled to be commemorated.

The *imago*, or image, was a funeral mask, a wax impression taken from the face of former magistrates – and only from them – at their death. The family of the deceased magistrate would keep the *imago* in a closed box shaped like a temple, which hung on the wall of the *atrium*. Below it would appear an inscription like those found from the second century onwards on funerary monuments. These inscriptions would give details of the birth and career of the man, his name and his honours. The following inscription belonged to a certain Scipio, a praetor in 139 BC: 'Gnaeus Cornelius, son of Gnaeus, Scipio Hispanus, praetor, curule aedile, quaestor, two times military tribune, decemvir in charge of justice, decemvir in charge of religions.'

On the wall of the *atrium* such *imagines*, held together by strips of cloth, formed a complex network since, on marrying, women would bring to their new home their own family masks and these would join the husband's masks on the *atrium* wall. Then there were also the masks of the family of the adopted children. These networks did not really constitute family trees since those who had never exercised any responsibilities, either because they had died too young or turned out to be incapable, did not figure on the wall. A grandson might therefore be linked directly to his grandfather.

If these masks were shut away it was because they constituted only a trace of the deceased and not a monument to his memory, as did, for example, an inscription. A waxen face only disclosed those trivial peculiarities that distinguished one man from the next. The honour of a man could not be read in his lifeless face, since his honour was not linked to his facial features, but to the fact that he had reproduced the virtues of his race, shouldered responsibilities in the manner of his forebears and secured the continuity of both his family and the republic: 'I have reunited in my practices all the virtues of my race: I have engendered a line of descent; I have equalled the lofty deeds of my forefathers; I have secured the glory of my ancestors so well that they may delight in having engendered me for their glory; by my honours I have brought fame to my race', said Scipio Hispanus. He had done his duty in terms of both social and biological reproduction.

The funeral of a former magistrate was the only public ceremony for which the masks were brought out. The family of the deceased would open the image boxes and entrust the masks to actors who, clothed in the insignia of the highest office exercised by the dead men, would wear them. In the funeral procession, these dead men, thus reanimated and mounted on ceremonial chariots, preceded a litter bearing the deceased; his family walked behind. The cortège proceeded to the forum, where a young relative of the dead man would mount the rostra, or speaker's platform, and deliver a funeral oration in praise of the deceased, developing what would become his funeral inscription. He would then praise each of the attending ancestors in turn. This second part of the speech had a dual function. First, it served to commemorate the glory of the ancestors and to afford them immortality by fixing them in the Romans' collective memory – for there was little point in striving for glory if it was to expire with the last witnesses to the deeds that had given rise to it. Second, it rehearsed the actions of the ancestors, thereby showing that down through the ages the men of the family had repeated the same achievements and displayed the same virtues, in circumstances that were similar.

In this way, each family passed on from generation to generation its exemplary actions, its model behaviour or even its own special rituals, so that when the time came they might be put to use for the republic. On three separate occasions the family of the Decii Mures, in battles whose outcome hung in the balance, turned to the ritual of the *devotio*: the general sacrificed his life in exchange for the defeat of his enemies by giving himself up to the infernal gods. Having thereby become *sacer*, untouchable, he threw himself on to his enemies' swords. Contaminated by the contact with him, they too fell under the spell of the infernal powers and sank to their deaths.

Family specialities were also recorded for posterity through the use of surnames, *cognomina*. A man's victory left a trace in his name: Scipio became 'the African' and Metellus, 'the Macedonian'. Their descendants, moreover, were free to revive the surname, by re-enacting the deeds of their ancestor. Scipio Aemilianus thus became the second 'African'.

Names summed up a man's nobility and a string of surnames expressed not only the past glory of the family by commemorating the

deeds of its ancestors but also the family connections and the breadth
of its noble kinship. Each nobleman therefore had three names: the
forename that his father gave him and which signalled his liberty; the
name that he shared with his father and that indicated his lineage; and
the surname or surnames of his father. If he had been adopted, the
Roman noble would keep the name of his natural father as a
surname. He would also bear those surnames that he had himself
acquired. Lastly, should he so wish, he might add a few surnames
from his mother's family. Scipio Aemilianus was thus able to style
himself Publius Cornelius Scipio Africanus Aemilianus.

DESERTERS OF THE CITY

Social life constantly reminded a Roman of his duties. To shirk them
was to betray oneself, the hopes of one's youth, one's family, one's
ancestors and those friends who had been unstinting in their support.
But no duty could ever be performed fully enough: even after years of
toil, the only excuses for retirement were sickness or age.

Sometimes, however, a Roman did plunge from glory to infamy.
Overcome with weariness, embittered by all the ingratitude he had
encountered, he might suddenly give up, his spirit splintered.

Lucullus was one of those famous Romans whose will to fight
suddenly snapped and who exposed himself to dishonour.[12] A
nobleman, Lucullus had been a consul, a proconsul of Asia, and had
won a glorious victory over Mithridates, the great king of the Orient.
The senate and the aristocratic party were counting on him to do
battle against Pompey and so curb the latter's suspect ambitions.
Lucullus, however, rejected what the future seemed to hold in store
for him. After the exertions of the war, the battles fought against the
enemy and the plots that his brothers-in-law hatched within his own
camp, Lucullus lacked the inclination and the strength to plunge back
into political wrangling. He collapsed almost overnight, sinking into
a life of idle luxury. No longer driven by ambition, no longer braced
for effort, Lucullus felt feeble and empty, with more time on his hands
and more gold than he knew what to do with. Now that he had no
reason to follow the strict regime enforced by political life, he
surrendered himself utterly to all the pleasures of life, gradually losing
the very will to live. It was fine at banquets to sing of how much
sweeter life would be if only one could spend it exclusively in the
bedroom, the dining-room or in transit between the two, but
everyone recognized that this vision was suitable only for a weary

warrior for whom a spell of banqueting provided a temporary respite. Woe betide anyone who wished, like Lucullus, to live out his banquet-hall dreams!

Lucullus spent fortunes on villas and parks which he thronged with statues and other works of art. He coiled marine hippodromes around his Naples residences and built palaces in the middle of the sea. He added new dining-rooms to his house in Rome, where the beds were hung with purple, and the tableware decorated with precious stones. The cuisine was complex and sophisticated. Yet the people he received there were of a vulgar sort: parasites and social climbers. His former friends from the senate, whom he had abandoned to their political struggles, had no inclination to dine at the house of Lucullus the deserter. The luxury in which Lucullus indulged was a mere empty gesture, for it was divorced from any proper social role: luxury, after all, should display the liberality of the master of the house towards his peers. But increasingly Lucullus shut himself away alone. The whole city sniggered about his sumptuous but pointless banquets. Most shameful of all, some said that Lucullus had his cook prepare him banquet dishes that he then ate in solitude, the only guest at his own banquet: 'Lucullus dines with Lucullus!' He had brought shame on his name: in Rome people referred to eccentric sensualists as 'leading the life of a Lucullus'. The most loyal of his friends were ashamed for him and sought in vain to check his fall. Yielding to those closest to him, he did appear one last time in the senate, to lend his support to a fellow senator. But he had become too easy a prey for his opponents. He was snubbed, and this compounded his disgust with politics.

Lucullus opened a library whose rooms and study areas were open to everyone. It was used mainly by Greeks residing in Rome. These Greeks became Lucullus' family, and he helped them whenever they needed assistance in the law courts, providing for foreigners what he refused his countrymen.

The Romans considered that you could tell a man's character by his public associates, and in their eyes Lucullus and his Greeks formed a sorry spectacle of moral degeneration. Unable to dodge the image of himself that the city held up to him and which even he found distasteful, Lucullus went further. He boasted of his disgrace, taking a morbid pleasure in it. Finally he escaped from his self-hatred into madness. The law decided that he was 'furious' – that is, out of his mind – and appointed his brother to manage his estate. Lucullus died raving. There was a rumour that a freedman had given him a love potion to drink, hoping that this would make Lucullus love him, and that it had proved fatal. Whether true or false, the anecdote illustrates the state of emotional bewilderment into which, in his solitude, Lucullus had fallen. No one could survive in disgrace after knowing glory.

THE PHILOSOPHICAL TEMPTATION

If the Romans were quite incapable of rejecting the image of themselves that their peers held up to them, this was because for them there existed no inwardness of thought, no autonomous consciousness of self that could serve as a bulwark against judgements imposed from outside by the community. The only way in which a Roman might escape such judgements was to place himself above the law – in other words, to adopt the stance of a tyrant. This was a dangerous course of action which generally ended in violent death. The fates of Catiline Caesar and Antony bore this out. People therefore tended, like Scipio Africanus, to resign themselves to the verdict of the majority. On his return from Asia in 189 BC, Scipio, already famous for his victory over Hannibal, had defeated Antiochus. This triumph should have sealed his fame, but his adversary, Cato, a staunch defender of tradition, was lying in wait. Rumours began to fly. During the campaign Cato had already charged Scipio with spending too much time in the gymnasium, at the theatre and the baths, and accused him of indulging in 'Greek customs'. At first these accusations failed to stick, since the delegation sent to investigate testified on their return to the sound morals of the general. But when Cato repeated his attacks, the people's tribunes grew restless. It was said that Scipio had lined his pockets during the campaign and had extorted fifty talents from Antiochus. Although Scipio won the ensuing trial, Cato had been so successful in tarnishing the general's image that Scipio withdrew of his own accord, his spirit broken, to his estate at Liternum in Campania. There he died in 183 BC, a year after his lifelong enemy Marcus Porcius Cato, was appointed censor, thereby fulfilling his highest civic ambition. Life was a contest with no holds barred.

Those who had been disappointed in public life, however, could achieve happiness in other ways, which, if symbolically no less costly, at least did not entail any sacrifice of morality. These alternatives were provided by two philosophies of Greek origin: Epicureanism and Stoicism. Both philosophies promised to rid the citizen of politics while enabling him to realize his full human potential. No longer *homo civilis*, he might at least aspire to be *homo sapiens*. Both Epicureanism and Stoicism claimed to stand in for culture and civilization, allowing the citizen to escape the judgement of the crowds whose fickleness and willingness to listen to demagogues they constantly denounced. But who then was to judge the citizen, to hold up a mirror to him?

The Stoics had a forthright answer to this. The philosophical man had no need of a political city, for he was a city unto himself, and his rational soul was its king. At the same time, he was a citizen of a world that was itself organized by divine reason. The entire Earth was spread before his philosophical ambition, with reason as its only law. Moreover, at least in theory, he could in his solitude gain full knowledge of this reason through the asceticism of his soul. The philosophical man might therefore be his own judge and remain detached from the world without sinking into madness. Happiness in the tranquillity afforded by his total mastery of himself and his image was the reward for his virtue. The Stoical man, even if he remained an active citizen in his city, would not seek to 'fit in', expecting the people to acknowledge his virtues. The Stoic school taught indifference to others, insensitivity to human feelings. It was a dangerous school, for in Rome the expression of feeling was the normal way of regulating the rigours of politics. *Humanitas*, which the Greeks termed philanthropy, meant a tenderness of the heart, an ability to weep, a capacity for compassion that characterized the civilized man, even the lowest of citizens, setting him apart from the brute or the tyrant who revelled in the blood he spilled and triumphed in the sufferings of a defeated enemy. The wise Stoic ran a grave risk of one day stumbling either into madness or into tyranny. The worst thing about Stoicism, and surely its least Roman feature, was its insensitivity to suffering, the indifference to the death of a father, a wife, a child, or to the ruin of one's country. If in private Romans might hide their pain, they generally gave it free rein in public, as at the forum, where they would willingly go to display their bereavement, proclaim their despair or pour out their entreaties. As children, Romans learnt reserve but they were never trained to be as unfeeling as stones in the face of suffering. Contrary to what has often been argued, Stoicism did not blend in well with Roman culture. Few people adopted it as a philosophy of life, even if many turned to it on occasion for consolation in the face of political setbacks.

Epicureanism started from the same premises but resulted in a quite different lifestyle. Like Stoicism, it provided a means of escape from the judgement of the people, but it did this by simply advocating abstinence from political life rather than indifference. For the civic community Epicurus substituted a community of friends bound only by the pleasures of the banquet and conversation, meeting in closed gardens beyond the reach of rumours or political cares. This form of social intercourse involved only shared pleasures and mutual indulgence (see p. 275). Any man who chose to follow Epicurus necessarily became, like Lucullus, loathsome to everyone except his friends. But he would learn to scorn the opinions of the vulgar crowd. Epicureanism, although it tempted many a noble contemporary of Cicero, was a desperate remedy, a kind of social suicide, hard to live out to the full. The first Roman Epicurean, Titus Albucius (born in around 200 BC), who came from a family of senators, was converted to Epicureanism as a young man while studying in Athens. He lived there surrounded by friends, without distinction of race or birth. On his return to Rome, however, he resumed the pursuit of honours and regained a taste for glory. Indeed, he became governor of Sardinia where, before leaving the island, he enjoyed a private triumph.

Those who persevered in their Epicureanism ran the risk of meeting with the same tragic end as the hedonist Lucullus. It is not surprising that Titus Lucretius Carus, a Roman citizen, no doubt of good family, and a popularizer of Epicurean philosophy in his poem *On Nature*, also fell victim to a love potion and committed suicide. There were, of course, more balanced characters, contented Epicureans like Cicero's friend Atticus the banker, or Maecenas, the noble descendant of Etruscan kings who was a friend and companion to both Virgil and Horace. But by the time of Maecenas, the republic had vanished and the imperial was beginning to replace the republican Roman.

2

Wealth and poverty

THE RICH, THE POOR AND THE WRETCHED

With its registers and finely tuned assessments, census-taking gave each citizen a civic and human identity. Yet the kind of classification that emerged from the census conjures up an abstract grid-like society that failed to take any account of people's lives. There were other fault-lines separating people and groups, and other points of connection too. Cities were more than a *populus* or a straightforward political or military entity. The Romans did not experience their society as a succession of classes gently shading into one another, from the richest and most dignified senator down to the lowliest freedmen who, as they said, had 'neither money-box nor slave'. The census certainly provided a numerical estimate of each citizen's wealth, but at Rome the difference between a rich man and a poor man was not a quantifiable matter of money. They were separated by an abyss: the very words 'rich' and 'poor' meant different things to each of them.

To grasp this, one has to picture what it meant in Rome to be wealthy, bearing in mind that there was no halfway house, no 'middle class'. There is no point in looking to the equestrian order for the equivalent of an *ancien-régime*-style bourgeoisie. Indeed, it is high time that anachronistic accounts of Roman society were discarded. As Moses Finley has written: 'Nothing has bedevilled the history of the later Roman Republic more than this false image of the *equites*, called businessmen, capitalists, the new moneyed class, *ad lib.*, resting on the large, deeply entrenched assumption that there must have been a powerful capitalist class between the land-owning aristocracy and the poor.'[13] For either a Roman was very rich indeed, rich enough to lavish wine, food and entertainment on thousands of guests at a single feast, to have hundreds of oxen, pigs and sheep butchered, to hire scores of carriages with their coachmen and horses, or his fortune was of no use to him whatsoever and he might just as well be poor. There was no point in economizing. Wealth was of no use except in public life. Any Roman who cherished political ambitions, for himself or for his son, had to amass a colossal fortune. But such ambitions were far beyond the means of the majority of citizens, for whom therefore it made no sense whatsoever to scrape together a smallish pile, while leading a wretched life as a miser.

Roman satire was relentless in heaping sarcasm on misers, as if Rome were peopled with skinflints and penny-pinchers. In fact, the Romans scorned money and all those who set too much store by it. At the same time, money played an increasingly important role during the republic. Hence the perpetual exhortations that money was to be spent and not to be hoarded in coffers or lent out at interest; it was to be used to bring people closer together, to help a friend in distress or to enjoy a feast in congenial company. Roman avarice was not, like its modern counterpart, a character defect: it was a social offence. To be miserly was to go without and to make others go without, to economize with the income from one's property instead of making the most of it with one's friends. The offence was all the more serious in that it removed the miser from his social milieu: he invited nobody to his house, lived 'like a savage', and starved himself into a sub-human condition. The crime of avarice was generally felt to be as bad as its opposite: uncontrolled spending and the squandering of one's fortune. Both the miser and the spendthrift courted social decadence and led wretched existences.

It was not easy to maintain a correct relationship with money, and fathers had to take care to ensure that their sons became neither spendthrifts nor misers.

Servius Oppidius, a rich man, divided his two farms at Canusium between his two sons. On his death-bed he called them to him and said: 'Ever since I saw you, Aulus, carrying your taws and nuts in a loose toga, giving and gambling them away, and you, Tiberius, anxiously counting them and hiding them in holes, I have greatly feared that madness of different kinds might plague you – that you, my son, might follow after Nomentanus [the spendthrift], and you after Cicuta [the miser]. I therefore adjure you both, by our household gods, the one not to reduce, the other not to increase, what your father thinks enough, and what nature sets as a limit.'[14]

The meaning of this fable is clear. Aulus embodies avarice and Tiberius prodigality, the two kinds of depravity that threaten the owner of a property that nourishes him and affords him a handsome living. Aulus' unrestrained appetite and his taste for betting fore-shadow the man of pleasure, while Tiberius, hiding his marbles, or rather the walnuts and knucklebones that Roman children played with, is doomed to turn into a miserable skinflint. But another, more serious, threat hangs over them: the temptation to pursue excessive political ambition. For if either of them had to organize games, or maintain a clientele with gifts and banquets, he would immediately be ruined. Their father therefore adds:

> Further, that ambition may not tickle your fancy, I shall bind you both by an oath: whichever of you becomes aedile or praetor, let him be outlawed and accursed. Would you waste your wealth on vetches, beans, and lupins, that you may play the rich man and strut about in the Circus, or be set up on bronze, though stripped of the lands, stripped, madman, of the money your father left: to the end, oh yes, that you may win the applause which Agrippa wins – a cunning fox mimicking the noble lion?

The political ambition of the 'poor man', if he set out to compete with the generosity of wealthy senators, was his downfall.

COMFORTABLE POVERTY

Unless you are immensely rich, it is best to live in poverty on your own property: so said the moral consensus. One could live happily surrounded by children and by solid and prosperous servants.

A life of rustic poverty meant that one had few needs. Whether one's property was large or small, one slept on straw, ate vegetables, bread and bacon, went barefoot and wore a simple tunic. There were few obvious differences between the owner of a seven *iugera* smallholding, considered by Romans to be the smallest viable concern (the *iugerum* was roughly one-quarter of a hectare, or three-fifths of an acre) and the owner of a fifty hectare farm, much of which might be given over to woods or meadows. Nothing was more foreign to the Roman way of thinking than the notion that well-being and creature comforts should increase in line with the earnings of the father of the family. On his property, the Roman consumed little, mainly what he himself had produced; he was wise, happy and healthy. His sleep was untroubled, and he awoke refreshed.

There were, of course, the temptations of the market, but these were very limited and concerned only such goods as were deemed to be inessentials: crockery; carpets; luxury foods such as fish; exotic wines; expensive slaves, selected more for their comely appearance than for their sturdiness, and destined for the pleasure of the master of the house. Besides, such 'extras', even if they found their way into the house of our 'poor' Roman, would only be brought out on feast days to honour guests. In normal circumstances, a Roman would have felt that he had everything he required and that he lived in a society of plenty. He was persuaded that any refinements that might be introduced into his everyday life would mark not progress in civilization but rather decline. The only occasions on which it was legitimate to spend money on unusual refinements were feasts and banquets; only the presence of a stranger could justify luxury and splendour. And then it was proper, indeed it was a duty, to consume every superfluous possession – wine, animals, money – always ensuring that one did not cut into one's inheritance. To fail in this duty was to behave as a niggard. Wine would then turn sour before it was drunk; oil would go rancid; moths would get into the clothes chests and eat holes in the blankets; corn would go mouldy; and money would be squandered by one's heirs. The miser cut himself off from other men, from civilization: he was *incultus*. He was as unable to maintain a correct relationship with himself as he was with others. Skinny and haggard, misers were viewed as depriving themselves of life's necessities, eating leaves, pears as hard as stone and wild berries, nibbling at five-year-old olives, drinking vinegar and wearing rags. Dire poverty made them stupid and hideous, like the nomads who, it was said, wandered through the forests at the edge of the world.

The 'poor' Roman peasant therefore lived with his family on a small farm that provided for everyone's needs. Nothing changed during the five centuries of the republic, and a seven *iugera* property remained sufficient to feed and raise a family. Caesar's veterans, even if they had three children, were granted only two and a half hectares of land.

These surface areas seem ridiculously small to contemporary historians. But Italy was cultivated like a garden, and the abundance of labour ensured excellent yields from these small plots of land. Modern agronomists find it hard to believe the figures advanced by the ancients, and take the view that cereal yields cannot normally

Plate 3   Roman store: food and household items
Reproduced by kind permission of the Ancient Art and Architecture Collection
(Ronald Sheridan)

have exceeded tenfold nor ever reached twentyfold even in exceptional years. The ancients, however, talk of hundredfold yields, even if, it is true, they proclaimed them miracles. The Romans took great care with the land, maintaining the soil meticulously. They ploughed it several times and manured it prior to sowing, regulating their work in accordance with the nature of the soil in order to get the most benefit without exhausting it. Once the corn had come up, the field was harrowed twice, and then weeded carefully, so as not to damage the roots or the plants themselves. The Roman peasant did sometimes leave the land fallow for a period, but more often he practised crop rotation of beans, corn and lupins, which gave several harvests in a year.

The Roman peasant's staple food was not corn but vegetables. He lived on the produce of his garden, which he was skilful enough to make productive all year round. Often, especially during periods of particularly arduous work, he would add to this diet bread, mashed beans, bacon and cheese. Everything was cooked with oil, herbs, garlic and salt. He would also have had a few vines, some fruit trees, a small herd of goats, a pig, a team of oxen grazing in the woods and on the stubble fields, and some farmyard poultry. Our 'poor' Roman could even afford to have guests and to make sacrifices on the household altar.

The standard of living of the 'poor' town-dweller was similar to that of the 'poor' peasant. He could be content with what he had, without working himself to death or going short of essentials in order to save money. The following are both examples of 'poor' Romans, one a peasant farmer from Sabine, the other a town crier in Rome. Both were friends of Horace.

Ofellus, a tenant-farmer from Horace's own region, summed up his life as follows:

> I was not the man to eat on a working day, without good reason, anything more than greens and the shank of a smoked ham, and if, after long absence, a friend came to see me, or if, in rainy weather, when I could not work, a neighbour paid me a visit – a welcome guest – we fared well, not with fish sent for from town, but with a pullet or a kid; by and by raisins and nuts and split figs would be our dessert. Then we would make a game of drinking, with a forfeit to rule the feast, and Ceres, to whom we made our prayer, would smooth out with wine the worries of a wrinkled brow.[15]

The poor man was happy and he was wise. He was almost self-sufficient. As the Stoics said, he alone was rich, for poverty is want and the poor man wants for nothing. If Ofellus was certainly not a realistic picture of the Roman peasant, he was at least its imaginary representation and that is what matters: he was an expression of the widespread view that to be poor was not to be needy and that poverty did nothing to hinder moral fulfilment. On the other hand, what Horace, belonging as he did to the empire, failed to mention was that this poverty, which enclosed men within the confined space of a few *iugera*, was balanced by the opportunities offered the citizen by public life and politics, whether in his local town or in Rome, and above all by war. The Roman was a peasant-soldier, and the dimensions of his plot of land were calculated not only to enable him to bring up children but also to allow him to feed his family for a month in the event of war and also to arm himself. In Rome, given that the economy was not a sphere in which one could demonstrate particular moral – that is, civic – virtues, it did not matter if one was poor. The only virtue that one could exercise consisted in giving generously but without excess: what Romans termed *liberalitas*. Not to be attached to money was the distinguishing feature of the man who had other, more honourable attachments, such as the love of glory. It was a crowning virtue and the mark of the free man. The countryside, which could only be the sphere for economic pursuits, was a place of happiness, but not a place for action. One could hardly make one's life there. It was because he was also a citizen that the Roman could be a poor peasant.

The following is a portrait of Volteius Mena, a 'poor man' of the city who lived at the beginning of the first century BC, which is given in an anecdote that contrasts him with a man of the nobility, Lucius Marcius Philippus, a consul in 91 BC.

> Philippus, the famous pleader, a man of vigour and courage, was returning home from work at about two o'clock. Being now somewhat advanced in years, he was grumbling at the Carinae being too far from the Forum, when (so the story goes) he caught sight of a close-shaven man, sitting in a barber's empty booth, who, with a pocket-knife, was quietly cleaning his own nails. 'Demetrius,' he said to his servant, a boy not slow to catch his master's orders, 'go and bring me word about where that man comes from, who he is, and what is his standing, who is his father, or his patron.' The boy went, and came back with the information that the man's name was Volteius Mena, and he was a crier at auctions, a man of modest fortune and blameless record, known to work hard and be idle as need dictated, to make money and spend it, taking pleasure in his humble friends and a home of his own and, when business was over, in the games and in the field of Mars.[16]

To appreciate the full flavour of this anecdote and the contrast that emerges between the rich man and the poor man, one has to conjure up contemporary Rome, at about two o'clock in the afternoon, towards the end of April. The sun is already overwhelming, the streets are deserted, people are resting and bathing prior to their evening stroll and dinner. Philippus, despite his years, is still a busy lawyer at the forum and remains there after everyone else has left. The short climb from the forum to the Carinae seems like a long journey to him and by the time he gets home he is exhausted. Mena, on the other hand, is already washed and refreshed. This Mena, who lives life at his own pace, is a smallish fellow and to look at him it is hard to say whether he is a citizen or a freedman, whether he has a father or a patron. Yet he is clearly at one with himself, occupying his rightful place in society; he is a sage and a man of good report with whom the censor has no quarrel. He performs the tasks that must be done in order to live, but keeps sufficient time free for social life. This takes him to different places and brings him into contact with different communities: he joins his family at his home; he dines with friends of his own age and rank, members of his century of town criers, to whose homes he is invited and whom he invites to his own home; he rubs shoulders with the entire populace on his visits to the circus and the theatre or while chatting with acquaintances during his afternoon strolls on the Campus Martius, along the Via Sacra or in other public areas.

VIRTUOUS POVERTY

It was military life that enabled poor men, peasants generally but sometimes townsmen also, to rise in the civic hierarchy by demonstrating their *virtus*, or manly valour. To these men war was extremely profitable, not to mention the spoils – even if they only received a tiny part of them. A man might leave for the wars with nothing but a small house to his name, and yet win renown and a position of affluence through his civic virtue alone. It was not a matter of social advancement, but rather the city's acknowledgement of a man's worth, as this emerged on the testing-ground of war. A citizen could thus rise to the rank that was seen to be rightfully his. The life of Spurius Ligustinus provides a clear illustration of this process.[17]

In 171 BC, during the Macedonian wars, four legions were levied, two of which remained in Italy while the other two were sent to fight in Macedonia under the command of Consul Publius Licinius. Many old soldiers and former centurions enlisted voluntarily in the army of the East, because soldiers who had fought in the previous wars against Antiochus in the eastern Mediterranean had brought back fabulous spoils and amassed considerable personal wealth.

Centurions were subaltern officers, in command of a century, usually around one hundred men. They were appointed by the officers, that is by the military tribunes, and their place in the hierarchy was in accordance with the position they occupied in the battle division. The highest-ranking was the chief centurion, who commanded the first century of the third division, the most experienced legionaries who had to stand their ground, come what might, when the enemy had broken through the first two divisions. These military ranks were never granted permanently, however; at each new enlistment it was up to the military tribunes and the consul to appoint centurions to the various positions available, and to redeploy them as required during the course of the war. Owing to the naturally high levels of mortality among the combatants and the retirement of old soldiers, the men would generally arrive at the appropriate level in the military hierarchy.

That particular year too many centurions volunteered for service, so some of them would have to fight in the ranks. A total of twenty-three chief centurions joined up, whereas the army, consisting of two legions, only required two. Feeling that they had been demoted, the centurions complained and lodged an appeal with the political authorities. Licinius, the consul, convened a people's assembly. The debate took place between Licinius and Marcus Popilius, himself a former consul, who acted as spokesman for the dissatisfied centurions, because only magistrates and senators were entitled to address the people's assembly. Then, departing from normal procedure, the consuls allowed one of the old centurions to take the floor. This gesture spoke volumes for the esteem in which this particular citizen was held, even though he did not belong to the political class. As he said in his speech,

> Fellow citizens, I, Spurius Ligustinus of the tribe of Crustumina, come of Sabine stock. My father left me an acre of land and a little hut, in which I was born and brought up, and to this day I live there. When I first came of age, my father gave me as wife his brother's daughter, who brought with her nothing but her free birth and her chastity, and with these a fertility which would be enough even for a wealthy home. We have six sons, and two daughters, both of whom are now married.

Four of our sons have assumed the toga of manhood, two wear the boys' stripe.[18]

Ligustinus had started out with nothing, a shack and a garden, scarcely one-quarter of a hectare in all. He was too poor to marry outside his own family, so he married his first cousin on his father's side – which was not normal practice. She was almost as poor as he was, and so this step hardly improved his lot. Had he decided to stick at farming, he would have had to rent some land in order to feed his family and himself, but at his death his numerous children would not have had the tax rating necessary to be enrolled in the honourable classes of land-owning citizens.

Having enlisted in 200 BC, at the age of twenty, Ligustinus spent a total of twenty-two years at war. By the time he was fifty he had attained an honourable rank, and war spoils had enabled him to enlarge his property and marry off his daughters. A summary of his career would consist of a series of advancements and rewards granted *virtutis causa*, for his courage and valour. He had played a part in all the most lucrative foreign wars. In Macedonia, during the war against Philip, General Titus Quinctius Flamininus raised him from a private soldier to the rank of centurion, with command of the last century of the first division. Later, Marcus Porcius Cato, the future censor, appointed him first centurion of the first division. 'No one,' commented Ligustinus, 'of all the generals now living, was a keener observer and judge of bravery.' Volunteering again for action, Ligustinus left for Greece and Asia with Manlius Acilius Glabrio, as the first centurion of the second division. He embarked on two further campaigns in Spain and took part in the triumph of Quintus Flavius Flaccus over the Celtiberians in 181 BC. He was by this time so well known that Tiberius Sempronius Gracchus, proconsul in Spain, asked Ligustinus to accompany him. He was then appointed chief centurion. His career was punctuated by glorious deeds. Thirty-four times he received personal rewards *virtutis causa* from the general; six times he was presented with the civic crown, awarded to soldiers who had saved the life of a fellow citizen on the field of battle.

With this impressive service record behind him, Ligustinus concluded that a man had no right to claim honours for himself other than the acknowledgement of his individual worth in the civil hierarchy. 'Of what rank the military tribunes think me worthy is for them to decide; I shall see to it that no one in the army surpasses me in bravery; that I have always done so, both my generals and those who have served with me are witnesses.'

He then turned to the centurions and advised them to submit to the decision of the tribunes since, he said, honour consisted in defending the republic. Honour and virtue were the values that Ligustinus respected. This supposed a state of permanent competition among soldiers, each man for himself and the dignity of each soldier subject to the relative assessment of all. Ligustinus' viewpoint was precisely that of the nobility. He therefore spoke to the assembly on his own behalf only and displayed no solidarity for the other centurions in their conflict with the military tribunes.

At first sight, the problem seemed to be an arithmetical one: how to find positions for twenty-three centurions when there were only two vacant posts. Ligustinus argued, however, that there was no such problem, because no one was ever appointed chief centurion for life. The only honour to which each of them could lay claim was to fight for the republic; everything else was a matter for the community to judge. No post had a guaranteed life tenure attached to it: each man's merits were always relative to those of his fellows and might be reassessed by any assembly of the people. The philosophy of rank was the same as electoral philosophy: the best man might win this time round, but next year the contest will start again from scratch. The glorious past of a particular individual granted him no more rights than the noble past of his family. Both might plead in his favour, but it was up to the people, through the censors and the military tribunes, to decide which rank he should occupy. There was no dishonour in not being a chief centurion if there was a better man to fill the post.

This speech, with its lack of demands, secured for Ligustinus the position of chief centurion *virtutis causa*. The other centurions admitted defeat and allowed the military tribunes to deploy them as they saw fit.

Spurius Ligustinus was the perfect picture of the peasant-soldier, as dreamt of by Cato, Ligustinus' general in Spain. His great fortune was to have reached manhood just as Rome had a pressing need for soldiers, for otherwise the low tax rating calculated on his single-*iugerum* plot would have kept him from entering military life. War enabled him to grow in *dignitas*. Enriched by war spoils, bathed in the glory of his valorous deeds, Ligustinus became a well-known figure, a man to whom one could give the floor at assemblies of the people.

Noble-mindedness was not confined to the higher classes. Through war, Ligustinus accomplished what the nobility achieved through politics. To fulfil its potential, his courage needed a broad scope and the regard of a general. War was the only way that the poor might reveal nobility of spirit; it put citizens to the test to see how they measured up.

OPULENT POVERTY

Last in this parade of 'poor' Romans comes the distinguished Cincinnatus, living proof that poverty was not in itself dishonourable. Men of noble descent who ruined themselves, provided it was done for a good cause, might yet retain their rank. It was, of course, vital that they hold on to the social network that glory had afforded them and that testified to their worthiness and furnished them with resources, *opes*, equivalent to the material riches they had lost. This situation is illustrated in the tale of Cincinnatus, the 'opulent' poor man.

Lucius Quinctius Cincinnatus, born of a distinguished patrician family, the Quinctii, had several sons. One of them, young Caeso, was a fiery supporter of the aristocratic party and always ready to engage in fisticuffs with the plebeians at the forum. This was the fifth century BC and struggles between the two parties were intense. Cincinnatus did not approve of his son's excesses but when Caeso was incriminated, no doubt falsely, for the murder of a young plebeian, and brought to trial, Cincinnatus stood surety for the enormous bail that was demanded by the court. Believing that the trial was unlikely to go his way, Caeso absconded to Etruria in order to avoid a capital sentence. Cincinnatus consequently had to reimburse those who had put up the bail money. Since the amount in question was roughly equivalent to a third of the senatorial tax rating, Cincinnatus sold the bulk of his property and retired to the other side of the Tiber to farm four acres (roughly one hectare).

None of this, however, prevented him from being elected consul in 459 BC, nor two years later from being called upon to become dictator – that is, to assume, for a short period, all civilian and military powers. A particularly serious situation had in fact developed that summer: the general who had been dispatched to lead an army against the Aequi had not been up to the task and, through cowardice, lack of *virtus*, had allowed himself and all his men to be completely surrounded by the enemy. The city therefore turned to Cincinnatus to save the army and Rome's honour.

The former consul was still scratching a meagre existence on the far side of the Tiber. The senate envoys found him hard at work, digging. Livy gives the following description of the scene, drawing on Roman imagery:

> What followed merits the attention of those who despise all human values in comparison with riches, and who think that great honours and worth are impossible without great wealth. The sole hope of the empire of the Roman people, Lucius Quinctius, cultivated a farm of some four acres on the other side of the Tiber, now known as the Quinctian meadows, directly opposite the place where the dockyards now are. There he was found by the representatives of the state. Whether bending over his spade as he dug a ditch, or ploughing, we do not know, but it is agreed, at all events, that he was intent upon some rustic task. After they had exchanged greetings with him, they asked him to put on his toga, to hear the mandate of the senate and expressed the wish that good might come of it to himself and the republic. In amazement he cried, 'Is all well?' and bade his wife Racilia to hurry and fetch his toga from the cottage. Then, after wiping off the dust and sweat, he put it on and came forth to the envoys. They hailed him as dictator, congratulated him, and summoned him to the city, explaining the army's alarming situation. A boat was waiting for him, provided by the state. When he reached the other side he was greeted by his three sons, who had come out to meet him, followed by other kinsmen and friends, and by most of the senate. Attended by this throng and preceded by his lictors he was escorted to his house. A great crowd of plebeians also collected, not at all overjoyed to see Cincinnatus' selection, because they thought that not only was the office too powerful, but the man was more dangerous than the office. That night nothing more was done than to post a watch in the city.[19]

Cincinnatus had become poor, but he had kept the minimum amount of possessions needed to maintain his patrician status. This enabled him to go through the various social rituals that in Rome were the essential counterpart of his political advancement. Livy's account invites readings on two different registers, private and public. The city had appointed Cincinnatus dictator; the decision was a public one and needed to become a social reality. This would be effected in a number of stages. First, the meeting with the senate envoys. Cincinnatus was in a position to receive them because he possessed that essential civic minimum, a minimum of worthiness: a wife to serve him; a plot of land to feed him; a toga in which to clothe himself as a citizen; and a house in Rome. The exchange of greetings between Cincinnatus and the envoys complied with protocol. They greeted him first, as visitors entering the property of a land-owner to whom they had to justify their intrusion. Cincinnatus' greeting acknowledged the visitors as representatives of the city, and this enabled them to give him an order: to go and put on his toga. Cincinnatus must not hear the will of the senate as a private individual, a poor ploughman, but as a citizen, in this case as a citizen of senatorial rank. For it was not the ploughman who was to be made dictator but the former consul. Properly attired, Cincinnatus returned to meet his visitors. The envoys' second greeting had a performative value: they created him dictator by greeting him as such. From that moment on Cincinnatus was dictator and would be treated accordingly.

As soon as he landed on the Roman bank of the Tiber, it was clear that the social network around Cincinnatus had remained intact. The procession that conducted him to his home included both public officials and private individuals. Leading the way, the twenty-four lictors, with their *fasces*, surmounted by the axe,* provided an impressive image of his dictatorial powers. But it would have been inconceivable for Cincinnatus to proceed with only the lictors as his escort. That would have presented the spectacle of an isolated tyrant. Those accompanying him in a personal capacity – his sons, his relatives, his friends, the senators – all represented Cincinnatus' social dimension, providing civilian backing for the public decision. They embodied his *dignitas*, his rank in the city, thereby justifying the senate's choice. The crowd that accompanied Cincinnatus was in Rome the essential auxiliary of every politician, just as much a part of his resources as were material riches. This crowd was the visible embodiment of Cincinnatus' civic value, his political weight, his *virtus*. Yet it was not consensus: the massed plebeians, attentively watching the procession, displayed neutrality, torn between dread of the Aequi and fear of dictatorship. But Livy suggests that in the end the plebeians placed their faith in Cincinnatus, for the city slept soundly that night, everyone relying on the dictator to save the Roman army.

Cincinnatus freed the Roman camp, crushed the Aequi and, to avenge the humiliation that Rome had suffered, forced them to pass under a yoke made of three spears, to signify their defeat. He demoted the weak general, appointing him his lieutenant, thereby placing the entire Roman army directly under his own orders. A twofold glory awaited him, part private, part public, each complementing the other, swathing him in social and political consensus. The ex-general's

---

* The *fasces* was a bundle of rods bound together, which was carried on their shoulders by lictors before important Roman magistrates as a symbol of their power. Under the republic only dictators were allowed to include the axe in the *fasces*.

soldiers, most of whom were plebeians (since nobles served in the cavalry), whom he had liberated, albeit while degrading their general, showed which side they were on by presenting Cincinnatus with a gold crown weighing one pound. And at his departure they addressed him as *patronus*, protector. They acknowledged that Cincinnatus had been a second father to them, and that they were bound to him by a personal obligation. They had become his clients, thereby extending his social range to include a legion of young men who would thereafter be ready to demonstrate in the street, follow him to the forum to support his candidature for public office, or crowd around the law courts on days when he was to plead a case. He would only have to lift a finger to have his son Caeso cleared.

Cincinnatus' triumph was official: 'At Rome,' wrote Livy,

> the senate being convened by Quintus Fabius, the prefect of the city, commanded Quinctius to enter the gates in triumph, with the troops that accompanied him. Before his chariot were led the generals of the enemy; the military standards were borne on ahead; after them came the soldiers, laden with booty. It is said that tables were spread before all the houses, and the troops, feasting as they marched, with songs of triumph and the customary jokes, followed the chariot like revellers.

Cincinnatus had made as much of a success of his dictatorship as any noble in possession of his entire estate. He had provided a treat for the people of Rome, filled the public coffers and gained a sizable clientele for himself. He could retire and, as was fitting, abdicate the dictatorship, now that the circumstances that had necessitated his appointment to such exceptional office had vanished. But first he made use of his newly won credit to settle a personal score: he had his son's accuser convicted of perjury.

Poverty clearly did not rule out opulence.

LANDLESS POVERTY

For the poor peasantry everything was fine as long as they held on to their land and that minimal social standing, those minimal resources, that enabled them to remain citizens, both in the eyes of the tax authorities and in terms of their ability to respond to demands that the city might make on them. But tragedy struck when a peasant lost his land. This might have happened as a result of enemy incursions, or debts contracted to allow him to pay his taxes or buy new seed or ploughshares. Or, after the reform of Marius, because the system of geometrical equality was no longer respected and the poorest peasants were dispatched for lengthy periods to fight wars in far-flung regions. Their farms in this case might not be pillaged by the enemy, but if in their absence their land was ill-managed or stolen by dishonest neighbours, the end result was the same. If, from the third century BC onward, poor peasants could no longer be sold as slaves by their creditors, ruined peasants could still be forced to sell themselves as gladiators, or to sell or desert children whom they could no longer feed. Whatever path they chose would lead to poverty and ruin. To a peasant, the loss of his land spelled the loss of his house, his family, his household gods, the tombs of his ancestors, and his dignity as a citizen-soldier.

This is why Roman history is continually haunted by the land question as it related to debt cancellation. In every period, plebeians could be heard crying out for land, and the forum would fill with hordes of dispossessed and grief-stricken peasants proclaiming their despair. In the second century BC, Tiberius Gracchus, whose political career was founded on his patronage of these plebeians, spoke on their behalf as follows:

> The wild beasts that roam over Italy have, every one of them, a cave or lair to shelter in; but the men who fight and die for Italy enjoy only the light and air that is common to all above their heads; having neither house nor any kind of home they must wander about with their wives and children. It is with lying tongues that their imperators exhort soldiers in battle to defend sepulchres and shrines from the enemy, for not a man of them has a hereditary altar; not one of all these many Romans has an ancestral tomb, yet they fight and die to maintain others in wealth and luxury. Though they are styled masters of the world, they have not a single clod of earth to call their own.[20]

To recover their dignity as men and as citizens, the plebeians demanded that the authorities allocate them plots of public land (*ager publicus*), land in those territories seized from the enemy that now belonged to the Roman people. The poorest and the richest citizens argued over such land. Was it to be sold to the state's creditors – swapped for debts – or should it be handed over free of charge to landless plebeians? The Roman state had paid off its debts with land after the Second Punic War, abandoning all public land situated up to fifty Roman miles (roughly seventy-five kilometres) from Rome. A few years later, however, this policy was reversed and under the laws of the Gracchi colonies began to be set up, in order to provide the plebeians with land. The first of these was Carthage.

A man without land could not become a soldier and could not therefore demonstrate his valour: a hunger for land therefore meant a hunger for honour.

POVERTY AND AGRICULTURE

The poverty of the peasantry was thus structurally necessary and profoundly civilized. It was defined not as a natural but as a cultural minimum. Such poverty could not be dissociated from a conception of man as a civic being. It also related to the way that the Romans thought about land cultivation. In their view, the best possible relationship that a man could have with the soil was that enjoyed by the ploughman. In Latin he was termed *colonus*, an occupant-farmer, indicating that his work on the land was one of numerous activities that contributed to cultivated life. The Latin verb *colo*, from which the English word 'culture' ultimately derives, covers all these activities: religious cults; the setting-up of a fixed dwelling; the care taken of one's body; the education of the mind; the art of cookery (if one follows the ancients' etymology of *culina*, kitchen, which, though no doubt mistaken, none the less indicates the kinship that they felt existed between *colo* and *culina*); and lastly, agriculture. Peasants who observed both technical and ritual farming procedures – of which the legitimacy and hence the efficacy was guaranteed by the gods – experienced their labour as a way of taking cultural possession of the soil. Romans even argued that arable farming was a form of religious observance.

This contrasted with livestock-breeding, a slavish activity which involved no real rapport between man and soil. Herd-driving was a nomadic practice that left both the land and the herdsman uncultivated. The term *prata*, meaning land intended for livestock-breeding, was also used to denote patches of waste ground, areas covered by religious interdicts where neither construction nor cultivation were permitted. Tiberius Gracchus claimed that one of the reasons he wished to parcel out public land was that he had seen how the vast stretches of land taken from the Etruscans had been left fallow and used as grazing for large herds driven by foreign slaves, barbarians belonging to patricians. Conquered lands had simply been abandoned to stockbreeding.

Traditionally, any man who failed to cultivate his land was publicly disgraced by the censor: 'It anyone had allowed his land to run to waste and was not giving it sufficient attention, if he had neither ploughed nor weeded it, or if anyone had neglected his orchard or vineyard, such conduct did not go unpunished, but was taken up by the censors, who reduced such a man to the lowest class of citizens.'[21] The terms employed to describe uncultivated fields were the same ones that were used to speak of a man who was slovenly, a man devoid of his dignity as a civilized being.

In the Roman mind, poverty, culture and agriculture were inseparable. Anything produced by the soil, at least by Roman soil, was of scant market value and its consumption was always therefore blameless. This is why sumptuary laws, designed to curb luxury, always exempted from their restrictions anything grown on Italian soil. Life in the country remained a moral ideal until the end of the republic. The good life was rooted in a rural smallholding that one managed oneself (or with the help of a steward) and from which one could obtain the bulk of one's food. 'This is what I prayed for! A piece of land not so very large, where there would be a garden, and near the house a spring of ever-flowing water, and up above these a bit of woodland.'[22]

SACRIFICE AND WEALTH

If peasants had known only the poverty of self-sufficiency, each confined to his own plot of land, with politics and war as the only unifying principles, Roman society would have shattered into an infinity of rural microsocieties, cut off from the town, held together by state centralism. From time to time the call of duty would have brought the heads of families and their adult sons to Rome, but the city would have been austere indeed, and perhaps hardly viable if this had been the only reason for people to visit it. In fact, the civic community had other reasons to come together: Roman unity was expressed in festivities on a scale befitting the dimensions of the city, celebrated at its geographical heart, in Rome itself. The city in its broadest sense would turn out: men, women and children would flock into town for orgies of feasting and music and mingling with the crowds. These entertainments were given by the rich and provided the *raison d'être* for their wealth.

In Rome the notion of the feast was inseparable from that of sacrifice. Sacrifice entailed, among other things, the collective consumption of food, and the association of a human community with one or more deities. The food served at sacrificial banquets was out of the ordinary. Animals were slaughtered on the altars and then eaten, and wine was drunk, while libations were made to the gods. The larger the community that was engaged in the sacrifice, the bigger and better were the sacrificial animals. At household sacrifices a piglet or kid would be offered, but civic sacrifices were more splendid, and there would generally be three larger victims: a bull, a sheep and a pig.

From an economic standpoint, Romans viewed sacrifice as a loss of revenue. No miser would ever make a sacrifice, because it meant wastage. The fruits of the earth could be eaten without depleting one's stock, but to eat the animals in one's herd or flock was to reduce their number; keeping them alive would lead to the herd's automatic increase. Unlike land, a herd was unstable: through natural reproduction and sacrificial consumption, it was forever growing and shrinking

Romans insisted on the kinship that, in their opinion, linked the words for livestock, *pecus*, and money, *pecunia*, thereby revealing that they thought of money and livestock in the same terms: things that brought in revenue and that could be spent.

'Money too,' as Pliny the Elder wrote,

> received its name of 'pecunia' from 'pecus', 'cattle'. Even today, in the registers of the censors, we find set down under the term of 'pascua' or 'pasture lands' everything from which the public revenues are derived, from the fact that for a long period of time pasture lands were the only source of public revenue. Fines, too, were only imposed in the shape of paying so many sheep or so many oxen.[23]

Indeed, the earliest Roman coins were said to have borne the image of a bullock's or sheep's head.

So to make money in Rome, one needed to go in for livestock rather than arable farming. At the same time, livestock was directly invested in feasts or exchanged for other luxury goods, with or without the mediation of money. Only nobility and the wealthy were involved in rearing large herds, and they employed slaves to act as herdsmen. For grazing land they took over large spaces 'borrowed' from the *ager publicus*, the kinds of extensive and desolate areas that had made such an impression on Tiberius Gracchus. There were, of course, other ways to get rich: usury, for instance. But livestock-rearing remained the cultural model. Until the days of the empire, the nobility kept thousands of hectares fallow for their immense herds to roam about in. Even Cato the Elder, whose treatise *On Agriculture* aimed to show how land could be cultivated for maximum profit, acknowledged that livestock-rearing was by far the best way to get rich. 'When Cato was asked, "What was the best policy in the management of one's property," he answered, "Good grazing." "What was next?" "Tolerable grazing." "What third?" "Bad grazing." "What fourth?" "Tilling." '[24]

Roman culture associated livestock with wealth and public feasting. The consumption of surplus produce reinforced social cohesion, as long as this consumption formed part of a collective ritual. Avarice, like solitary consumption, disrupted social cohesion and diverted wealth away from its proper function. To maintain social cohesion the city needed both rich and poor and plenty of livestock to consume at feasts.

SPECTACULAR WEALTH

The rich gave generously, as was their duty. In reward they gained public recognition. Should they fail to shower largesse, public opinion would drag them through the mud and call them misers. As we have seen, in Rome this term spelled social disgrace.

Generals returning at the end of a campaign, heads of families at the funeral of a family member or, simply, the magistrate responsible for games, would spend more money (including public money) on such feasts, triumphs and games than a small farmer could save in a thousand years.

On such days, there was too much of everything. The waste was wilful and wanton: when people could gorge themselves no more, whole sides of meat as yet untouched would be heaved into the Tiber. The entire populace, all classes jumbled together, would delight both in the favour of the gods and in the opulence flowing from the wealth of the nobility and from the spoils of war, two sources of happiness that were often hard to distinguish. The fecundity of the nobles' livestock and their good fortune on the battlefield bore the same name, *felicitas*; and whether they were the spoils of war or had been reared in herds on public land, the succulent meats that ended up in Roman stomachs had always been properly fattened. At their feasts, Romans staggered under delicacies, experiencing divine bounty at first hand in the streets of their own city. It was proof that the austerity of the Romans' everyday lives was not a matter of shortages, or lack of necessities, but rather their view of the proper way to live. It would not do for every day to be like a feast day, spent in wasteful idleness, or in what the Romans called *luxuria*. That would soon lead to shortages and dire poverty. Hence the continual denunciation in Rome of the inroads made into the daily lives of the nobility, or even the urban plebeians, by *luxuria* – a vice as worrying as avarice. Those who ruined themselves in this way were condemned as dishonourable by the censors, driven from their order and heaped with public contempt. Such people, it was said, were destroyed by their *gula* (literally, gullet) – that is, by their sensuality.

City-wide feasts were more than mere rituals of consumption; they were spectacular entertainments that the community organized for itself and that gave expression to its social cohesion. Each large-scale feast was preceded by a procession through the town. The people watched themselves stream past, or rather watched their youth and their constituent bodies, *senatus populusque romanus*, on parade, along with all that their hearts could desire: livestock to be sacrificed; drivers with their carts; actors and dancers; musicians. If a triumph was being celebrated, the people would stand and gaze as the spoils of war passed before their eyes. And spoils were precisely the surplus that everyday labour could never hope to create. Triumphs celebrated wars not only as instruments of individual glory, but also as a source of collective riches. War was not economically essential to Rome, but it was culturally essential since the surplus that it brought into Rome was itself necessary not only to furnish collective festivities but also to maintain the city's level of expenditure, to finance the construction of public monuments, the upkeep of the temples, the building of roads and to pay for public sacrifices; it was essential, in other words, to the *res publica*, the precise meaning of which might be rendered by 'public property'. Taxation, which disappeared in any case in the second century BC, was quite unable to cover such expenses.

War contributed to public wealth and it seemed natural to the nobility, who were in a way the depositories of collective wealth, that they should have the lion's share: just as it seemed perfectly natural to them to use public land for rearing herds of animals destined for feasts.

The best surviving account of a triumph is that of Aemilius Paullus over Perseus, the last king of Macedonia, in 167 BC.[25] Thanks to this victory Romans never again paid taxes. The splendour of the triumph signalled to everyone that Rome had vanquished Alexander's successor, that the eastern Mediterranean was now, like the western Mediterranean, subject to Rome, and that the riches of the eastern kings would now flow into the hands of the people of Rome.

The people erected structures in the circuses, where equestrian contests are held, and round the forum, occupied the other parts of the city that afforded a view of the procession, and watched the spectacle arrayed in white garments. Every temple was open and filled with garlands and incense, while numerous servitors and lictors restrained the thronging and scurrying crowds and kept the streets open and clear.

The victory procession lasted three days.

The first day barely sufficed for the exhibition of the captured statues, paintings and colossal figures, which were carried on 250 chariots. On the second, the finest and richest of the Macedonian arms were borne along in many wagons. The arms themselves glittered with freshly polished bronze and steel, and were carefully and artfully arranged to look exactly as though they had been piled together in random heaps, helmets lying upon shields and breast-plates upon greaves, while Cretan targets and Thracian wicker shields and quivers were mixed up with horses' bridles, and through them projected naked swords and long Macedonian spears planted among them, all the arms being so loosely packed that they smote against each other as they were borne along and produced a harsh and dreadful sound, and the sight of them, even though they were spoils of a conquered enemy, was not without its terrors.

The triumph was a spectacle constructed and calculated to arouse contrasting but mutually reinforcing emotions. The terrifying clamour of weapons, echoed in the military music, brought home to the Romans the dangers that their soldiers had faced and made those hearing it feel as though they had been personally delivered from Macedonian violence. Added to the happiness of victory was the euphoria of having been released from anxiety.

After the wagons laden with armour there followed 3,000 men carrying silver coins in 750 fifty vessels, each of which contained three talents and was borne by four men, while still more men carried dishes of silver, drinking horns, bowls and cups, all well arranged for show and excelling all others in size and in the depth of their carved ornaments. On the third day, as soon as it was morning, trumpeters led the way, sounding out . . . such a strain as the Romans use to rouse themselves to battle. After these there were led along 120 stall-fed oxen with gilded horns, bedecked with fillets and garlands . . . After these came those carrying golden coins, which, like the silver, were portioned out into vessels containing three talents; there were 77 of these vessels. After these followed the bearers of the consecrated bowl, which

Aemilius had had made of ten talents of gold and adorned with
precious stones, and then those who displayed the bowls known as
Antigonids and Seleucids and Theracleian, together with all the gold
plate of Perseus' table.

All such fine tableware, mainly consisting of drinking vessels
captured from the Macedonian kings, was, like the oxen led to the
sacrifice, a foretaste of the feasting to come. In its triumph over a
king, Rome would drink and eat as befitted a king.

These were followed by the chariot of Perseus, which bore his arms,
and his diadem above them. Then, after a short interval, came the
children of the king, two boys and one girl, led along as slaves; with
them came a throng of foster-parents, teachers and tutors, all in tears,
stretching out their own hands to the spectators and teaching the
children to beg and supplicate. The children were too young to grasp
the fate that had befallen them, and the thought of their future sorrows
evoked great pity in the Romans. Perseus walked along almost
unheeded, while the people, moved by compassion, kept their eyes
upon the children, many of them shedding tears, and for all of them the
pleasure of the spectacle was mingled with pain, until the children had
passed by.

Here one can glimpse Roman *humanitas*, as the people shed tears
for the misfortunes of the enemy and were temporarily disarmed by
their sorry fate. Such tears, however, made no difference to the fate of
the vanquished, who would still have to live down their defeat.
Besides, the tears of Roman *humanitas* were inspired less by the
misfortune of individuals than by the general sadness of the human
condition. The Roman people, in their display of compassion,
showed that victory had not gone to their heads, that they remained
fully aware of the vicissitudes of the human condition of which they
partook.

Behind the children and their train of attendants walked Perseus
himself, clad in a dark robe and wearing the high boots of his country.
He appeared to be utterly dumbfounded and bewildered by his ill
fortune . . . Perseus had sent word to Aemilius begging not to be led in
the procession and asking to be left out of the triumph. But Aemilius,
apparently in mockery of the king's cowardice and love of life, had said
that Perseus himself had had the power to grant his own request, and
'still had it, if he should wish it,' signifying that he should have chosen
death in preference to disgrace. For this, however, the coward had not

the heart, but was made weak by who knows what hopes, and became a part of his own spoils.

Perseus was no child and inspired no pity. His presence at the triumph was a mark of his cowardice: he had preferred to live as a slave than die as a king. But this was hardly surprising in a Macedonian prince who, to Roman eyes, was nothing but an Oriental barbarian.

Aemilius Paullus made his appearance at last. The sight of his victory procession had struck all the right emotional chords: the Roman spectators could now gaze on the begetters of such glory and such woe.

Next, mounted on a magnificently adorned chariot, came Aemilius himself, a man worthy to be looked upon even without such marks of power, wearing a purple robe interwoven with gold, and holding forth in his right hand a spray of laurel. The whole army also carried sprays of laurel, following the chariot of their general by companies and divisions, and singing comic songs, as the ancient custom was, and others paeans of victory and hymns in praise of the achievements of Aemilius.

King Perseus was banished to Alba where he died. Only then did Rome show him any *humanitas*. The senate dispatched a quaestor (a magistrate responsible for financial affairs) to Alba to bury the former king at state expense. Rome wanted to grant Perseus' remains this last honour and to spare him the humiliation of a pauper's burial.[26]

THE SCRAMBLE FOR RICHES

Triumphs were feasts of an exceptional kind. But private and public games were held every year, supplied by wars and the spoils of war. The Romans sought more from war than the heady but fleeting enjoyment of proving themselves the better fighters. Victory had to be final; plunder was not enough. Rome's policy of annexation and conquest turned enemy peoples into perpetually vanquished tribute-payers, at least until they gained the right to Roman citizenship. This had a certain legitimacy: the Romans regarded submission as something entirely voluntary. War was waged until either victory or death ensued, and the Romans therefore felt entitled to bring pressure to bear on slave populations. The Romans believed that regular feasting confirmed their status as world conquerors and provided them with the opportunity to enjoy their conquests. Spoils were luxury and luxury was spoils. The people became accustomed to festive wealth and demanded more and more.

While the conditions of the poor remained unchanged, the number and opulence of Roman feasts increased the more Rome extended its empire. On embarking upon a political career, therefore, the wealthy had to spend more and more just to keep up with their predecessors and rivals. This continual one-upmanship had perverse effects. The nobility contracted debts at the outset of their political lives and when at last, towards the end of their careers, they obtained a province, they would burden their Gallic, Spanish or Sicilian subjects with crushing taxes, and use any border incident as an excuse to pillage foreign towns and so pay off their debts. What other reason had Caesar, when he was proconsul of the Gauls, to wage war against a handful of miserable Helvetians who were merely trying to escape from their native Switzerland where life was much too hard for them?

The wealthy soon embarked upon a non-stop quest for funds, and to save their honour would stoop to any dishonourable expedient they thought necessary. After Rome's initial territorial conquests, they merely set their herds to graze on public land. But they soon turned to usury, trade, shady deals and even outright swindling. Two illustrious and contradictory figures – Crassus, a man devoid of scruples, and Cato the Elder, a paragon of virtue – demonstrate that the Roman nobility's search for money was liable to become a desperate duty beyond the reach of good and evil.

Marcus Licinius Crassus, born into a noble family in the first century BC, was none the less born poor, in the Roman sense: his family's small house was equipped with only one dining-room. From his childhood he had sober tastes and kept regular habits. But his political ambition demanded means, and he would do anything to get money: he bought up the property of people outlawed in Sulla's time; tricked women into letting him have their land at less than its value; extracted money from people whom he had helped by intervening in the senate; harboured criminals for a consideration; pressurized allies in the provinces; and even developed an ingenious form of protection racket. Rome at that time was plagued by fires, and had no public fire-fighting service. Crassus paid arsonists to set fire discreetly to houses that interested him, while he waited round the corner with a team of firemen. As soon as the owner arrived on the scene, Crassus would offer to put out the fire, on condition that the owner agreed to sell him the building. If the owner refused, Crassus would prevent the fire from being extinguished while his firemen held onlookers at bay.

The more damage the fire did, the lower Crassus would drop his price. It was therefore in the owner's interest to give in as soon as possible. Crassus demolished the burnt-out shells, replacing them with low-cost buildings that he then rented out floor by floor to Roman plebeians.

He became notorious for his greed and avarice, yet Crassus' true passion was honour not money. When he finally gained control over the province of Asia, he was so intoxicated with joy that he set off at once despite dire omens announcing his death and oblivious to the curses hurled at him by a people's tribune at the Capena gate.[27]

It might be imagined that no one could be more unlike Crassus than Cato the Elder, the austere censor. Born poor – that is, without the means to engage in politics – he too turned to questionable methods to amass a fortune. As a young man he tried his hand at agriculture, but soon realized that even using rational land usage methods and employing skilled farmers it was not a profitable business. He then turned to industry, purchasing some ponds, some hot springs and some plots of land on which to build laundries. He also set up some pitch factories. Above all he practised usury, although senators were barred from so doing, by lending money to merchant ship-owners. He gathered together fifty businessmen and persuaded them to found a company to commission fifty vessels. Using his freedman Quintio as front-man, Cato himself took a share in the company capital, thereby spreading the risks across all the ships. He also carried on business with his servants. He lent them money to buy slaves whom he then had trained at his own house for a year before they were resold. Cato would thus recover the price of the slaves while keeping a few for himself as 'interest'.[28]

Towards the end of the republic it became harder and harder to be wealthy, as it demanded ever more colossal fortunes. The nobles – even those who could rely on vast networks of clients – thought of nothing but how to get money. Feasts devoured everything. It was becoming impossible to maintain one's position. In some years no one could be found to stand for election to the post of aedile, for whoever took on the job was expected to organize games that had now to feature not only the traditional horses and floats but lions, elephants, theatres decorated with ivory and gold, star actors, and floating displays. There were few who could afford to throw parties on such a scale.

3

Slaves and freedmen

WHAT SLAVES WERE FOR

One cannot talk about Roman citizens without mentioning their slaves, though not for the reasons generally given. Slaves were not an economic necessity, enabling Roman citizens to engage in politics by freeing them from work. Roman civilization was a society of plenty not of penury. As we have seen, Roman peasants and townspeople worked without undue strain and the small size of farms meant that working days were not over-long, either for the master or for his slaves. Rome was a leisured society and for the majority of its citizens those few mornings taken up with assemblies paled in comparison to the amount of time devoted to feasts or to gossiping in the public square. Because they knew how to be poor, Romans had a wealth of time. The only people who grumbled that they had not a second for themselves were busy politicians like Philippus who constantly dashed from his home to the senate and back home again, while the poor town crier lounged in the shade.

Slaves were, of course, to be found hard at work everywhere in Rome – in the countryside and in town; in the fields; in the houses; in the shops; and in every corner of state administration – but neither to a greater nor lesser degree than freedmen or citizens. Except in the army and in political positions, wherever slaves were employed citizens were at work also. Slaves, freedmen and citizens all belonged to the same professional associations, without any distinction on the grounds of status. Although degrading or demeaning jobs, such as collecting rubbish, turning grindstones, working in the mines, acting in the theatre or prostitution, were generally earmarked for slaves, they were not reserved exclusively for them. Often such jobs were very lucrative, as in the case of acting or rubbish collection, and freedmen might not turn their noses up at them. It was, in fact, only to safeguard their honour that citizens avoided such work.

Slaves did not therefore form a labouring class or a pariah caste or even a pool of cheap labour that, as Aristotle had argued, could be used as 'living tools'. Many enjoyed considerable wealth, and occupied key positions in the economy or in the administration. Slaves might be bankers, managers of estates or high-ranking government officials; they might hold sway over other slaves, semi-skilled workers, scribes, bookkeepers, archivists, farmers, and so on.

Slaves were defined by their legal status: like movable goods, they were objects of property, whereas men, *homini*, were free subjects. In Roman society, women, children and freedmen also had a dependent if quite distinct status, even though legally they were free.

Historians have spent too long hunting for the hidden reason behind the existence of slavery in Rome. Rather than rehearse the traditional view that the Romans required a cheap workforce to run the economy and that all the Latin disquisitions on servitude and freedom were mere smokescreens designed to hide an economic infrastructure, let us take a look at what the inhabitants of Rome actually felt and said. The Romans bore no guilt for keeping slaves and therefore had no reason to attempt to disguise the truth. When a Roman states that a slave has a servile spirit, we should take him at his word while seeking to reconstruct the moral environment to which such an assertion belongs. In Roman eyes a slave that cleaves to his master throughout the latter's life, who only acts on command and who is a mere extension to the citizen's body, although certainly a man, is a man bereft of moral independence; he is cut off from his past and his will is broken. We can see that a slave, therefore, is a man with no *animus*.

SLAVES AS DOUBLES

Unless poverty-stricken, every free man owned at least one slave, the daily companion of his life. A house, a field, a slave: such were the possessions of even the poorest peasant as imagined by Virgil in *Moretum*. Romans of good family were brought up by slave nurses, and as children played with slaves of their own age. An old servant watched over them day and night. Their teachers and their coaches for rhetoric and fencing, their first loves and last helpers, were all slaves. Their warmest loyalties were to their secretary and equerry. Yet one cannot speak of friendship in the term's ancient sense, as this presupposes equality and the liberty of both friends.

Slaves were not confined to Roman houses like worker bees to a hive, forever cooking, sewing, washing, carrying letters, bearing torches, but as invisible as the fixtures. Rather they formed a permanent human presence, a warm environment that the Romans found indispensable. A special sentiment that was neither friendship nor love but a sort of grateful compassion bound citizens to their slaves. This is borne out by the numerous funerary inscriptions expressing a master or mistress's regret and sadness over the loss of an old and devoted servant or a child of the house.

Hounded, fugitive, left to die of thirst in the middle of a desert, a Roman's slave would be on hand to carry out his last requests, and to kill him if commanded so to do. *Statius*, 'he who waits', was a common nickname for slaves and accurately defines the life of a slave spent at the beck and call of his master. The Romans were appalled by the prospect of ending their lives totally alone, in an empty house that resounded with soldiers' steps, and without a slave to come between the master and the assassins' knife, to help him commit suicide. A man without a slave was as naked as a soldier without a weapon.

But slaves never left their masters; they were their shadows, their doubles. This was how both slaves and masters saw the situation. A slave had a sole *raison d'être*, a sole source of social recognition: the bond that tied him to his master; a single virtue was open to him: loyalty. Roman memoirs are full of edifying accounts of slaves who remained faithful to their masters in times of trouble. Reading them makes it quite apparent that such loyalty was founded on an identification with the master.

'To avoid falling into the hands of his enemies, Gaius Gracchus ordered his slave Philocrates to take his life. Having done so, with one stroke of his sword, Philocrates then plunged the weapon, still dripping with his master's blood, into his own heart.'[29] Nothing impelled Philocrates to kill himself after taking his master's life, except that if there was no room on earth for his master, Philocrates would judge that there was none for him either.

The story of Urbinus Panopio and his slave is yet more revealing of such faithfulness and identification. For in this instance the slave actually took the place of his master and through death attained the only glory to which a slave might aspire: that of linking his memory to his master's salvation.

> Urbinus Panopio was proscribed; his servitors had denounced him to soldiers who were coming to his villa in Reate to kill him. Hearing of what was afoot, Urbinus' slave immediately changed clothes with his master, even placing his master's ring on his own finger. He then ushered his master out of the house by a side door and withdrew into Urbinus' bedroom, where he lay on the bed and let himself be mistaken for Panopio and killed.
>
> It does not take many words to outline the bare facts of what happened, but what a wonderful subject for an orator the story makes! One can just imagine the soldiers rushing in, breaking down the doors, shouting threats, then bursting into the bedroom, their faces distorted by hatred, their weapons flashing. Imagining the horror of the scene gives some idea of the slave's character. Dying in someone else's place is easy enough to talk about, but not so easy to do.
>
> To acknowledge his debt to his slave, Panopio dedicated to him a large tomb, bearing an inscription in praise of his devotion.[30]

When citizens were banished from the city, the personal loyalties of friends, relatives and slaves were put to the test. Panopio's story clearly illustrates the two possible and contrasting attitudes that slaves might adopt towards their masters. Slaves never left their masters' sides and knew all there was to know about them. Either they turned them over to their enemies, or they abetted their flight: betrayal or loyalty. When they betrayed their masters, it was generally out of self-interest, to secure a reward or to get a chance to pillage the house, cupidity being a slave's passion. But slaves would never betray their masters for political reasons or sacrifice their personal ties on the altar of superior state interests. Slaves were incapable of the independent moral judgement characteristic of free men: if there was one thing that slaves could not fathom it was the nature of the state. They were involved only in vertical relations and personal ties, having no inkling of either Roman patriotism or solidarity with other slaves. The only social bond known to them was with their masters, and thus their only moral imperative consisted – as it did for citizens – in being true to themselves, the slaves of their masters.

An occurrence that took place during the course of the Second Punic War provides an illustration of what one might term 'Sempronius, or a slave's limits'.

Following the massacre at Cannae in 216 BC at the hands of the Carthaginians, Rome was short of soldiers, even after calling up the last centuries of the lowest class. It was decided to enlist slaves.[31] The state accordingly purchased 8,000 slaves, after asking them if they were willing to serve in the army. Rome sought their consent – seemingly an odd way to deal with slaves – because of the conviction, shared with the Greeks, that only armies that were free could win battles. Roman soldiers did not fight because they had to obey their generals; rather they fought because they chose to obey them. Military discipline did not involve submission, and the power of a general over his soldiers was not that of a master over his slaves. Roman soldiers were bound to their generals by an oath that they took as soldiers and not as individuals and from which they were freed at the end of a campaign. It was only Oriental kings who drove their armies forward under the lash, and it was for that very reason that their vast expeditions could so easily be routed by a handful of free men.

The Roman state therefore armed its slave-soldiers, surrounded them with free men and placed Tiberius Sempronius Gracchus, the grandfather of the Gracchus family, at their head. The result was a valorous army that faithfully followed its general. After a two-week campaign in 214 BC, at the battle of Beneventum, their courage won them their freedom.[32] But psychologically and morally, these freedmen were still slaves and continued to do battle not for the republic but for the general whose name they thenceforth bore. The following year, on Gracchus' death, the Sempronians no longer felt bound by oath to the military and so deserted. The Roman state had them traced and they were re-enlisted, but care was taken to avoid punishing them, in the belief that former slaves could hardly be expected to understand that freedom from slavery entailed loyalty to one's city.

Masters responded with compassion to the loyalty displayed by their slaves. Both qualities were revealed in situations of crisis, such as banishment, which provides the background to the following story.

Gnaeus Plotius Plancus, of senatorial family, had been outlawed by the triumvirs, and was in hiding near Salernum. He was no politician, more of a sensualist, and his luxurious habits, the purchases made on his behalf and the style of living enjoyed in his home, betrayed him. His slaves were cruelly tortured to make them reveal his hiding-place, but they refused to talk. Plancus, however, unable to endure the sufferings inflicted on his slaves, gave himself up and bared his neck for the soldiers.[33]

Plancus accepted death out of pity, *misericordia*, the effect of his *humanitas* towards his slaves. But the sensitivity that he displayed was also a sign of weakness and betokened a somewhat effeminate man, a man of pleasure who valued private life and domestic attachments above civic duties. He balked at the suffering of his slaves' bodies as he would have balked at the suffering of his own. Plancus' voluntary death was quite unlike Cato's suicide at Utica: there was nothing glorious about it. Like all family relations, those with one's slaves often clashed with political duties. The Romans admired those who put their city before their home.

The torturing of slaves to obtain trial evidence against their masters would scandalize modern sensibilities but was a logical consequence of the position of slaves in Roman society. As witnesses to the deeds and actions of citizens, slaves knew everything that went on in Rome, but at the same time were totally dependent on their masters and would only speak at their command. Interrogating slaves about their masters was like asking the masters to incriminate themselves. Torture could free slaves from submission to their masters by enslaving them to their own bodies. They would then speak not to obey their master but to obey the dictates of pain. Slaves, as we have seen, had no *animus*, were devoid of moral autonomy, and if they were no longer guided by their masters' will then they could be led only by their sensuality and natural instincts, *impulsus*. And as everyone in Rome knew perfectly well, men instinctively sought to escape pain. Only culture, moral education and strength of spirit enabled men to resist their instincts. That was why it would be pointless to torture a citizen.

However, loyalty to the master was sometimes stronger than fear and pain, as strong as the free man's passion for honour.

Mark Antony, the famous orator, had been accused of adultery. During the preliminary enquiry, his accusers insisted on interrogating one of his slaves under torture because, they said, he had often accompanied Mark Antony and at night had carried the lantern for him, when Antony went to one of his amorous assignations. The slave, who was still a child, had come with his master to the hearing and heard the debate and understood that he might be tortured. He made no attempt to escape, however, and when they got back home he told Antony, who was much tormented by the scandal, that he should hand him over to the judges so that they might question him, assuring Antony that no word would pass his lips to damage his master's case . . . He kept his promise and his resistance to pain proved extraordinary. Whipped mercilessly, placed on the rack, burned with red-hot irons, he said not a word, thereby ruining what the accusers hoped would be their prime piece of evidence against Antony.[34]

The purpose of slaves, quite simply, was to be there. Liberty was inconceivable without servitude. The world was as it was because of the existence of both life and death, day and night, land and sea, peace and war, free men and slaves.

Slaves were human, but they were the lowest kind of humans, because they were not free, either in their bodies or in their hearts. The adjective 'servile' in Roman usage degraded everything it qualified: hunting was a servile occupation, love a servile passion, Egypt a servile nation, because the hunter, the man in love and the Egyptian failed to behave as free men, impelled by honour alone, with no masters but themselves. They had given up their freedom to chase after an animal, a woman or life.

FROM SLAVERY TO FREEDOM

Recently the bold thesis has been advanced that slavery in Rome was not conceived of as a final state. Every slave was therefore a potential freedman and servitude a station on the route from foreign prisoner-of-war status to citizen status. Slavery was, so the argument goes, a way of swelling the population of the city by gradually integrating foreigners over a span of two or three generations. Prisoners-of-war were sold as slaves along with war plunder, then set free by their masters after ten or twenty years. If, after a slave's emancipation, he was still young enough to father a son, that son would be a full citizen. If, however, a slave's son was born into slavery, his grandson at least would be a free man.

The proponent of this theory has advanced two reasons, one economic and the other sociological.

Slaves were expensive to buy and eventually died of sickness or old age, entailing a heavy loss for their owners. If, on the other hand, a slave bought back his freedom, his former master could afford a replacement. In Rome, any slave might, providing his master gave his consent, build up a *peculium*, or nest egg, that he could then use to buy his freedom. The Latin word *peculium* seems originally to have denoted a small herd or part of a herd that a master could set aside for his slave to rear for his own profit. It is possible that slaves were only allocated those lambs that were surplus to the strict requirements of herd renewal. To find livestock-farming tied in once again to the making of money comes as no surprise. But this pastoral practice in classical times was merely a model for a more widespread arrangement: *peculium* came to denote any form of enterprise entrusted by the master to his slave which afforded the latter a personal income. Often the slave would be able to keep part of the sum amassed, after paying the agreed price for his freedom. The *peculium* might also take the form of intellectual and artistic training. A master might send his slave to school to become an actor, a poet or an accountant. The master could then profit from the slave's professional skills either by hiring him out or by using his labour directly. Once the slave was free, he could practise his profession for his own personal gain. The vast majority of artists, intellectuals and people of fashion were freedmen who had received their training when slaves.

The longing for freedom provided the Romans with a way of averting slave revolts and diffusing the hatred of domestic servants who might otherwise poison family life – either literally or meta-phorically. Many slaves were indeed prisoners-of-war and not a few of them, even the barbarian captives, had been brought up in freedom, as had for example the Gauls, the Iberians and the Thracians. Romans feared their slaves' despair. After all, citizens ate food prepared by slaves, tendered their throats to a slave barber, drifted off to sleep in a house staffed by servants. It was not enough to mete out exemplary punishment to the comrades of Spartacus, to line the Appian Way with grisly crosses, to deny burial to the rebellious slave, or to send him to die in the mines. Such punishments were useful in so far as they set an example, and fear certainly sharpened servile minds. But it was also essential to reward loyalty and to ensure that the slave's aspiration to freedom, alive even in the breasts of wild animals, found an outlet other than desperate rebellion.

A third line of reasoning, relying on demographic considerations, might be added to these economic and sociological explanations. It is generally agreed that emancipation, along with the granting of Roman citizenship to Italians, enabled Rome to achieve a steady rate of demographic growth at a time when the populations of other Mediterranean cities were at best stable and in many cases declining. It has been calculated that the Third Punic War resulted in the capture of 200,000 prisoners-of-war and that Caesar enslaved one million Gauls. Emancipation was also therefore a way of addressing the problem of a 'people shortage' that had so debilitated Greek cities. It was, of course, essential that this integration of foreigners be ideologically acceptable and that appropriate cultural circumstances prevail in Rome.

Emancipation should in fact be viewed alongside adoption. These two practices, so characteristic of Roman life and offering such a clear contrast with Greece, were founded on particular conceptions of time, human nature and servitude. One might state quite baldly that in Rome birth counted for nothing and education for everything. At first sight, this notion seems paradoxical, given the aristocratic nature of the city. Yet it was not the high birth of the nobleman's child that mattered but the education he received within the patrician household. It was nurture rather than nature that was decisive. Romans were the inheritors of the culture, the goods and the moral values of their parents over one, two or even three generations, but their nobility was not hereditary. As we have seen, blood in Rome soon ceased to accord any privilege and the collective memory of noble families had nothing to do with genealogy: they sprang from neither gods nor heroes. The same may be said for citizenship. Whether adoptive son or freedman, you bore the name, indeed you *were* the name, of whosoever had enrolled you on the census register.

Unlike many Mediterranean civilizations, Greece and Egypt being two examples, in Rome divine genealogies or genealogies of ancestors had never been recited. Blood did not count, bodies had no memory, the son of the freedman inherited nothing of his father's servile past, of his blemishes or of his submissions. Children were brand-new beings whose bodies would assume the form imposed upon them by their soul; they were as soft clay on which education left its stamp. Equally, a child born free but brought up to servility was irremediably lost to the republic. He might regain his freedom but could never become an honourable citizen.

This had a curious consequence. In the process of becoming Roman citizens, freedmen lost their ethnic characteristics. As slaves they might have been swarthy or light-skinned, frizzy- or curly-haired, bearded or beardless, according to their origins, and indeed often were purchased on account of these things. As soon as they were free, however, these characteristics were suddenly no more than personality traits. A Roman of Libyan origin was not a 'negro', he was simply black-skinned. We would indeed be astonished if we could see a Roman crowd: an ethnic rainbow about which the Romans themselves were quite unconcerned. No one worried that Terence had been born a Berber and Catullus a Gaul. Indeed, many of the great politicians of the republic had not been born in Rome. Cicero himself was Volscian, and Pompey from Bruttium. The legend of Rome's earliest origins speaks tellingly of a jumble of shepherds, fugitive slaves and outlaws whom the laws and statutes turned into citizens. The Romans were neither local aboriginals, sprung from the land, nor noble scions of some godlike forebear: they were children of the law.

One might add that freedmen were children of Roman culture or of the Roman *cultus*. They emerged from a system of reproduction not unlike cultural 'cloning'. There was after all a direct link between the *fides* of the slave and his future identity as a citizen. It was the slave's loyalty, his faithful obedience, that the master would reward. But this faithfulness also denoted an identification with the master of the period of slavery. This identification is recorded in the emancipation itself: having been his double and his shadow, the emancipated slave would bear his master's name and become his client.

It is debatable whether Rome had always cherished this conception of nobility and hence of citizenship and slavery. The key period seems to have been the fourth century BC. In the space of a few decades, Rome suppressed the hereditary patriciate (367 BC), increased the number of emancipations (first tax on emancipations), abolished slavery as a punishment for indebtedness (326), enabled sons of freedmen to enter the senate (312), while launching a campaign to conquer Italy and purchasing slaves, mainly barbarian prisoners, Etruscans, Samnites and Gauls. From this period onward the slave was the 'other', a strange foreigner, coming from abroad to be turned into a Roman. Conversely, never again could a citizen fall into slavery, unless by his own volition. Roman society no longer generated slaves from within: it now imported them to make citizens of them.

THE STATUS OF FREEDMEN

The condition of the freedman in Rome makes the difference between the image of the city provided by the census and actual civil society. There were in effect two ways to be free: as free-born Roman and as freedman. The free-born Roman had a right to accede to honours providing his tax rating, *cense*, was sufficiently high, whereas freedmen could not gain such access whatever their wealth. In a city where honour was all-important, the freedman was closer to the slaves, his companions up until his emancipation, than to the citizens among whose number his name now figured. Until the third century BC, funerary inscriptions celebrating the *nomen* of the deceased did not distinguish in any way between slaves and freedmen: both were called *servus*. In everyday conversation, right until the end of the republic, people continued to refer to them as slaves.

If freedmen had no access to honours, it was because they lacked *honos*, the sense of honour, a direct relation with civic values, unmediated by either master or patron. In their hearts, freedmen remained slaves, men of broken spirit, and this barred them from all honourable and honorary activities.

Although free, the freedman remained in a relation of dependence *vis-à-vis* his former master, now his *patronus* – literally 'he who takes the place of the father'. He owed him *obsequium*, as a son his father; in other words, he had to join his retinue in public places and generally support him in public life. He could not bring legal proceedings against him. He also owed him *operae*, a certain number of days of work. If the patron was a craftsman, the freedman had either to work under him or to set up shop in a different town.

Romans expected freedmen to show their patrons the same loyalty as slaves showed their masters, with the subtle difference that to the slave's *fides* was now added *pietas*, the sacred respect that a son owed his father. Nor was the emotional bond broken, for the patron was the only free-born person whom the freedman could get to know intimately. Freedmen were otherwise restricted in their relations to a circle of other freedmen or slaves. Although freedmen might have professional relations with free-born Romans, they could not vote with them, go to war with them or dine with them. Maecenas, however Epicurean he may have been, would never have invited a freedman to dine at his table.

SONS OF FORTUNE

The fate of every freedman was a matter of divine chance. As the ancients said, freedmen were sons of Fortune. Depending on the luck of a sale, a slave might spend his life hoeing beans, watching over herds of sheep on a mountainside, or he might become his master's or mistress's favourite, be given an education, pampered and enfranchised. He might even inherit.

Such was the happy fate of Ctesippus the fuller, a contemporary of Cicero, whom a stroke of luck propelled from a lowly and menial job to giddy opulence. Ctesippus had been a fuller, or launderer, a particularly repellent occupation that involved wading around in urine. However, at a closing-down sale, Ctesippus had the good luck to be 'thrown in' as a free gift to a lady called Gegonia who had purchased a candelabrum. Ctesippus became Gegonia's lover, she enfranchised him, and on her death she left him her entire fortune, which was enormous.

However fantastic it may appear, this story was not unique. Q.

Metellus, an ally of the noblest families in Rome, left all his possessions to a certain freedman, Carrinas. Whatever the precise nature of the bond of affection that tied a freedman to his former master, it was of vital importance. One can see why freedmen might resort to any means, including magic and love potions, to retain the affections of their patrons.

Freedmen whom Fortune had kissed ruined themselves as quickly as they got rich. As Horace put it: 'One morning he steps out of a palace, the next out of a hovel.' More than anyone else, the freedman was susceptible to *luxuria*, ill-considered expenditure on pleasure. Like slaves, freedmen were in thrall to their sensuality but, more important, the only social life that they knew consisted of the banquets they gave in their houses. The freedman was a Lucullus devoid of civic nostalgia, indifferent to the image he projected of himself. Publius Syrus, a famous actor and mime artist whose theatrical successes had made him fabulously rich, dined every day on whatever was most luxurious. He had even coined a new word for a sow's vulva, a dish considered particularly succulent in Rome.

Plain-living freedmen were more numerous but less well-known: amazing feats or flashy luxury alone could set the town gossiping. Sober freedmen merged into the free-born population whose way of living they imitated, and within a generation everyone had forgotten that the owner of the neighbouring farm was the son of a man born into slavery. And if the said neighbour made a success of his business, no one was surprised if he or his son were candidates for honours.

One such obscure freedman is known to us thanks to Cicero's correspondence. Tiro, Cicero's librarian and confidant, was born in around 94 BC in the orator's own house, hence his Latin nickname Tiro, 'the beginner'. Tiro was ten or so years younger than Cicero. Between 94 and 54 BC, when Tiro was enfranchised, one can only guess at his life. As a young man, he was given a literary training, doubtless with a view to making a secretary of him. He soon rendered himself indispensable and won Cicero's trust. He knew how to do everything, manage the estates, recover debts, draw up guest lists. He acted as librarian and record-keeper and above all he knew how to listen to Cicero, put up with his unbelievable conceit, and provide him with cues during literary and political conversations. Cicero could no longer manage without him. Tiro, however, was delicate, and prone to bouts of fever. Cicero kept a nervous and affectionate eye on Tiro's health, and insisted that he look after himself properly. When Cicero left for Cilicia to become proconsul, he took a still-convalescent Tiro with him. Tiro had invented a rapid writing system, a kind of shorthand, known as Tironian notes, in order to jot down the great man's slightest public pronouncements. When, following Caesar's rise to power, Cicero's career declined, Tiro was on hand to console him and to assure him that he was still the greatest politician in Rome and the saviour of the fatherland. In the meantime, Cicero had finally been persuaded to enfranchise him. This had not been an easy decision for Cicero to make, and after years of promises, he only agreed to enfranchise him when he thought that Tiro was at the point of death. Perhaps owing to the tonic effect of freedom, Tiro's health improved; he outlived his benefactor and was over one hundred years old when he died. From 54 BC onwards, Tiro piously devoted himself to the publication of Cicero's complete works and compiled a catalogue to them. After Cicero's assassination by Anthony's soldiers in 43 BC, Tiro wrote the orator's biography.

Tiro had salted away a small fortune and had bought an estate in Campania at Puteoli. He managed his small Roman farm like the good Roman peasant that he had become. Cicero's son poked fun at him and his claims to be leading a simple life, the life of a citizen:

> That you have bought a farm is a great joy to me, and it is my sincere wish that the transaction may turn out happily for you . . . Why, you are now a land-owner, and will have to drop your city ways. You have become a Roman country gentleman. I call you up before my eyes this very moment – and a very charming picture it is. I seem to see you buying rural implements, hobnobbing with your steward, or keeping the pips after dessert in the corner of your cloak.[35]

What can the worthy Tiro have thought of the Tullia family? His biography of Marcus, unfortunately lost to us, was not flattering. In it he gave what he believed to be the true reason for Cicero's divorce from Terentia, which preceded a swift remarriage. Cicero had run up debts and was tutor to a young heiress. He divorced Terentia and married the young girl in order to use her dowry to pay off his debts. This was all the easier for him since it normally fell to a young girl's tutor to protect her from the cupidity of a spouse. Shortly thereafter Cicero repudiated his new wife on the pretext that she had rejoiced at the death of his daughter Tullia. Once Cicero was dead, Tiro the complimentary mirror to his patron was no longer bound to submission and so became Tiro the sharp observer.

Cicero had even less luck with another freedman whose betrayal he felt most bitterly.[36] Several years after enfranchising Tiro, he freed a slave of Greek origin of whom he had grown fond. This Chrysippus was well-educated, with a 'smattering of culture', and Cicero enjoyed chatting to him. He had assigned him to his son, hoping perhaps that he would turn into a second Tiro. But as soon as he was free, Chrysippus left Cicero's house with a workman, a comrade in slavery, in whose company he had been enfranchised. Cicero was furious. He accused Chrysippus of every possible misdeed, including theft, but what he could not pardon was Chrysippus' abandonment of him. He even thought of compelling him to return by neglecting to register the enfranchisement. He appears not to have implemented this plan for fear of the ridicule and hatred that such petty jealousy would have aroused.

THE FREEDMAN AND THE LIMITS OF CITIZENSHIP

Slaves and freedmen were essential to the Roman citizen's perception of the world. Slaves provided a source of comfort that owed less to their actual work than to the feeling of security that they gave. Roman citizens were constantly surrounded by men and women who served as complimentary mirrors and as intermediaries between themselves and others. The existence of slaves made Roman citizens feel bigger, stronger, more handsome, more intelligent and more sure of themselves.

Slaves also supplied Roman citizens with a living example of a quite different and utterly contemptible kind of humanity, one tossed about by Fortune and incapable of honour. They embodied everything that the Roman citizen must never become – subject to the whims of others and at the mercy of their own sensuality. Freedmen and slaves traced for Romans the limits that they must never overstep, beyond which lay a hateful existence, confined to personal relations and private activities.

Part II

Places and Lives

4

The organization of Roman space

The Romans thrived in company and were happiest away from home. Most of their day was spent outdoors: in the fields; on the roads; in the squares; or at the public baths. Often too they went off on military campaigns or on journeys to far-flung provinces, staying away for months at a time. The Romans lived most of their active lives in the open air.

Even when they returned home, Roman citizens did not spend much time with their families. The main part of the Roman house was entirely given over to social life, to receptions and banquets that brought the outside world into the heart of the Roman's home. The Roman house, like the Roman citizen, looked outwards. It was more a site of anchorage on Roman soil than a sphere of action.

In Roman minds, space was divided into quite distinct and contrasting sites: town and country; Rome and the world; fields, meadows and forests; provinces and barbarous lands; the inhabited earth and the outermost fringes of the world; land and sea; house and army. And a range of specific activities was associated with each place.

MEMORY, TIME AND SPACE

The Romans lived and thought in spatial rather than in temporal terms. Like all peoples who do not produce mythological poetry or long genealogies, who do not trace their origins back to heroic times, they regarded places as sacred. Roman memory, lacking any anchorage in the inspired works of ancient poets, was rooted in the sacred ground of the city. To walk around Rome was to travel through its memory, past Romulus' cabin, Cacus' rock and Egeria's wood. What had happened in these places in former times was not precisely known: there were plenty of stories about them but they differed enormously from one version to the next. What mattered was that these places were sacred, the reasons were less important.

Right in the middle of the forum one could see the coping of a well surrounding a hole brimming with water, a sort of pond known as the Curtian Lake. Three stories circulated about this place, which was protected by a religious taboo. The two versions that have come down to us from the ancients have little in common.

According to some writers,[37] Curtius was the name of a Sabine, a certain Mettius Curtius who, during the war that followed the rape of the Sabine women, had become bogged down with his horse in what was at that time a swamp and had had to abandon the animal to save his life.

Another version cast Curtius as a young Roman hero.[38] When a gaping chasm appeared in the forum, Romans turned for guidance to the Sibylline books, which stated that the earth would close up once it had received that which the Roman people valued most highly, and that from that day on the earth would produce an abundance of what it had received. People threw sacred cakes and silver into the hole, but it failed to close up. At last Marcus Curtius, a young cavalryman and renowned warrior, begged leave to address the senate. He declared that in his view it was the courage of its soldiers that Rome held most dear, and that if one could be found willing to sacrifice himself, the earth would then produce courageous men aplenty. Clad in his armour and astride his warhorse, Curtius then hurled himself into the chasm. On top of him the crowd cast animals, cereals, silver, precious fabrics and manufactured objects. And the earth closed over.

As far as Roman memory was concerned, it mattered little whether Curtius was a Roman hero or a Sabine enemy. The main thing was the religious respect that attached to this sacred place in the middle of the forum – as to so many other sacred places. What was known with certainty was that this spot had to be surrounded by a fig tree, an olive tree and a vine. And it was essential that each year without fail this and every other sacred site received its due of offerings and prayers.

POLYTHEISM AND RELIGIOUS SPACE

The city was peopled with gods who had left their marks in ancient holy sites or who continued to live among men in the temples dedicated to them over the centuries. The number of Roman gods continued to grow as did the number of sanctuaries built within the city. These gods, however, did not dwell just anywhere. Each god was linked to a particular human activity and had its appropriate place. There were gods of war, gods of home life, gods of cultivated soil, garden gods, forest gods and gods of the hunt, gods of pasture: each imposed his or her own rites and duties in the place where he or she held sway. The Romans thus spent their lives moving between one religious space and the next, switching god and appropriate behaviour as they went. This was the form assumed by polytheism in Rome: a proliferation of religious spaces.

Each human activity was an act of worship to the deity that watched over it. On starting to plough, on sitting down at table, or at the outset of a military campaign, it was wise to make a sacrifice to the god in whose space one intended to take up temporary residence. A sacrifice would be made to the deities of the earth that one was about to cut through, to the gods of the house where one was to dine, to the god of war who would then throw a magic circle around the army to protect it. The actions themselves – ploughing, eating a meal, waging war – were ways of acknowledging these gods; the Roman made the gods present by performing the activities over which they presided. To some extent, the gods *were* the activities. When it was all over, the Roman would then give the god his or her due: the first fruits of harvesting or the weapons captured from the enemy.

If in poetic diction bread was referred to as Ceres, after the goddess of corn, or if 'to worship Venus' meant 'to make love', these were no mere figures of speech. Mars *was* war, and waging war was to worship Mars by making him present among men. Every action was performed with the authority of a particular god and had to be carried out in the space proper to that god. To transgress would be an act of impiety. It was a profanation to make love in the open air, in the forest or on a lawn: the darkness of a bedroom lit only by an oil lamp, the traditional auxiliary of Venus, was the essential backdrop. Similarly, warlike violence had no 'place' in the city, for violence belonged to Mars and the city was Jupiter's territory.

THE CITY AND THE WORLD: *URBS ET ORBIS*

The two main poles of the Romans' mental universe were the city and the world: *urbs et orbis terrarum.*

The city – that is, Rome – was the centre of the world. Rome was *the* city *par excellence*, the domain dedicated to Jupiter Optimus Maximus ('most good, most great'), whose temple stood at the top of the Capitol, dazzling all onlookers with the brilliance of its golden roof. Rome was the city of power, of temples, of pleasures and social life, of wealth, culture and refinement. For the wealthy of the political orders, to own a house in Rome was not a luxury – it was a legal obligation.

Everything that happened began in Rome and to Rome everything returned. When the red flag fluttered from the top of the citadel, Romans flocked to the city to enlist. Similarly, it was to the field of Mars, the Campus Martius, that returning soldiers came to lay down their weapons before going home to their land.

It was at Rome that some soldiers might choose to remain after demobilization, to pursue a career in entertainment. Ennius, a southern Italian, became a dramatic poet after acquiring glory and fortune while serving in Sardinia under Cato. And it was to Rome that an ambitious provincial, provided that he belonged to the equestrian order, could, like Cato and Cicero, come to seek a patron to help launch his political career.

It was to Rome too that the Roscius family, far too wretched to care about glory or infamy, sent a young son in the hope that his beauty would open doors for him into high society. Which, indeed, it did. Winning the heart of several distinguished citizens, Roscius became a fashionable actor, founded a theatre school, commanded high fees for his services and lessons, and became wealthy enough to provide his sister with an honourable marriage, despite his own infamy. Rome, the centre of festivities, required artists and poets, even if it never ceased to confine them to the inferior classes of society.

Rome received all the plunder that its armies managed to capture from the enemy, the wealth of the whole world, strange animals and thousands of prisoners sold off as slaves to the highest bidder. Some slaves soon left for the country to work as farm labourers or shepherds; others, if they had one of the skills in demand in Rome, stayed in the city as cooks, hairdressers, perfumers, masseurs or doctors. The youngest, most talented and most beautiful were sent to

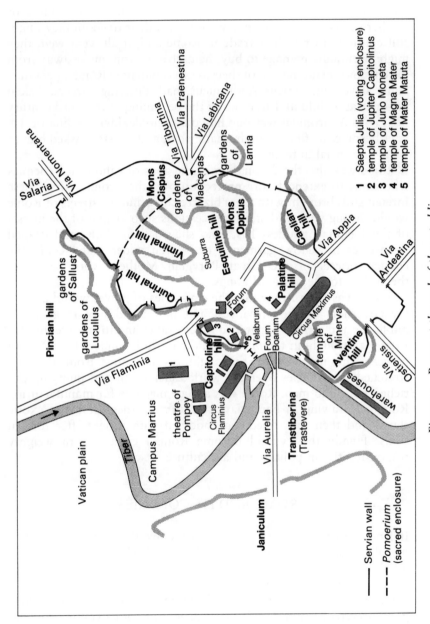

Figure 1   Rome at the end of the republic

1   Saepta Julia (voting enclosure)
2   temple of Jupiter Capitolinus
3   temple of Juno Moneta
4   temple of Magna Mater
5   temple of Mater Matuta

——— Servian wall
- - - *Pomoerium*
(sacred enclosure)

school to study poetry, music, dance, theatre, accounting, agronomy, architecture, philosophy or rhetoric. With luck they might become their master's favourite, his steward, the keeper of his purse or teacher of his children. If they were to win their freedom they might still continue to ply their trade in Rome and, if all went well, they might eventually manage to buy themselves a farm, move away from the city and spend the rest of their lives as contented Roman peasants. Some slaves, like Livius Andronicus, had glittering careers. Taken prisoner as a child at Tarentum at the beginning of the third century BC, Livius Andronicus was purchased by a noble, Livius Salinator. He later become the first Latin dramatic poet, and the state asked him to write an official anthem.

Rome was also the destination of the gods of vanquished enemies who came to extend future protection over their conquerors. These foreign gods brought with them bizarre cults, and the streets of Rome would throng with outlandish processions such as that of the priests of the Egyptian goddess Isis, who shaved their skulls and draped themselves in yellow garments, or – even odder – the *Galli*, the eunuch priests of the Great Phrygian Mother, who flagellated themselves to the music of gongs.

And it was from Rome that the emissaries of power would depart, the governors of the provinces, and the armadas of magistrates, publicans and scribes dispatched to levy taxes and to enforce the *Pax Romana* throughout the *imperium*, the territory subjected to Roman power. The network of thoroughfares radiating from the city stretched its tentacles over the world, sucking in and pumping out riches, gods and men. Rome was a huge machine for manufacturing Romans, drawing in barbarians and turning them first into exotic slaves and then into freedmen endowed with sought-after foreign skills. Finally they would become Roman citizens with weighty responsibilities in politics and agriculture.

ROME AND ITS COLONIES

If Rome became a metropolis – indeed by the first century BC a megalopolis, a city with a population of close to one million inhabitants – it was because Rome was unique. As far as the Romans were concerned, it was the only city in the world.

Greek cities had burgeoned and swarmed. Whenever one of them grew overcrowded, it despatched a generation of its young people to set up home somewhere else in a colony: in Asia Minor, in Africa, in

Italy or even in Gaul. The new colonial city would then become the equal of the founding city, even if it maintained privileged links with it. It would be independent and possess its own government, army and politics. It would be situated far from Greece, in a barbarous country: Greece never annexed a neighbouring city in order to resettle its own citizens. This form of colonization was known as Greek liberty. Other Italian cities may have adopted it, but Rome did not.

Rome proceeded in its own highly original way. It swelled but did not swarm. For the Romans, there was only one city, established on the Capitol and the hills that ran down to the Tiber. Rome was unique because its setting was unique: it could not resprout elsewhere. The Greeks did not link their culture to a specific territory. To be Greek was to be of Greek culture, whether in Africa, Italy or Gaul. Hellenism had no capital. In contrast, Latin culture did not on its own make a Roman; one also had to be a citizen of the eternal city.

Roman colonies were therefore quite different from Greek colonies. Rome spread out gradually from its own territory, annexing the free cities of Latium, then the Italian cities and finally the peoples of Spain, of southern Gaul, of northern Africa, of Greece and of Asia Minor. A Roman colony was a settlement of Roman peasants, generally former soldiers known as veterans, on a piece of conquered territory. The ancient town would be razed to the ground, as in the case of Carthage, and in its place a new urban centre would be built. The new town would reproduce the grid pattern of the military encampment, with its two main thoroughfares, the *cardo* and the *decumanus*, crossing at right angles in the centre of the town, and all the other roads running parallel to one of these two main axes. Ancient cities traditionally placed their urban centres on hills, and built outwards from a citadel; Roman colonial towns were located on plains, at crossroads. In some details they did, of course, reproduce the topography of the mother-city: Arles or Timgad have their Capitol, their forum, their curia where local elected representatives would meet, their circus and their theatre. But these were ghost towns where public life was a pale imitation of public life in Rome, just as their Capitol was a man-made molehill. They had no political or military autonomy, no genuine citizenship.

A scaled-down Rome, a Rome stitched together in *trompe-l'oeil*: the Romans could not conceive of a city as anything other than Rome writ small. There was no abstract legal or religious definition, no founding ritual sufficient to create a city. The material image of Rome had to be reproduced, because the city of Rome provided a model for every city.

There was therefore a permanent process of exchange between the city and the world since the very notion that the Romans had of their city (*the* city) destined it to become the centre of the world. The Romans imposed this viewpoint on others: before Rome became the queen of cities, as early as the middle of the second century BC,[39] the Greeks already saluted Rome as the all-powerful city.

MAPS OF THE WORLD

The Romans pictured the geographical sweep of their empire with the help of a sketched representation of space that gave them an intellectual grasp of the world that surrounded them.[40] When triumphs engulfed the city, behind the parading chariots and lines of men loaded with loot, and behind the columns of prisoners, marched soldiers bearing placards listing the victories and conquests. Some of these placards displayed the names of the towns and mountains and rivers that had been conquered. Others took the form of maps showing the shape and extent of the countries subjugated. These maps, projections of the earth on to a flat surface, were on too large a scale to be of any practical use. (Travellers and generals used another kind of document known as an 'itinerary'.) The maps served rather as a prop to thought, a way of giving form to Roman power. Once the triumph was over, the maps were reproduced and painted on the walls of the temples. In 174 BC Tiberius Sempronius Gracchus displayed a map of Sardinia in the temple of Aurora, Mater Matuta, in memory of his victories.[41] Around 59 BC, there was a map of Italy in the temple of the Earth.[42]

Rather than celebrate their mastery of the world in song, the Romans tended to visualize it, and the representations that they produced acted as springboards for political and philosophical speculation. At the time when Rome held sway over the entire perimeter of the Mediterranean, when Augustus was establishing the empire, he ordered Agrippa to have a universal map set up in the Vispianus portico in the Campus Martius in order to reassure the citizens of Rome. This map showed Rome as the physical centre of the world. Standing at the mid-point between the frozen North and the burning South, between the violent barbarians of the West and the spineless barbarians of the East, Rome seemed the geometrical site of every kind of balance, the legitimate queen of the world.

TOWN AND COUNTRY: *URBS ET RUS*

The Romans felt a violent love for Rome. They loved the superb spectacle offered by its hills topped with temples, they loved its intense and sophisticated social life. They loved Rome almost to the point of hatred and reproached it for devouring them, body and soul. Against this unbearable and irresistible paramour, they could set no other town, for there existed none other: Rome's only rival was the country, that calm and faithful wife.

Town and country were inseparable; Romans came and went between them, along the roads and in their heart: 'At Rome you long for the country; in the country, you extol to the stars the distant town.'[43]

In fact they needed both. Town and country were paired opposites, like wealth and poverty, public life and private life. Two abstract nouns reveal the essence of town and country. Urbanity, *urbanitas*, stood for refinement and culture, social life, banquets, courtesy, wit and fashion. Rusticity, *rusticitas*, signified austerity, grumpy harshness, squalor, ignorance, doltishness, inelegance.

Yet such values might be reversed and the countryside might prevail over the city. The frugal routine, the narrow horizons of the farm, the thankless labour on the land, the heavy plough, the drudgery of wood-chopping, the unrelieved boiled vegetables for supper, could easily yield to a country idyll. The country was then viewed as a place of rest and happiness far from ships that sank or electors that proved fickle. A faithful wife, respectful children, friendly slaves with whom a peasant could feast on thick bean soup and a fat slice of bacon: what else could one require? Night would fall on a household already tucked up in bed and assured of the sound slumber that was their due. The family counted on the father and the father did not have to rely on anyone but himself.

The town, by contrast, became a jungle, a rallying-point for every vice, full of corruption and the site for fate's bitterest blows. Today's millionaire merchant might be tomorrow's bankrupt eager to hurl himself into the Tiber. His ships might founder, his partners betray him. The orator deafened with adulation one day might be booed the next. In town either you were rich and powerful or ridiculous and a prey to swindlers. A condescending patron might invite you to sit at the far end of his table where insolent slaves would haughtily pass you scraps that you then had to fight over with a collection of grasping social parasites. While the well-to-do stuffed themselves with lobster sluiced down with exotic wines, you would be handed a prawn and some rough local stuff. The din at night made it impossible to sleep, and consider what would happen if you fell ill. Attended by a charlatan charging astronomical fees and robbed by one's innkeeper, the only way to avoid untimely death would be to flee headlong from such a place of perdition.

To lead a full life, the Romans needed both the city and the country. In the countryside, the Roman would turn himself into a horny-handed peasant, rediscovering the rude and tranquil life of his childhood. Every Roman child was after all brought up in the countryside on a simple farm. It was in the countryside too that a Roman would end his days, tending his leeks and lettuces. They needed to draw sustenance from the poverty, the rigour, at a safe distance from sophistication and parties. If, however, a Roman spent too much of his youth or his prime in the countryside he would languish and fade, like Scipio in voluntary exile from politics and the city.

Rusticity was not a feature exclusive to peasants living on remote smallholdings. Largish Italian villages and provincial towns were also deemed more or less rustic. Any Roman not from Rome itself was always somehow redolent of the 'provinces'. Even Cicero, hailing from Arpinum, was vulnerable to this reproach. Provincial idiocy was one of the effects of centralization. Since the eternal city was the only city, every provincial was to a greater or lesser degree a peasant. Those whose entire lives were given over to politics felt that local postings were a ridiculous waste of time and effort. In these miniature Romes, with their tiny Capitols and curias, the principal magistrate was nothing but a petty praetor, with derisory powers; a ghost of a praetor, a comic opera praetor. Like a certain Aufidius Luscus whom Horace encountered at Fundi and was delighted to leave, 'laughing at the crazy clerk's gewgaws, his bordered robe, broad stripe, and pan of charcoal,'[44] of use to him in his religious offices.

Rome and the countryside grew to maturity, as it were, side by side. At the beginning of the republic, the Roman countryside extended no more than fifty kilometres to the south and to the south-east of the City. But from the fourth century BC onwards, Latium, and thereafter Etruria, and then the whole of Italy, were occupied by Roman colonists, while the former inhabitants were gradually granted Roman citizenship. As a result, the Romans found they had to spend a disproportionate amount of time travelling to Rome to participate in political life. Some colonists complained that they were systematic- ally dispatched ever further from Rome to make it hard for them to vote in elections. By the end of the republic, some electors had given up coming to Rome altogether, and therefore only assumed their civic identity when in the army. Others abandoned their provincial posting altogether and rubbed along at Rome, in the keep of some wealthy politician who thereby held in his grasp a clientele that could be quickly mobilized. The extension of rural territory contributed therefore to the collapse of republican culture.

BOUNDARIES, FRONTIERS, GATES: JANUS AND TERMINUS

Every Roman space was defined by a boundary that took the form not of an abstract line clearly marking off different territories, but rather of an intermediate zone at which people had to perform rites of passage: it was here that the god Terminus stood guard. In some cases, however, there were physical boundaries or fences, which might or might not be interrupted by gates: these were dedicated to Janus.

Terminus was the god of the boundary-stone, sunk in the earth, that marked out a piece of land or a territory that was occupied or cultivated, and identified its owner. Such stones were to be found at the edge of private estates, but also at the outer limit of the Roman people's territory, the *ager Romanus*. The rituals that surrounded Terminus made him a neighbourhood god. At the annual feast of the boundary-stones celebrated on 23 February, the Terminalia, owners of neighbouring fields would advance towards one another, each from his own side, and would lay a wreath on the boundary-stone, with the offering of a cake. The neighbours would then hold a banquet together, where they would eat the lamb or piglet that had just been sacrificed.[45]

Terminus acted therefore as a god of separation and proximity. By making the sacrifice, neighbours clearly distinguished themselves one from the other, but the symmetrical quality of the ritual also asserted their similarity. For the ancients, only two kinds of relation could exist between two similar men: one of confrontation by duel or a bond of friendship. The banquet offered in honour of Terminus forced friendship upon neighbours who, living in the country, might all too easily grow to hate one another. Roman law gives one a rough idea of the law-suits and mutual suspicions that constantly arose between peasants with neighbouring farms. Some peasants had even been accused of using magic to switch harvested crops from one field to another – a crime punishable by death. Terminus guaranteed the demarcation of fields, prevented boundary conflicts, and also made sure that boundary-stones were not moved during a land-owner's absence. He constrained neighbours to banquet and make merry in each other's company, in other words, to play host to one another, a process likely to cement trust and friendship.

The same applied to the territorial boundaries of cities. To cross a territorial limit guaranteed by the god Terminus, unless one came from the city to which that territory belonged, could only be done as a guest or as an enemy. Indeed, both words in Latin (*hostis*, enemy; *hospes*, guest) were formed from the same root, which had the meaning 'the other who is similar to you'.

Any hostile seizure or invasion of land bounded by Terminus had to be put right by war when two cities were involved, or by a trial if the conflict arose between two neighbours. But the boundaries marked out by Terminus could be crossed even where there was no gate: the god did not trace out sacred areas on the ground. The nature of the space remained the same on both sides.

A town, a territory or an estate could also be ritually enclosed, however. Mars, the god of war and of the sacred circle, would be invoked, and he would throw a magic wall around the site to protect it. Each year, the head of an estate, at the Ambarvalia ritual, asked Mars to spare his family, slaves, herds, fields and himself from all the calamities that might otherwise strike them: illnesses, hailstorms, droughts or parasites.

Rome was ringed by the most famous of all sacred walls – the *pomoerium*. Jupiter reigned within this wall, guaranteeing peace, life, culture and social harmony, and expelling death and its cemeteries, war and its armies, and fields and their ruggedness. The *pomoerium*, drawn at the very moment at which the city itself had been founded and taking the form of a furrow ritually traced by a plough drawn by a white heifer and ox, could not be crossed. Indeed, the city could only be entered through one of its gates, at the place where the founding ploughman had lifted his ploughshare to break the line of the furrow.

The gate, *janua*, was to be found at every point of transit between different kinds of space: on arrival in the city from the countryside, or on entering one's home from the street. Even to mark the transition from war to peace, when soldiers sought to become plain civilians once again, they had to pass beneath symbolic gates, one form of which has survived in the triumphal arch. Janus, the god of the gate, was a god with two faces, Janus Bifrons. He demonstrated that time could be thought of as a sequence of isolated noments. Janus oversaw the passage from one year to the next, and the first month of the Roman calendar was named after him. As a gate-god, he indicated that the coming year would be essentially different from the year that had just passed and that the Roman conception of time was not cyclical. For the same reason, Janus was the god of the beginning of the month, and also of the beginning of the day: he was the 'father of the morning'.

Safely to cross the boundaries that Terminus guarded, one had to be free of any hostile intent. To pass through a gate, however, was always dangerous. It was wise first to gain a proper mastery of the passage in question by pronouncing the right words and performing the right actions, otherwise, one's enterprise was doomed to failure. A good beginning must be made: to one's day, to a war, to a speech. The first actions performed and the first words spoken were highly significant. When leaving one's home, entering the forum, departing from or returning to the city, or entering a foreign country, to stumble on the threshold or enter left foot first could presage disaster. It was essential to avoid unfortunate remarks and birds of ill omen and instead seize on any favourable sign that might appear. 'Woodpecker and raven to one's left, crow and eagle to one's right, together they urge us to act,' as the proverb said.

If there were too many unfavourable signs it was best to postpone any action, to return home and await a better opportunity.

> Tiberius Gracchus was preparing to introduce a number of revolutionary laws. On the way out of his house, he stubbed his toe so hard that he fractured it. A little further on, three crows cawed as they flew towards him and then broke off a piece of tiling and dropped it at his feet. But he took no notice and before long was chased from the Capitol by the *pontifex maximus* Scipio. He died as a result of a blow from a piece of bench.[46]

Tiberius' mistake lay in his failure to take such portents into account, either by abstaining from action or by seeking to overcome them. The main thing was to be extremely careful at the moment at which one entered the new space, exercising strict control over one's body and over the words one spoke in the dialogue that developed between oneself and the space. If a sign told you that 'Here a misfortune will befall you!', and if you really wished to proceed, you would be wise to stumble, rip your toga and cry out: 'My god, what a misfortune!' The portent could thus be fulfilled at no great cost.

In the same way, a careless word could signal success or failure, depending on whether or not one knew how to interpret it.

The consul Aemilius Paullus had just received the command for the campaign against Perseus. He left the curia and went home. There he found his young daughter Tertia in a flood of tears. He took her in his arms and asked her why she was so sad. She replied, 'Persa is dead'. Persa was a little dog that Tertia adored. Aemilius Paullus seized on this omen to predict with certainty a brilliant triumph.[47]

In this story Aemilius Paullus was storing up, as it were, situations of transition. He was about to receive his military command: he had been appointed by the senate but not yet ritually commissioned. He had left the senate and was returning home. The first person he encountered was his daughter, the first thing he heard was 'Persa is dead'. This return home, following hard upon his appointment to a position of command, invested Tertia's otherwise anodyne phrase with the quality of an omen. It was, of course, up to Aemilius Paullus to interpret it in this light. He had to hear behind the name of the dog Persa that of the king against whom he was to fight: Perseus. This he did, thereby assuring himself of victory. Everything was a question of will, courage, caution, and self-possession.

Pompey, defeated by Caesar at Pharsalus, arrived at the island of Paphos in search of help. From a distance he sighted a superb palace standing on the shore. He asked the ship's captain to tell him its name. 'It is known as the house of the wicked king,' his guide replied. Far too dejected to counter this omen, Pompey heaved a sigh and accepted what it appeared to portend: 'Pompey will receive a poor welcome here.'[48]

THE ALIEN WILDERNESS

At the outer limit of the world the Romans set a fabulous and divine stretch of water, an ocean that encircled the universe with expanses that could never be crossed. Logic dictated that the area between the ocean and the inhabited world should be occupied by intermediate beings, half human and half divine, roaming over lonely wastes that no man could travel.

If things were somewhat more more complicated than this, it was the fault of the Gauls. The Romans had long enjoyed a tranquil existence in the shelter of the Etruscans against whom they waged incessant wars but by whose presence they were protected from the incursion of the creatures from the edge of the world. Then, at the beginning of the fourth century, the Etruscan safety barrier gave way and in poured the northern hordes, hurtling down the Alps, chasing out the Italians and settling on their land. These savages, according to rumour, were Gauls, one of those peoples from the furthermost bounds of the universe, on the very edge of the ocean. They advanced invincible, a horde of giant warriors that nobody could halt. Armies fled without a fight. The Romans sent a legion to do battle with them, but at their first glimpse of the enemy the Roman soldiers scattered, killing one another in their scramble to run away. The Roman army's unaccustomed panic aroused an appalling doubt: what if these men were divine warriors, messengers foretelling the end of the world?

These Gauls were people who marched straight ahead, with neither discipline nor citizenship, knowing nothing of war's legal niceties. They didn't even know what a route was. They advanced along a single line, a rabble of horses and men, and they took Rome without baring a sword. Rome was wide open, its population had sought refuge in Veii with their sacred objects and had left only a handful of men to guard the Capitol. The Gauls entered the city, pillaged, killed and burnt. Then, wearied by their unsuccessful attempts to take the Capitol, they made for the countryside to raid farms, leaving a few men behind them to maintain the siege. For the Romans it must indeed have seemed like the end of the world.

Yet it would not take much for such godlike giants to be recast as miserable and semi-human beasts that could be shooed away like pigeons. It was a question of attitude, of looking at them in a different way. Camillus, a Roman noble, was bold enough to feel contempt for the Gauls. He demonstrated to the Latins, among whom he was living in exile at the outbreak of the Gallic hostilities, that a few determined men could dispatch hundreds of Gallic enemies. 'A handful of men in the citadel and the Capitol are holding them at bay; already . . . they are departing and roaming aimlessly through the countryside. They greedily gorge themselves with food and wine, and when night approaches they erect no rampart, and without pickets or sentries, throw themselves down anywhere, besides a stream, in the manner of wild beasts.'[49] Camillus gathered together a few handpicked men, surprised the Gauls as they slept, and slit their throats like so many sheep. Roman fear was a thing of the past. The Romans no longer saw the Gauls as supermen but rather as subhumans whom they would soon repel from their territory for ever.

This was how Rome discovered the barbarians that lived between civilization and the peoples on the edge of the ocean. They never again feared them, whether they were Gauls, Carthaginians, Iberians or Illyrians. Rome deemed it possible to subjugate them and did just that, bringing the conquered peoples into the society of inhabited and civilized lands. But Rome never ventured beyond the barbarian countries. If the Gauls were not themselves the peoples of the ocean, the latter surely lived at a distance that placed them out of reach: it was best to leave the edges of the universe to them. One might talk about such peoples, but one never actually caught sight of them.

The Greeks told many a far-fetched tale about such peoples.[50] They recounted that the most remote of the Scythians, who lived on the shores of the Black Sea, ate human flesh as though it were ox meat. Still further to the north lived the Arimaspi, who had one eye in the middle of their foreheads. In the mountains, to the north of India, there were men with the heads of dogs and others with no necks, who had eyes in their shoulders and ran at great speed on a single leg. There was a tribe in India whose bodies were covered with feathers and who ate no food but drew sustenance by inhaling the perfume of flowers. In Albania, though no one knew where that country lay, children had white hair and could see better at night than during the day. The Sauromatae, who lived beyond the river Borysthenes, were gluttonous eaters although they took food only every other day.

The world as seen by the Romans was shaped like an onion: in the centre was Rome; around Rome were civilized peoples; then barbarous peoples, then wondrous savages and lastly the end of all things: the ocean, reaching up to the sky and down to the land of the dead.

WHAT GLADIATORS WERE FOR

If savages peopled the periphery of the world, a link was forged between this periphery and the centre of Rome through the practice of gladiatorial combat. It is no accident that gladiators were introduced to Rome at a time when the city had just embarked upon an expansionist policy that changed the way in which Romans pictured the universe and when Rome was assuming its position at the centre of the world and of civilization.

Gladiatorial combats were obligations rendered to the dead. They were held in one of the city's public places, often the forum.[51] Blood had to flow to slake the thirst of the *manes*, the deceased ancestors of the Underworld. Gladiators were always barbarians, though not necessarily by birth, birth being of no consequence to Romans. It was in their souls that gladiators were barbarous, and in their manner of combat. Whether captured barbarians or Romans who had become degenerate, gladiators would be decked out with exotic and systematically strange weapons of varying degrees of authenticity. Indeed, the more far-fetched the weapons, the more barbarous did the gladiators appear. Gladiators never used the weapons of the legionary. There were Gauls, Thraces, Samnites, all sparkling in their metal shells; naked *retiarii*, each with a helmet, a net and a trident; and *andabatae* whose helmets acted as blindfolds and who fought on tiptoes. Asymmetrical pairs were selected for combat, though an effort was made to ensure a fair match. One might be very light, but with nothing to protect him; the other iron-clad from head to toe, virtually invulnerable but pinned down by the weight of his armour.

Each gladiator, in other words, was either too heavily or too lightly armed. Combat never took the form of a duel between two equally armed braves. When a *retiarius*, his net aloft, pursued the *mirmillo* in his sparkling coat of mail, the Romans followed a struggle between fisherman and fish. Gladiators made mediocre soldiers. When the republic called them up to fight a war, not one of them could stand up to a real soldier. Gladiatorial fencing was a dance, a body art, rather than a discipline of the spirit. 'Samnite, refuse of humanity,' Lucilius once said. The value of gladiators was that of barbarians or of men who had fallen from social grace: they were fighting machines, of scant worth.

The spilling of blood marked a separation just as the offering of blood, through marriage, created a union. Gladiatorial combats thus dramatized the difference between the civilized living and the barbarous dead who, like savages, were thought to drink human blood and were therefore confined far from the living, in the Underworld. Such combats also served to differentiate and separate extremes from each other: Gauls from Numidians; Thracians from Spaniards; the overweight from the underweight; the skittish from the sluggish. For a fleeting instant the edges of the world would meet at its centre, immediately to be hurled back, separated by blood, to the far ends of the universe. Romans, creatures of equilibrium, remained in the centre, at an equal distance from every excess and from every margin.

5

Roman houses

Although the Romans were not often to be found in their houses during the day, during peacetime they returned home every evening. Latin usage contains the paired expression 'at home and at war' just as 'in the town and in the country' or 'on land and on sea'. At home and in the army represented two different ways of sleeping, two ways of eating, two kinds of community.

The life of the Roman citizen was shaped by both. On the one hand, there was the camaraderie of fellow soldiers, the dangers of the pursuit of honour, the stale bread, the nights spent under canvas, the cold, the heat, the war weariness, the pain, the journeys to the ends of the earth, the looted gold; on the other hand, the love of one's children, the peacefulness of home, the fine meals enjoyed on soft couches, the ancestral roof, the familiar landscape, the reassuring presence of friends, clients and household slaves.

THE HOUSE AS SHRINE

As far as the Romans were concerned, to be civilized was to be settled in one place: a genuine Roman was rooted by his house to the territory of his city. Just as Rome possessed its public hearth, established in the round temple to Vesta near the forum whose eternal flame was fed by young maidens, the Vestals, so too the citizen had to have a private hearth and women to watch over it – his wife and his daughters. Here the fire of Vesta burned beneath a roof, rather than in the open air, outside a temple.

Constructed around this domestic hearth, the Roman house linked the head of the family, the *paterfamilias*, who inhabited it to the land and to his lineage through the household cults that were celebrated under its roof. Three kinds of deity were venerated. The *lares* were offered fire, the *genius* pure wine, and the *penates* incense. The *lares* were the gods of settlement, and resided wherever men had taken possession of land and cultivated or civilized it: there were garden *lares*, crossroads *lares* and house *lares*. The *genius* was the god of the agnatic or male line – all the ancestors and descendants, via male kinship links, of the head of the family. Each citizen had received from his father, who in his turn had received from *his* father, the blood that he would one day pass on to his sons and to his sons' sons. This line of descent was present in the name of the father and, if he had one, in his surname. The *penates* were the gods of the larder; they turned the house into a food store, a place where one could preserve from one year to the next the fruits of the earth: corn, beans, wine, as well as bacon and salt meat.

The household fire at which offerings were made created links between these deities. The fire must never go out: every evening it was banked up, every morning rekindled. Only when the master left the house for the last time, if, for instance, he had been exiled, would the fire be ritually extinguished with wine.

BETWEEN COURTYARD AND GARDEN

Roman houses were four-sided, often rectangular. They had two floors but no cellar. The material used to build the walls varied over the centuries. For a long time Roman houses were built with cob (clay mixed with gravel and straw) on stone foundations. Later, however, they were made wholly of brick. Concrete, which made its appearance in the last century of the republic, was used mainly in public monuments but also in the substructures of the large villas that people began to erect on the outskirts of Rome and in the gulf of Naples, and even in a number of private houses at Rome. At that time, however, it would have been faced with stone or brick. On a steep slope, concrete could be used to build powerful vaulted foundations that could hold a series of houses hanging, as it might seem, above the sea.

Roman houses were in two main parts, the functions of which were quite different.

At the rear was a collection of windowless rooms seeming to turn away from the outside world and leading to an enclosed garden (see figure 2). All the light that entered the house came from this garden which in the most splendid of houses was arranged as a peristyle, or a square patio surrounded by a canopy resting on pillars (see figure 3). Where there was no peristyle, the garden would be bounded by a portico on one or two of its sides. This part of the house was reserved for family use and included bedrooms, food stores, kitchen and baths.

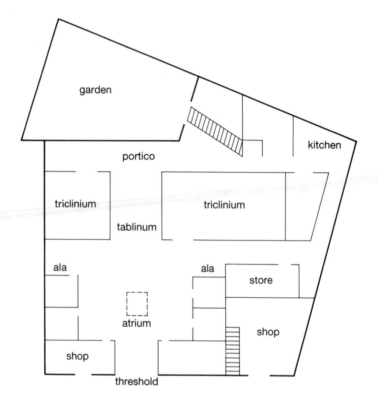

Figure 2   The surgeon's house, Pompeii; a traditional Roman house

The front part of the house opened out on to the outside world, though again there were no windows. But the *atrium*, a large entrance hall, was in part open to the sky. At the front of the house all the rooms served to receive outsiders to the household. The social standing of the head of the household was immediately apparent. It was in the *atrium* that the *paterfamilias* would exhibit his wealth

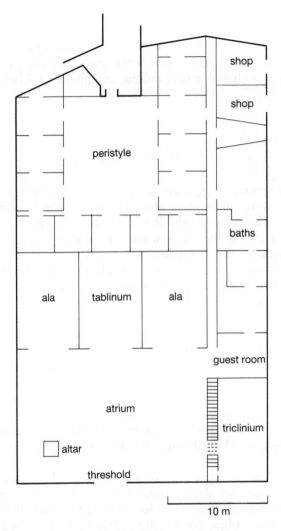

Figure 3 Livia's house, Palatine (simplified plan). The house was made of concrete clad with reticulated stone

through the luxury of the decor, and his nobility by way of the wall cupboards containing the wax masks of his ancestors.

The relative importance of the two parts of the house varied from one citizen to the next and from one kind of house to the next. Those who lived in town and were active in politics required large and sumptuous reception rooms, whereas the tradesman would set up his shop adjoining the *atrium*. A poor client who never received any visitors at all could make do with a tiny *atrium*.

Roman houses also had a third part, consisting of lodgings and shops. These were turned towards the street and away from the rest of the house, with which they did not communicate. They were let to strangers.

ROOF AND GARDEN

The private rooms ranged around the garden, in the rear portion of the house, were small, uncomfortable and sparsely decorated. This was where the women, children and slaves lived. Free men only entered this area of the house when they wished to sleep, to wash or to eat a quick cold breakfast. On the odd occasions when they lingered, talking with their closest friends, known as their *familiares*, they kept to the garden itself or to the portico. The design of the portico was so calculated that it provided shade in the summer but let in the warm slanting rays of the winter sun.

Everything complied with the austere daily regime that constituted the general rule of Roman life, luxury being an exception. Bedrooms were tiny, with just enough space for a bed and a few chairs that could be fetched if required. The bed itself consisted of a wooden bedstead on trestles, a straw mattress, woollen blankets and some cushions. Some houses also had small anterooms from where slaves could keep a watch over their masters' slumbers. Night-time, when a Roman slept, was the only time he was ever alone – and some found it distressing.

Some of the small rooms in this part of the house served as workrooms for the slaves, other still smaller ones were used as general storerooms. Not many Romans had clothes chests and even fewer had wardrobes. For furniture they had tables, beds, benches, chairs and armchairs: a civilized man would never sit, lie or eat on the ground.

The kitchen was situated in a corner, at the very back of the house, and was always tiny, even in large houses that had huge dining-rooms. It contained a sink and a fireplace with an opening in the wall for the smoke to escape. This fireplace might contain a built-in oven, and would be used for heating water for the bath, which would normally be situated next to the kitchen.

It was in this part of the house that everything requiring a roof or a covering of some sort – eating, sleeping and washing – was performed. Even if a dining area were built in the garden, with grassy couches, a canopy would be spread above the guests' heads.

This private part of the house was ruled over by the *penates*.

THE *ATRIUM*

Luxury, frescoes, mosaics, candelabra made from precious metals, vast halls with coffered ceilings and inlaid tables, golden tableware, Greek vases: all of these were to be found in the ceremonial rooms that led to the outside world.

The main room in this part of the house, at once the most ancient and the largest, was the *atrium*. The word was often used as a general term to denote this entire part of the house. The plural might be used, or (as in this book) the singular, 'the *atrium*', to indicate both the *atrium* and its adjoining rooms. It was after all a single system.

The proper definition of the term *atrium* is controversial. Some would define it as a hall with its roof open at its centre, others as a partly covered courtyard. The question is not mere sophistry. Upon the answer depends whether or not the *atrium* is seen as a symbolically covered area, a 'roof over one's head'. It is perfectly true that the *atrium* had at its centre a large opening to the sky, known as a *compluvium*. Below this stood a basin, called an *impluvium*, to collect the rain that fell through the *compluvium*. The purpose of this hole in the roof is also in question. A number of modern historians, haunted no doubt by a fanciful notion of primitive times, believe it was to let smoke escape. Such historians presumably picture Romans as a hirsute race clad in goatskins, squatting around bonfires in square one-room huts. The roof opening above the fireplace would preserve such hut-dwellers from being asphyxiated by the smoke. A strange practice indeed considering that to place the fire under the hole in the roof was the surest way of guaranteeing that it went out at the first drop of rain. According to this view, this one room served as kitchen, place of worship and parents' bedroom. That is why, our historians explain, the *atrium* contained the *lares* and a symbolic conjugal bed.

Regrettably for such prehistoric speculations, neither the *lares* nor the conjugal bed were ever kept in the *atrium*, but in a room that led into the *atrium*. Indeed, the *lares* were sometimes kept in the inner part of the house. There is therefore no choice but to discard the oft-repeated hypothesis that the *atrium* was initially the Roman house's only room, that the rest of the house developed behind it at a later date and that the *atrium* was retained solely as a ceremonial room. The final objection to such a view could not be more straightforward: if the hole in the roof was designed to let smoke out rather than rain in it ought surely to be have been called a 'smoke-hole' rather than a 'rain-hole' (*impluvium*). Why also did the hole, at all costs, have to be square in shape? If any smoke did exit through this hole, it was not smoke from a household fire – which was in any case covered – but sacrificial smoke that was destined for the gods above and *had to* rise vertically towards the sky.

The word *atrium* in Latin in fact meant 'court': the *atrium* was a semi-covered court. If the *compluvium* had been preserved it was not in memory of its former utilitarian purpose but because it had some significance. A house was by definition a roof, but an *atrium* open to the sky had no roof. Falling rain could symbolically strike its floor, a square of sky could be glimpsed, and the *atrium* thus formed a site of transition like a court in front of a house. It was here that the master of the house in his toga would receive visitors each morning.

The *atrium* was a vestibule-court that allowed strangers to the house to 'begin to enter'. They had crossed the *threshold*, they were already *inside*, within the private domain of the master of the house, but they were not yet *under his roof*.

At the rear of the *atrium*, facing the entrance, slightly raised above the level of the ground, was a room called the *tablinum*, also known as the 'floor', because it was a kind of balcony, usually made of wood. On either side of the *tablinum* were the *alae*, side-halls, two reception rooms which often contained the shrine to the *lares*. The *tablinum* was separated from the *atrium* by a curtain or by an open door; a visitor could normally see into the *tablinum*, which formed a sort of theatre stage. It was there, and not in the *atrium* itself, that one found the symbolic conjugal bed and the masks of the ancestors enclosed in their boxes over inscriptions giving a brief summary of each career.

It was in the *tablinum* and the *alae* that the master of the house would receive visitors and attend to his business, in the company of his secretary, his overseer, his political friends and his associates. This is therefore where his records and library would be kept.

The *atrium* with its adjoining rooms formed the social façade of the house and it was this part that varied most from one house to the next. The architect Vitruvius classified houses according to their *atrium* – that is, according to the social standing of the master of the house:

Magnificent vestibules and alcoves and halls are not necessary for the common people, because they pay their respects by visiting others, and are not visited by others.

But those who depend on country produce must have stalls for cattle, and shops in the forecourt, and, within the main building, there must be cellars, barns, stores and other apartments designed for the storage of produce rather than for an elegant effect.

He also gives a description of the *atrium* of one of the great men who were soon to seize the republic for their own personal gain:

For persons of high rank who hold office and magistracies, and whose duty it is to serve the state, we must provide princely vestibules, lofty halls and spacious peristyles, plantations and broad avenues finished in a majestic manner. Further, there must be libraries and basilicas of similar grace, and as magnificent as the equivalent public structures, because, in such palaces, public deliberations as well as private trials and judgements are often performed.[52]

There was no clearer way of stating that the house of the noble citizen would thenceforth receive a clientele as vast as the Roman people itself. It is worth noting that in this kind of residence, the front part of the house would eat into the back part, since the garden and peristyle would also become reception rooms. Such high-ranking Romans did not actually throw open their private lives to visitors, even if they pretended to do so. Instead, the house split into separate parts again: behind the public peristyle was a second peristyle and the various private rooms. It was this pattern that Augustus followed when establishing the palace on the Palatine hill.

House-owners displayed in the *atrium* their conception of life and their political preferences. Converts to philosophy would exhibit in a prominent position the busts of Socrates, Cleanthes or Epicurus instead of images of their ancestors and inscriptions recording their mighty deeds in the service of the state. Others would set up statues of allegorical Greek deities representing their favourite occupations, the Muses of history, tragic poetry or astronomy. Those who as yet had nothing to show but their wealth, for instance freedmen relying on their sons to dignify a future family, would lavishly decorate their *atrium*, amassing costly vases, Oriental tapestries and skilful paintings. By these means one's place in society could be conveyed: philosophers would claim to be the heirs, irrespective of national boundary or social origin, of their philosophical mentor; freedmen who had become rich would demonstrate that they were the sons of Fortune.

The two parts of the house were linked in two different ways. In practice a small narrow corridor was used to pass from one to the other. But the *tablinum* often had a door that led to the back of the house. This door was a clear signal to visitors that privacy began at that point. A door was a threshold, a point of passage from one world to another. To open it wide was to welcome someone into one's private domain. Performed by a nobleman it was a democratic gesture, even if the privacy was fraudulent and the peristyle ceremonial.

THE DINING-ROOM

Ambiguous in character, the dining-room might be situated in either part of the house, since meals were sometimes taken in the intimacy of the family but could occasionally provide the setting for a reception. Often therefore there were two dining-rooms: a smaller one at the rear and a larger and more sumptuous one at the front of the house (see figure 2).

This ambiguity was apparent in the room's layout and in the way it was furnished. The dining-room was called a *triclinium*, a 'room with three couches'. The three couches in question were arranged in a horseshoe shape around a central table, each couch normally accommodating three guests (see figure 4). Roman men ate lying

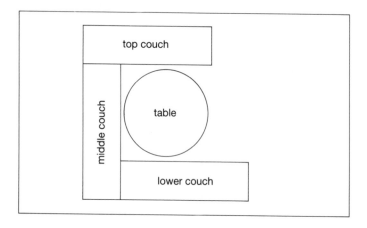

Figure 4   Plan of a triclinium

down, leaning on their left elbow, ranged like sardines, their heads nearest the table. Women and children, when they dined with the men, would remain seated.

The reclining position adopted by the men signified the unwinding and relaxation that went with intimacy. Yet at the same time, together with the *atrium*, the dining-rooms were the most luxuriously furnished rooms in the Roman household. The banquet to which one invited one's friends formed the terrain for an expression of sociability that opened on to the outside world through a shared intimacy.

The ancients related that to comply with tradition dining-rooms should remain open (that is, open to scrutiny) during the meal. This was held to exert a degree of social control over the sumptuousness of the repast and the behaviour of the dinner guests. It would also mean that the dining-room would have had to be situated near the entrance to the house and to open on to the *atrium*. Perhaps the *tablinum* had formerly been a dining-room. The Romans, however, sought to escape any social restraint by locating their dining-rooms on an upper floor, over the *tablinum*, or further inside the house itself, close to the garden. These shifts in the location of the dining-room account perhaps for the spate of sumptuary laws enacted from the second century onwards to regulate the lavishness of banquets.

The Romans had a passion for gardens. Even wretched landless ex-peasants living in city-centre housing blocks kept pot plants on their terraces or balconies. To explain this in terms of 'peasant atavism' would be rather over-hasty. For a start it presupposes that one understands what atavism is. But it begs another, larger, question: why was it that the Greeks, subject to the same 'atavism', did not combine house and garden in the same systematic way? Indeed, at the Adonia festivals, when Greek women sprinkled tepid water on seeds in pots, it was to kill off any premature shoots that might have emerged. Not exactly good gardening practice!

It is the structure of Roman household space that explains why Romans were attached to their gardens. Legally, religiously and culturally too, gardens were part and parcel of the territory of the house. The very etymology of the word *hortus* appears to indicate that, like the *atrium*, the garden was situated inside the house. It was always closed in, either by a wall or by a dense cane hedge. It shielded the family from view and allowed women to work there undisturbed. The fact that the *lar* watched over it indicated that the garden was an entirely cultivated area. Unlike fields, gardens were never left fallow, nor were they ploughed. They were productive all year round and were tended by hand, manured and carefully protected from cold winds or the scorching sun.

The Romans said that the garden was a second 'salting-tub': one could always find food there. Gardens were used to grow the staple vegetables of the Roman diet: brassicas, greens, marrows, sorrel, cucumbers, lettuces, leeks – to mention only those that are familiar to us, for at that time a much wider variety of species was eaten. Another patch of the garden would be given over to those plants that add savour to food and appease hunger: garlic, onions, cress, chicory. Several medicinal herbs would also be grown for use in herbal tisanes, infusions and poultices. Lastly, the Romans grew flowers that were of use in the worship of household deities, for at festivals it was considered proper to crown the altars with flowers.

The gardens of well-to-do houses, when rearranged as peristyles, were no more than pleasure gardens, with flowers and evergreen shrubs, that could be treated architecturally as an extension of the house. The house-owner would have another garden on the outskirts of the city which would produce the necessary vegetables. One final change should be noted: from the first century BC onwards, the innermost part of Roman houses opened out on to large gardens that were themselves enclosed. These gardens, with their blend of stone constructions and topiary, were really landscaped parks.

FARMHOUSES AND COUNTRY HOUSES

There is a distinction to be drawn between farmhouses and city houses.

First of all, there was the traditional farm on which a Roman peasant family might live, this being their only property. Such farmhouses were rather like the more traditional city houses: the *atrium* was in this case really a courtyard and the rooms leading on to it were stables, cowsheds and outhouses for farm equipment. At the back of the house would be huge halls, exposed to dry winds, where wheat and other products, such as pulses, fruits and wine, would be stored. Bacon was kept in a special cool and well-aired storeroom, and cheeses were set to dry near the fire. Around the farmhouse there would be a threshing floor, a manure pit and a garden. These would be sited in appropriately dry or damp places and care was taken to prevent one from having a harmful effect on another. Gardens required the putrid dampness of the manure pit but had to be sheltered from any dry chaff that might blow across from the threshing floor. Wheat that was contaminated by rotting matter from the pit might not keep.

But this was not the only kind of farm. All politicians owned not only a house at Rome, their main residence, but also one or more farms which would be put to a variety of uses. First, they would have most of their provisions – wheat, vegetables, wine, oil and pork – brought in from these farms as well as wood, wool, leather and chickens and kids needed for feast days. Also, they would send their children to the farm so that they could be brought up away from disease, the corruption of city life and the temptations of the flesh. They would themselves make regular visits to the farm to take the air and live the good life. In old age, they would retire to a farm and take pleasure in overseeing farmwork and in digging their garden.

Farms close to towns could be turned to profit, as long as one concentrated on non-staple, luxury produce: snails, dormice, thrushes, peacocks, farmed fish, asparagus, fatted boars and chickens, or regional specialities, fruits or wines. Such farms were mere places of work, where crops were grown to be preserved and where they were stored. Everything was sacrificed to business. The farm was operated to produce the staple food for the men and animals while at the same time specializing in a specific profitable crop. Business transformed the farmhouse itself. As well as numerous and spacious storerooms, there would also be an oil press, a wine press or huge fishponds. One large farm not far from Pompeii, known as the Villa of Boscoreale, specialized in wine production. The farmhouse was a large building covering 800 square metres, with a living area on the first floor for the master. On entering the courtyard, one found on one's left everything to do with the day-to-day life of the animals and people who lived on the farm: a kitchen, a dining-room, baths, a stone for milling wheat, a bread oven, bedrooms and sheds for the livestock. The rest of the house, the central section and the area to the right, were given over to the production and storage of wine.

Every farm was run by a couple, the farmer and his wife. They might be citizens, freedmen or slaves. One rule, however, was strictly observed: a single man could not manage a farm on his own. But the farmer and farmer's wife did not undertake productive work: their job was to manage the farm and to ensure that all technical and religious rules were enforced. Another rule compelled the farmer to be something of a homebody: little or no entertaining was done on the farm and visits were not returned. There were some exceptions to this: religious festivals like the Terminalia obliged neighbours to invite each other round.[53] Only farm-owners who intended one day to go into politics would invite their neighbours to dinner. The farmer's main duties were to celebrate rituals and to demonstrate to his workers how each job of work should be performed. He had to have knowledge of every job on the farm even if he did not do them all himself. He was the only person who could make sacrifices or command sacrifices to be made: neither his wife nor any of the workers could take this initiative. He alone could order land to be cleared for cultivation, harvesting to commence or tracks to be laid.[54]

The farmer's wife also had a specific role: she made sure everyone was well-fed and oversaw the regular purification of the house.

> She should be neat herself, and keep the farmstead neat and clean. She should clean and tidy the hearth every night before she goes to bed. On the Kalends, Ides and Nones, and whenever a holy day comes, she should hang a garland over the hearth, and on those days pray to the household gods as opportunity offers. She should keep a supply of cooked food on hand for you and the servants. She should keep many hens and have plenty of eggs. She should have a large store of dried pears, sorbs [fruit of the service-tree], figs, raisins, sorbs in must, preserved pears and grapes and quinces. She should also keep preserved grapes in grape-pulp and in pots buried in the ground, as well as fresh Praenestine nuts kept in the same way, and Scantian quinces in jars, and other fruits that are usually preserved, as well as wild fruits. All these she should store away diligently every year.[55]

The sense of plenty that was provided by a farm's brimming lofts, the good life without guests or business visits and love of the garden, that ideal place for unalloyed privacy, meant that country residences in the last years of the republic were turned into holiday resorts, warping their original character. Farms along the shores of the gulf of Naples became luxuriously appointed country villas fit for entertaining on a lavish scale. As in the city, parks were added to buildings so that people could live encircled by artificial fountains and dine under bowers or in pavilions.

6

The family

A HOUSE, A FAMILY AND A FATHER

The combination of the *lar* and the *genius* in the cult celebrated by the Roman *paterfamilias* shows that at Rome family and house really were indissoluble. At Rome, everything led back to the soil, even paternal power and kinship.

Family in its Latin sense, *familia*, covered every member of the household subject to the power of the father of the family, the *paterfamilias*: children, slaves and sometimes (depending on the type of marriage she had contracted) the wife. A house consisted of a family and a father, joined together in veneration of the *lar familiaris*. The authority of the father was not defined piecemeal in terms of property or genealogy but more comprehensively in terms of residence, even if he was in fact the father (or grandfather or great-grandfather) of the children and the owner of the slaves that lived in the house.

The *genius* was the god of household genealogy. It was in the house that children were conceived and born. The model family assembled under one roof three generations of men all of whom remained subject to the authority of the great-grandfather. Upon his death, the family would split into as many new families as there were men of the subsequent generation. Ideally a house was inhabited by all the sons, grandsons and great-grandsons, along with their wives, of a common surviving progenitor.

Three generations was the sweep of time that corresponded to what

Romans called *memoria*, or 'memory'. It was the amount of time deemed to be within anyone's living memory. The average length of Roman life was such that few survived beyond the appearance of their third-degree descendant. At best a man might in his lifetime know his great-grandchildren and his great-grandfather. These six generations amounted to what Romans referred to as *parentes*. At the Parentalia, the festival of the dead, the family venerated all those of its deceased that any surviving member had known, including all the dead *parentes* of the youngest member of the family as well as all those of the oldest. Beyond that the thread of memory was broken, there being no living direct witness. All other forebears joined the undifferentiated mass of *majores*, or elders.

This same measure of three generations crops up in legislation to regulate inheritance or prohibit incest. All the daughters of the household were 'sisters' and therefore, as far as the men of the family were concerned, unmarriageable.

Thus defined in terms of a three-generation span, the Roman family extended horizontally as far as sixth-degree relatives – that is, to include second cousins (see figure 5). In Rome it was only the male line of descent that counted, only relatives on the father's side were deemed family, and the ban on incest only extended beyond brothers and sisters to cover uncles, aunts and cousins on the father's side. The rule was clearcut: one might not marry a woman with whom one was already sharing a roof unmarried. This rule changed somewhat during the second century BC. The family was narrowed down to fourth-degree relatives, and it became customary for men to marry the daughter of their father's sister – that is, their patrilateral cross-cousin – with whom, of course, they were deemed to have no bond of kinship, since her father was from a different family.

At the head of the family stood a single authority, the male parent, the father of the family who reigned over his children, grandchildren and even great-grandchildren. Whether or not the children continued to live in the house, they depended economically and legally on their father, grandfather or great-grandfather, as long as these senior men of the family were alive. No Roman who was subject to the authority of a father could do business in his own name or take possession of any good, unless the said father chose to emancipate him, which in fact happened quite frequently. A father might even grant his son a *peculium*, or nest egg, as to a slave, though it would involve a much greater sum. After all, his son might be an aedile or praetor in great need of money.

Women who married into such a house necessarily came from

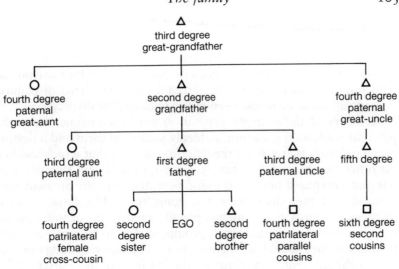

Figure 5 illustration labels:

third degree
great-grandfather

fourth degree
paternal
great-aunt

second degree
grandfather

fourth degree
paternal
great-uncle

third degree
paternal aunt

first degree
father

third degree
paternal uncle

fifth degree

fourth degree
patrilateral
female
cross-cousin

second
degree
sister

EGO

second
degree
brother

fourth degree
patrilateral
parallel
cousins

sixth degree
second
cousins

△ male
○ female
□ male or female

Figure 5   The Roman family, spanning three generations, taking account only of agnatic kinship; the patrilateral female cross-cousin has been added From: *Yvan Thomas*, Histoire de la parenté, *Armand Colin, Paris, 1987, p. 202.*

outside, and their status varied according to the kind of marriage they contracted. If they changed house, leaving that of their father and going to live in that of their husband, they assumed the status of a daughter. If they remained attached to the house of their father, they did not belong to the new house, but were merely 'passing through' in order to provide their husband with children.

This patriarchal household was no figment of the Roman jurist's imagination or fossilized imprint of archaic customs. The Romans loved to live surrounded by their relatives and there were, at all periods and in every social class, many large families living under the same roof. The striking example of the Aelii Tuberones is often cited: 'For there were sixteen members of the family, all Aelii; and they had a very little house, and one little farm sufficed for all, where they maintained one home together with many wives and children',[56] but it would be wrong to imagine that they were an exception to the rule.

Before launching himself into his career, Crassus lived with his two married brothers at the house of his father, a former consul and triumphant general. Everyone ate at the same table. Cicero had a friend at Brundisium, Marcus Laenius, who lived in the same house as his father, brother, sons and nephews. The women appeared to have vanished from this family of men, a dream-come-true for the Romans who found a woman's presence around the house hard to endure. Perhaps all these men had been either widowed or divorced.

Members of the younger generation would sometimes leave the paternal household if fortune suddenly smiled on them and a destiny presented itself that was markedly different from that which awaited the other members of their family. Cicero, Crassus and Sulla all went out and purchased houses to found new dynasties the moment they realized that their lives were not going to be like those of their relatives – as provincial knights, penniless patricians or low-ranking nobility. Ambition would often prompt such sons to make an early break, and they would set themselves up in temporary lodgings – at an exorbitant rent, but close to the forum. At the outset of his political life, Sulla lodged in a tenement. Caelius, Cicero's young friend, rented a small lodging on the Palatine hill in a house belonging to Clodius. This was how he met Clodius' sister, the bewitching Clodia, the root of all his troubles. Far from their father and their house, these young people were easy prey to loose women and usurers and could be inveigled by people like Catiline into dubious political scheming. Caesar collected around himself many such penniless boys, weary of paternal supervision and dreaming of their father's death and their own inheritance.

FAMILY, CLAN AND NOBILITY

Every Roman family belonged to a much wider community, their clan, or *gens*. But this community had neither spatial anchorage nor much social importance. The clan only appeared in one's name. One spoke of the *Fabia gens* or of the Fabii, sometimes adding a surname in order to distinguish, for example, the Cornelii Scipiones from other Cornelii.

But since names were passed on by birth, adoption or enfranchisement, and since there was a considerable degree of social mobility in Rome, the mere fact of belonging to a clan could not be advanced as a claim to either nobility or dignity.

That clans existed as communities was only apparent on two kinds of occasion: the assignment of inheritances and the performance of cult obligations. When a Roman left no heir, not even a sixth-degree

Plate 4   Roman family, second century BC
Reproduced by kind permission of the Ancient Art and Architecture Collection
(Ronald Sheridan)

relative, the clan would inherit. The clans moreover were the guardians of rites and observances that it was their responsibility to celebrate in the interest of everyone.

The Fabii, for instance, had each year to perform a religious ceremony on the Quirinal hill. Being very scrupulous, they felt obliged to fulfil their duty, even when the Capitol was being besieged by the Gauls:

A young Roman attracted the wondering admiration of fellow citizens and foes. There was an annual sacrifice to be made on the Quirinal hill by the family of the Fabii. To celebrate it Gaius Fabius Corso, in the Gabinian cincture [a mode of girding up the toga traditional in religious ceremonies], with the sacred vessels in his hands, descended from the Capitol, passed out through the midst of the enemy's pickets and, regardless of any words or threats, proceeded to the Quirinal, where he duly accomplished all the rites. He then returned the same way, with the same resolute countenance and gait, in the full assurance of the favour of the gods whose service not even the fear of death could cause him to neglect.[57]

Nobility was not a question of a clan or a name: it was built up or torn down within the setting of the household and family. 'Three fathers' was the duration required to establish a man's noble status: a father, grandfather and great-grandfather had each to have exercised a higher magistracy. In other words, for a child to be noble it was essential that he had been subject solely to the authority of relatives who were magistrates. The nobility of Octavian, whose great-grandfather had been a freedman, was called into question.[58] It mattered little that a man's family had been noble in times past; an interruption of three generations was all it took to deprive him of his noble status. Thus Marcus Aemilius Scaurus, consul in 115 BC, was regarded as a 'new man' because no one in his family had obtained a magistracy since his great-grandfather. The house of a noble family would contain men all of whom would have occupied higher magistracies.

The symbolic conjugal bed enthroned in the *tablinum* was a reminder that the house was also intended to accommodate a woman destined to become a mother. Whether the marriage really brought the wife into the household, for instance through the ritual sharing of a cake in the presence of Jupiter's *flamen*, or priest, and the *pontifex maximus*, or chief priest, or whether the marriage merely involved the couple living under the same roof after the signature of a contract, its function remained the same: to change the woman's status from that of young maid, *virgo*, to that of mother, *mater*. The marriage itself was not regarded as having been fully consummated until the first child was born in the house. Marriage was about procreation and nothing else, so it was essential that children should be born inside the house, but irrelevant whether the mother was under the authority of her father or her husband.

The bride's age varied greatly depending on whether it was her first marriage. Roman girls tended to marry very young, though the law prohibited them from marrying below the age of twelve. Such early marriages were even more premature than they might first appear, since girls reached puberty at a later age than they do today. In noble families, the wedding was often preceded by a lengthy engagement in order to bring the two families closer together. Prior to the wedding the young bride-to-be might go to live with her future husband in his house.

Whether or not it was a first marriage, and whatever kind of contract was involved, the ritual never changed. The bride would be dressed in her own house by the women of her family, who would disguise her under a fire-coloured veil and dress her in a simple white smock, gathered by a belt tied in a special knot that the groom would have to untie. Her hair would be separated into six separate tufts, arranged with a spearhead and held by ribbons. The groom would go to the bride's father's house and take in his right hand the right hand of his wife, thereby ratifying the vow of marital fidelity.

The wedding banquet would then take place, bringing together the relatives of both families and declaring their new-found amity. At the end of the banquet, the bridegroom, wresting the bride from her mother's arms, would pretend to abduct her. A procession would then lead the young girl to the husband's house. She would carry a spindle and a distaff and would hold the hand of a child whose parents were still living, while a third child, waving a torch of hawthorn, would clear the way for them. The people in the procession would laugh and hurl obscene jokes at the couple. Arriving at the threshold of the house, the bride would bedeck the door with strands of wool and smear it with lard and oil. Her husband, waiting indoors, would ask her to tell him her forename. Since Roman women did not use the forename, she would reply: 'Wherever you are Gaius, there shall I be Gaia.' She would then be lifted over the threshold so that her feet would not touch the ground beneath it. The only people who entered a house for the first time were strangers to it, family members having all been born there. The following morning, the bride, wearing the matron's costume – worn by mothers and women in a position to become mothers – would make an offering to the *lares* and the *penates*.

From then on, two different fates beckoned the bride. If she was lucky enough to be fertile and gave birth to three children or more, she would be a respected mother, a wife to be envied and would gain acceptance in the community. If, however, she proved infertile, she would soon be threatened with repudiation. This was not as bad as it might seem. Having returned to her father's house with her dowry, she might upon his death become an almost free woman who, in time, might even forget her failure as a matron by throwing herself into business affairs and amorous diversions.

Many wives died before either of these destinies could be fulfilled. Childbearing and its aftermath carried off huge numbers of women between the ages of sixteen and thirty-five. The young mothers who died in childbirth form a long list, even though the lives of so few Roman women are known to us. Tullia, Cicero's daughter, died when she was thirty-three, shortly after having given birth to a son by her third husband, Dolabella. Emilia, Sulla's daughter-in-law, compelled to divorce in order to marry Pompey when she was already pregnant by her husband, died in labour. Julia, Caesar's daughter and another of Pompey's wives, after suffering one miscarriage, died giving birth to her first child. Pomponia, the mother of the first Africanus, died after submitting to a Caesarian so that her son might live. But the fate of most Roman women is quite unknown. Funerary inscriptions add a few names to the list, but not enough to provide us with statistics. The evidence provided by Roman men complaining of the dearth of wives, however, is more eloquent than any statistic – especially when we take into account the Romans' general unwillingness to marry. Childbirth killed more women than wars did men. The balance was temporarily restored by massacres of men at the hands of Hannibal or the Gauls.

SURROGATE MOTHERS

From the second century onwards, as a result of this imbalance between the number of men wishing to get married and the availability of women capable of becoming mothers, there was in every section of society a sharp increase in the number of divorces and remarriages of fertile women. A wife who had proved herself a good childbearer might thus pass from one home to the next, providing children. Of course, frequent marriage was also a way for the nobility to enlarge the network of its relations and its political backing. But that did not apply to the families of the *plebs* or of the small provincial notables, where divorce and remarriage were just as common as among the Roman nobility.

Marriage assumed the character of an undertaking between men who lent one another their daughter, sister and even sometimes their wife as a way of ensuring that children were produced. In earlier times, the Romans had practised adoption. Divorce and remarriage came to be preferred because this enabled a man whose wife was fertile to supply children to men who would otherwise remain childless, instead of merely sharing such children with him. After all, an adopted son did not switch fathers; he had two of them. This was why many divorces took place when the divorcee was pregnant, like that of Sulla's daughter-in-law. Cato likewise gave his pregnant wife to Hortensius, and Octavian obtained Livia, six months pregnant, from her husband Claudius Nero. It was then simply a matter of deciding to whom the resulting child was to belong.

MARRIAGE AND FAMILY STRATEGIES

The Romans proclaimed to anyone prepared to listen that there was nothing worse than marriage, and that were it not for the necessity of producing children, no one would ever get married. A rich wife was a tyrant and a poor one would spend all your money. So the only Romans who married were those who could not avoid it, men burdened with the responsibility of continuing the family line or those who decided to found one.

An old and noble family, the Claudii, furnish an instructive example from the middle of the first century BC. The father had died leaving three sons, three daughters, of whom only the eldest was married, and very little money. The eldest son became head of the family. He married off his sisters, which was not too difficult, even though they had no dowry. Both of them made excellent matches. One married Lucullus, the other Metellus Celer the consul, her cousin on her mother's side. The first of these two sisters, owing to her ill-conduct and involvement with her brothers in political skullduggery, was repudiated childless by Lucullus. The other sister, the notorious Clodia, beloved of the poet Catullus, was soon widowed – it was rumoured that she had given Nature a helping hand – and had no thoughts of remarrying. Free at last, she held a salon, seduced the young and engaged in politics on the side of her brother Clodius, the tribune, an adversary of Cicero, who was eventually assassinated on the Appian Way. Appius Claudius, the eldest brother, got married but, remaining childless, arranged for his brother Gaius also to marry. Gaius' first son was given the forename Appius, which marked him off as his uncle's successor. Gaius then had a second son, whom he gave to his elder brother; he named him Appius. Appius Junior thus gained from his elder 'cousin' the role of future head of the family.

Publius, the youngest of the three brothers, who assumed the name Clodius because it sounded more democratic, had been adopted by a plebeian so that he could be elected tribune of the *plebs*. He left the paternal household, broke with the rather conservative family tradition and decided to throw in his lot with the popular party. He purchased a house and got married with a view to founding a noble family. He married Fulvia, an enviable match, who by the time he died had given him two young children. Fulvia later married Gaius Scribonius Curio, a friend of Clodius, by whom she had a son, despite the brevity of the marriage. Curio left shortly afterwards for Africa. In 45 BC, she married Mark Antony, a friend of Curio, by whom she had two sons. She died in Sicily in the summer of 40 BC. Like so many Romans, she had fallen ill in Greece and had not survived the journey home. She must have been about thirty years old, at most thirty-five. She had married in 58 BC between the ages of twelve and seventeen.

Fulvia had a fine matron's temperament. To each of her husbands in turn she was faithful in the Roman sense of the term. She actively took their part when they became embroiled in political difficulties and she headed Clodius' funeral procession with great skill and helped to convict his assassin, Milo. She supported Mark Antony's followers in Italy while he was away in Egypt playing the ladykiller with Cleopatra.

Those Roman women who had any children at all generally had several, four or five each, even if they had not all been born in the same house. They were not, however, the only maintainers of demographic stability: a great many children were born out of wedlock. Those Roman men who did not get married, and for that matter those who did, generally lived with slaves or freedwomen 'as husband and wife'. The children resulting from such unions could bear their natural father's name if he chose to enfranchise them, but they would not automatically adopt his social position. One might sire numerous children and still fail to reproduce oneself socially.

CONJUGAL LOVE

As far as Roman married couples were concerned, whether a marriage was loving or loveless was quite irrelevant. Love did not come into it. The public display of affection, however, was considered indecent. Cato the Censor expelled Manilius, a prospective candidate for consul, from the senate on the grounds that he had embraced his wife in broad daylight in front of their daughter. Manilius' career foundered on a kiss.[59] Commenting on the event, Cato said that for his own part he never embraced his wife unless it was thundering loudly, and he would sometimes joke that he was a happy man indeed when it thundered.

Men in love were thought laughable, especially old dodderers who married young girls. Yet this is precisely what Cato eventually did. Being a sensible old man, on losing his wife he had married off his son. Cato himself assiduously frequented a certain slavegirl, who came to see him every evening in his room, but his son felt that this carrying-on was rather shocking in a house where there was a young bride, his wife. Cato went straight to the forum where his friends gathered around him, forming an escort. Among them was a scribe, Salonius, who had worked at Cato's house when the great man had been a magistrate and who had since remained his client. Cato called him over and asked whether he had found a husband yet for his daughter. Salonius replied that he had not, and that he was reluctant to do so without asking Cato for his opinion. 'Well then,' said Cato, 'I have found a suitable son-in-law for you, unless you find his age an obstacle. He is a worthy man in all respects, but he is very old.' Salonius could hardly object. Cato then declared that he was himself the fiancé. Astounded but honoured, Salonius rushed to put his signature on the contract. Cato's young wife gave him a son who assumed as surname the name of his maternal grandfather, Salonius.[60]

Pompey was famous for his un-Roman conjugal sentimentality, which considerably damaged his reputation. He was unfortunately always in love with his current wife.

Pompey married Caesar's daughter Julia, his third wife, for strictly political reasons, yet their love was idyllic. At the beginning of their marriage, he spent all his time with her in the countryside on his farm at Piacenza, enjoying a somewhat inane bucolic contentment. They took the air in the gardens and watched the peasants working in the fields. In the meantime, Caesar schemed and plotted. Pompey, for his part, sought out every possible excuse not to leave Italy. The whole of Rome laughed behind the backs of the two love-birds: she seemed even more smitten than he was, despite the difference in age. Perhaps it was the charm of his conversation. It was certainly said that Pompey had broken many a heart. Flora, one of his ex-mistresses and an illustrious courtesan, declared that Pompey was irresistible in bed, and that she never 'left his embraces without bearing the marks of his teeth'.[61] Unfortunately, Julia soon died giving birth to a child who scarcely survived her. At the time Pompey seemed inconsolable.

Shortly thereafter, however, Pompey married Cornelia, the daughter of Metellus Scipio, recently widowed by the death of Crassus' son, who had died with his father on an expedition against the Parthians. This was a shrewd marriage in that Metellus Scipio, through his natural father and his adoptive father, had been the most noble Roman of his time. Cornelia was delightful and highly cultivated, being well versed in literature, philosophy and geometry. Pompey forgot everything and spent his time at banquets conversing with her about body, soul and the squaring of the circle. His exasperated friends had to wrench him from such delights and force him to turn his mind to politics. Cornelia gave him a son.

Thankfully for the republic – for politics might otherwise have been seriously affected – Pompey was an exception. Roman marriages were generally characterized by indifference and a succession of daily irritations. Married couples avoided meeting one another in private, for privacy was a constant source of friction.

Aemilius Paullus had married Papiria, daughter of a former consul. Papiria was the perfect wife and gave her husband two sons, both of whom proved exceptional men, who bore the names Scipio Aemilianus and Fabius Maximus Aemilianus. Socially, Papiria was everything that was expected of her: she was beautiful, virtuous and fertile. Aemilius Paullus, however, decided to divorce her. 'Why?' he was asked. 'Is she not discreet? Is she not beautiful? Is she not fruitful?' Aemilius Paullus then held out his shoe, saying: 'Is this not handsome? Is it not new? But not one of you can see where it pinches my foot.'[62]

So he married another woman, who fitted him better and with whom he had two sons and two daughters. Being so well blessed, Aemilius Paullus decided to have the sons of his first marriage adopted, hoping thereby to avoid the conflicts that regularly arose at Rome between the children of a man's first marriage and their stepmother. Unfortunately, the two sons of the second marriage both died, one aged fourteen and the other twelve, at the moment of their father's triumph over Perseus.

Married couples rarely shared the same bedroom: the bed in the *atrium* was purely symbolic. The physical relationship between the two would be confined to the essentials required for procreation. Pregnant wives abstained from sexual relations altogether and mothers nursing small children did likewise for the two or three years that they continued to breast-feed.

Conjugal love at Rome entailed neither physical intimacy nor closeness of feeling. It was more a form of social behaviour. In ordinary circumstances it worked in a restrictive way. Conjugal love was a *fides*: a good wife observed the loyalty that she owed her husband. She must not betray him, or behave badly in public, or ally herself with his political adversaries. But it was in times of crisis that conjugal loyalty was revealed. As with slaves and freedmen, a number of edifying tales circulated about wives.

The story of Sulpicia was set against the background of the wave of proscriptions at the end of the republic:

> Sulpicia, although spied upon by her mother Julia, who sought to prevent her from following her husband Lentulus Cruscellio to Sicily – he had been proscribed by the triumvirs – disguised herself as a serving-woman, took four slaves with her, two men and two women, and managed to escape and rejoin Lentulus. She was not afraid to risk her own proscription by displaying such loyalty, such *fides*, towards her proscribed husband.[63]

Such faithfulness always contained an element of ostentation. A decent woman, when her husband was in difficulties, was duty-bound to weep and wail in public in order to excite compassion for herself and her children. Bereavement was the high point: while the men sang the praises of the glorious deceased, his wife would scream and tear her cheeks. His household wept for him, his city honoured him, everything was just as it should be: the deceased received his due.

Wifely loyalty attained its most handsome expression when a wife happened to be infertile. Those who were then able to withdraw discreetly, yield to a repudiation that might prove only temporary, and welcome into the house a more fruitful womb, were celebrated as heroines, as were those who showed no jealousy to concubines, freedwomen or slaves, and took no advantage of their position to persecute them.

There existed, however, a malaise and a reciprocal distrust between Roman married couples. Wives were avid for the slightest sign of affection but this their husbands generally refused to show them. There were not many husbands who, like Pompey or Antony, behaved romantically towards their wives,[64] for such conduct was thought dishonourable. Cicero did not fail to go into minute details about Antony's amorousness in his diatribes against the triumvir. Men were afraid of falling under the spell of a woman with whom they might be in love, and what frightened them most was the thought that they might be seen as henpecked. Cato the Elder, who perhaps knew what he was talking about, was often heard to repeat this maxim: 'All other men rule their wives; we rule all other men, and our wives rule us.'[65] Antony, indeed, proved unable to resist Cleopatra.

To Roman men women seemed an unknown quantity, and this could make them panic. In 331 BC there was an abnormal surge in the mortality rate among the principal citizens of Rome. They were all succumbing to the same sickness. A serving-woman at last revealed to Fabius Maximus that there was nothing natural about the deaths: the men were being poisoned by their wives. A search was conducted and some twenty matrons were caught in their homes busy brewing potions. The matrons were led away and everyone reassembled at the forum before the tribunal. Two women swore that the concoctions were medicinal and not poisonous. The suggestion was then made that they should demonstrate their innocence by drinking the so-called medicines. Upon brief consultation, the wives did as proposed and all died. A torrent of denunciations ensued that led to the conviction of 170 women.

Society was thrown into a state of near-crisis. The last thing that the Romans wanted to do was to seek an explanation for such a widespread phenomenon. It was decided that the wives had fallen prey to insanity, that it had been a sort of divine plague and that the case called for not justice but religious atonement. The trials were halted and a nail was driven into the wall of the temple of Jupiter, as was the custom when the city was visited by plagues or by serious social conflicts between the *plebs* and the senate.[66]

This was not the end of the matter, however. At the beginning of the second century BC, a huge investigation throughout Italy led to the conviction for poisoning of 2,000 wives, including the wife of the consul, Calpurnius Piso.[67]

What were these potions? Love philtres? Cures for infertility? There was an entire female art of cookery deployed by wives in order to improve their marital relations. It is unlikely that all the women wanted to murder their husbands. Philtres and magic potions were frequently used at Rome by those who, like women and freedmen, had no access to power. Unable to persuade their husbands or patrons by force of argument, since the said men were wilfully deaf to their words, they perhaps sought to act upon them without their knowledge. But these philtres, brewed by witches who had commerce with the dead, were evidently extremely dangerous, capable of causing madness or death.

HOUSEHOLD SEX

The Roman household was a hotbed of sexual activity – except between married couples. Every slave was a potential sexual partner for the free men of the house.

It is hard for us to understand Roman sexuality. First, what made a particular sexual liaison taboo had nothing to do with gender or age and everything to do with legal status. Second, Roman sexuality did not create any relationship between partners; it was neither a service rendered nor a form of communication. It founded no obligation or bond on either side. In Roman society, where eating, working, going to war or living under the same roof with somebody automatically created a close relationship, sex played no such role.

The conjugal bond entailed signing a contract and having children together, but did not extend to sharing acts of love. To the Romans, sexuality had nothing to do with culture; it was a pure manifestation of natural life, like the need for sleep or food. Moreover, sex, unlike food, never became drawn into the cultural realm. One simply did it, without shame, though it was not proper to talk about it.

Sex was prohibited outside marriage only if one's partner was free-born – and this prohibition was waived if one could demonstrate that she or he had done it for the money. It made no difference whether the forbidden partner was a young girl, a woman or a boy, the crime of *stuprum* was abhorrent and punishable by death. Otherwise, everything was permitted without distinction as to gender or age. There were just two reservations: first, over-indulgence in the pleasures of love, like every other form of excess, was deemed a moral fault; second, the less that was said about sex the better. On no account should it be turned into one of the fine arts, as the Greeks had done: that was downright perversion.

As for the actual manner of love-making, no forms of behaviour were particularly prescribed or prohibited. It was not so much the act itself that mattered as what it revealed about the man in question. At Rome the greatest insult was to call someone 'effeminate'. A man who was effeminate was one who had become soft through being steeped in pleasures, especially the pleasures of love. He was both a womanizer and a homosexual – the two went together: it was said of Caesar that he was the 'husband of all women and the wife of all husbands'. It is quite mistaken to claim, as does Michel Foucault,[68] that the Romans distinguished between a morally good active sexuality and a morally bad passive sexuality. Sexual pleasure was always passive and as such morally suspect. Sooner or later, in fact, every Roman was accused of being effeminate. In the middle of his idyll with Julia, Pompey was met at Rome with taunts about both his lecherousness and his effeminacy.[69]

Slaves (whether male or female), freedmen and freedwomen were all bound by *fides* to submit to the desires of the master, as was his wife, and they had the same duty towards the sons of the house. Free men might well have made a show of respect for the other's desires, but if that other were then to have rejected his advances it would have been at their own risk. When a Roman did choose to accept a slave's refusal, it was not out of respect for that slave as a human being; he would do so in order simply to learn how to discipline his own passions, just as he would struggle to overcome his anger against a negligent servant. Always the most important relationship was that between a man and his brutish instincts, which needed self-control and discipline, rather than that with another person.

The outcome of all this domestic licentiousness was that the inhabitants of the house lived in a state of considerable confusion regarding blood relations. The children of the family were surrounded by people, many of whom were, might be or had already been their father's mistress or male lover. What we would consider to be acts of incest were frequent occurrences. The father's mistress might well be his servant's daughter, while her son might be his lover – and he might well be the father of both of them. The son of the family would also go to bed with both his 'brothers' and his 'sisters'. Yet whatever else it might be, such sex was discreet and quick. Sexual relations might sometimes coincide with close bonds between a slave and a master that led eventually to the enfranchisement of the slave, but they did not form a basis for such links. What mattered in a house was neither love nor desire but loyalty, *fides*.

LOVE OF CHILDREN

Women at the centre of Roman families lived hard lives. Only those women who escaped the wife's lot through widowhood or through infertility and consequent divorce could expect to lead a different kind of life. Such women would take young nobles as lovers and manage their own affairs with the aid of serviceable tutors and freedmen who would let them use their names in contracts. The wealthiest of such women could come and go at their leisure between their country villas and their gardens at Rome. They would hold salons, patronize poets, receive foreign guests and intervene in political alliances. But without a child such a life was not one of happiness. At Rome neither man nor woman could be happy without a descendant.

Romans loved their sons and daughters passionately, and their loss was said to be a sorrow that gnawed at one's heart. The greatest and most unbending of Roman generals had been utterly broken by such bereavements. The dictator Camillus, conqueror of the Gauls, lost one of his sons to an illness. Paralysed with grief, Camillus retreated into close seclusion with the women of his household.[70] The worst misfortune that ever befell Aemilius Paullus, the conqueror of Perseus, was the simultaneous loss of both his adolescent sons, on the very day of his triumph. He none the less celebrated the victory feast as if nothing was amiss so as not to cloud the happiness of the Roman people. Everyone admired such force of spirit, though it bordered on the inhuman. The *pontifex* Quintus Fulvius Flaccus did not possess the same moral fibre. On learning that one of his sons had died in the war and that the other was fatally ill, he hanged himself.[71] Cicero never really recovered from the death of his daughter Tullia whom he cherished so dearly[72] that he decided to dedicate a little temple to her memory.

MOTHERS AND SONS

The love that mothers and sons bore for each other was particularly strong, for many a Roman woman was left after the death of her husband to bring up a son on her own. Many of the great men of the republic had never known their fathers and had been brought up the hard way by a mother resolved to prepare them for a life of exertion and honour. Such mothers were stern tutors.[73] They well knew that too much indulgence would sap a child's future ability to face the fierce demands made of citizens. Julius Caesar, himself a fatherless child, was brought up by his mother Aurelia, and it was this early education that later enabled him, after years spent in a life of pleasure, to prove as firm, as tireless and as frugal a general as any Roman of earlier times.

Cornelia, the daughter of Scipio Africanus, was given in marriage by her father to his political opponent, Tiberius Sempronius Gracchus, in order to establish a truce in their quarrels. Sempronius was much older than Cornelia, had twice been consul, twice celebrated the victory procession and had been elected censor. He died before his wife – of his own free will, as Plutarch relates. He had found two snakes in his bed, and asked the soothsayers what this meant. They told him that he would have to kill one of them: if he killed the male, he would die, but if he killed the female, his wife would die. Being much older than his wife, he killed the male snake. Cornelia had had twelve children, only three of whom survived: two sons, who became the tribunes Tiberius and Gaius, and one daughter. Cornelia brought them all up on her own, taught them morals and eloquence, married her daughter off to her brother's son, a Scipio who would later become the second Scipio Africanus – that is, Scipio Aemilianus. Everyone in Rome considered Tiberius and Gaius to be the two most talented men of their generation and attributed this entirely to the education that they had received from their mother.[74]

When her two sons were assassinated, Cornelia bore her sorrow with nobility. This woman who rejected luxury – she remarked that her finest ornaments were her children – enjoyed a busy social life. She retired to Misenum, on the gulf of Naples, without making the slightest change to her customary way of life. She held banquets, entertained men of letters, Greek intellectuals and foreign kings. She would willingly recount the exploits of her father, Scipio Africanus, or the political careers of her sons, but with such a detached air that one might think she was talking of figures from history. Some believed that grief and bereavement had made her mad, others that her advanced age had robbed her of the memory of her family. There were a few, however, who understood that Cornelia possessed all the virtues of a Roman man, and that she knew how to resign herself calmly to adversity.[75]

The children brought up by such widows retained a powerful attachment to them. Sertorius, exiled in Spain, at the head of a rebellious army, pined for his mother who, a widow, had brought him up. On learning of her death, he took to his bed for a week, saw no one and refused to issue a single command.

In the fifth century BC, the fatherless Gaius Marcius Coriolanus bore his mother an absolute love. He got married at her command but continued to live with her – even when he had children. A brilliant general, Coriolanus attributed all his victories to her. Political setbacks eventually forced the proud Coriolanus into exile, whereupon he entered into an alliance with the enemies of Rome and led a Volscian army right up to the gates of the city. Rome was within his grasp. The Romans sent him an embassy that included all the city's priests, but he would not listen. The citizens, downcast, awaited the final assault.

Valeria, the sister of Publicola, assembled the mothers of the city and led them to the house of Volumnia, the mother of Coriolanus. There they found her with her daughter-in-law, sitting with her grandchildren on her knee. Shame had shut the two women up at home, in internal exile. Valeria prevailed upon Volumnia to go and speak to her son. A long procession of women made its way to the Volscian camp, bearing supplicants' branches. The enemy, taken aback, respectfully let them pass. Coriolanus was seated at his tribunal when he saw his mother approach. Overcome with emotion, he descended from the platform and walked towards her. He embraced her and wept as he hugged his wife and children to him. In front of the Volsci and the Roman women, Volumnia delivered a forceful speech and appealed to Coriolanus' filial piety, the religious veneration that children bore their parents. Coriolanus bowed to his mother and withdrew with the Volscian army. On his return to Antium, the furious Volsci assassinated him.[76]

Coriolanus had not only given way to the love he bore his own mother; it was to all the mothers of the city that he had sacrificed his vengeance and his triumph. The bond that united a Roman man with his mother was the only close and trusting relationship with a woman he would ever have. When a Roman's mother remarried there was often a degree of complicity between mother and son against the new husband.[77] Conversely, stepmothers often persecuted the children of a first marriage, and fathers, when they remarried, often preferred to have their children adopted, as Aemilius Paullus for example had done.

7

The army

There were two ways of leaving home and of escaping the narrow confines of domestic and rural life: politics and the army.

BECOMING A SOLDIER

'It is from the farming class that the bravest men and sturdiest soldiers come.'[78] The Roman citizen, when impoverished, turned to warfare for self-fulfilment. For the army, just as much as politics, provided an alternative to his home environment. He would return bathed in glory, with a bit of land and some gold coins which would slip rapidly through his fingers.

Army and warfare was one and the same thing; there was no Roman army except when the city was at war. There was no peacetime conscription or standing army in Rome. As long as peace held, there was not a soldier to be found anywhere on Roman soil.

To move from peace to war, the same procedure had to be followed as when entering a foreign territory: a gate had to be passed through. When the senate decided upon war, the temple of Janus, the god of openings, was itself opened:

There are twin gates of war (so men call them), hallowed by religious awe and the terrors of fierce Mars: a hundred brazen bolts close them, and the eternal strength of iron, and Janus their guardian never quits the threshold. Here, when the sentence of the Fathers is firmly fixed on war, the consul arrayed in Quirinal robe and Gabine cincture, with his own hand unbars the grating portals, with his own lips calls forth war; then the rest of the warriors take up the cry, and brazen horns blare out their hoarse accord.[79]

The citizen of Rome needed a war in order to become a soldier, to become a different man, to leave his cramped farm and to meet an unknown challenge.

When the red flag fluttered over the citadel, the message would be broadcast throughout the whole territory of Rome: all those subject to enlistment had to report for duty within thirty days. To serve as a soldier a man had to be free, a householder, liable to taxation, between the ages of seventeen and forty-six, and with fewer than sixteen previous campaigns to his name if he was an infantryman, fewer than ten if he was in the cavalry.

At the Capitol, the consuls with the help of the military tribunes – that is, the superior officers – made a selection from among the men. They needed approximately 4,000 to form each legion. They would start with the wealthiest, but avoid using up all those available from a single tribe or class. Whether or not a man was selected would depend on his physical attributes. The few exemptions that were made (see p. 159), were as a reward for outstanding deeds. Military duties were not in themselves a heavy burden – although they might become so if a campaign dragged on too long, keeping soldiers too far away from Rome – they were more a trial of a citizen's worth. Once a man had proven his worth elsewhere, further demonstration in the army was unnecessary. Conversely, and for the same reason, anyone carrying the taint of civic infamy was barred from the army.

Once selected, citizens had to turn themselves into servicemen. To do this they would take an oath. In Rome there existed several kinds of oath, the soldiers' oath being of a particularly fearsome variety. It was a *sacramentum*: only death or the end of the war could release them from it.

To become a soldier was to join a community that lived and acted in accordance with rules that differed from, and sometimes even ran contrary to, those of civilian life. It was a community in which the chief, whether consul or praetor, held the soldiers' and officers' lives in his power and where the said power was symbolized by the axes that surmounted the lictors' *fasces*. The *sacramentum* subjected the soldier to the power of the general but released him from the prohibitions of civilian life: he might kill and injure other men, enemies or even comrades-at-arms, if the general gave him the order to do so, without bearing the stain of their blood. He would not purify himself until he returned to the world of peace. This was why at war the citizen would wear neither the toga, civilian dress *par excellence* (see pp. 258–9), nor light-coloured clothes; instead he would wear a dark red tunic that would not show the bloodstains. The general would also wear a loose red coat, the *paludamentum*. Unless he took the *sacramentum*, the Roman soldier could not fight, not even if he was armed from head to toe: he remained a civilian.

Having taken the oath, the soldiers would return home to collect their weapons and make ready their provisions. The general would have told them when and where to assemble on the battlefield, the chosen rendezvous being close to the theatre of operations. It was up to the soldiers to make their own way there. At the start of the war against Philip, for example, the consul Manlius Acilius told his troops to rendezvous on the Ides of May at Brundisium, on the heel of Italy, before embarking for Greece. The consul himself left Rome on the fifth day before the Nones – that is, about twelve days before the date fixed.[80]

THE SOLDIER'S LIFE

From the moment the army was assembled to the day it was demobilized, the soldier lived a life apart, in a camp, at a distance from any town. Even if hostilities were slow to break out he would wait in the camp, sometimes for more than a year, never returning to live in a house, 'under a roof'. He would sleep 'under hides', Roman tents being made of leather. The Roman soldier had neither roof nor toga. All he had to protect and clothe himself with were his weapons and the camp itself.

The camp was one of the distinguishing features of the Roman army. Every evening the soldiers would enclose themselves in their camp and, if they were on the move, they would build a new camp each day. This would have been a hard task, after marching all day long, weighed down by their weapons and by the stakes they carried that would be used to build the palisade, and was an extra test of the endurance that was the cardinal virtue of Roman armies.

All Roman camps were identical. Whether square or oblong, they were built around two axes that crossed at right-angles running north–south and east–west and terminating at four gates. At the crossroads of the two axes stood the *praetorium*, the general's tent, and alongside it a forum where the entire legion could gather. The camp would be encircled by a ditch, the earth from which would be used to build an embankment on which the soldiers would plant the stakes of a palisade. The soldiers' tents were lined up along the roads parallel to the two main axes, the *cardo* and the *decumanus*.

The camp certainly fulfilled a vital utilitarian need in that it enabled soldiers to recover their strength in complete safety. But above all it served through the life he led there, to keep the soldier within the framework of civilized society. Civilized men did not, after all, sleep under the stars; they required a shelter over their heads. Only barbarians and wild beasts fell asleep on the bare ground wherever they happened to drop. The tent was not, of course, a proper roof, and homesick Romans were forever repeating: 'Oh, for a roof over my head!' Yet the strict regulation of camp life and the rites performed during its construction made it a place of civilization. The general's tent was a *templum* in which he could consult the auspices. The harsh day-to-day life of the soldier was never savage or rustic.

Army food provides an illustration of this. Legionaries ate only bread and drank only water, plus a little vinegar when the weather was particularly hot. Army supplies tirelessly rehearsed the same formula: wheat, *frumentum*, for the men; forage, *pabulum*, for the horses. The soldiers crushed their wheat and shaped it into biscuits which they cooked unleavened in the fireplace under tiles spread with charcoal embers. Wheat was the only food fit for a soldier, 'hard' food for hard men. It was also the only food sufficiently civilized for them. Every other kind of food was demeaning. To make them eat barley in the place of wheat was a terrible punishment. If the wheat ran out, as happened under Caesar's command in Gaul, and the general distributed barley or, worse still, if the barley ran out, beans or – and this was a sign of dire penury – meat, the troops would grumble and mutter. Such 'soft' foods failed to fortify them sufficiently and were unworthy of them. If they agreed to eat them it was out of loyalty and devotion to their commander. But the men did have one weak point: plunder. To conciliate them, the general would let them loose in the towns captured and they would make a dash for any gold or precious tableware they could find.

In the eyes of the Romans, only barbarian warriors would clothe themselves in animal skins and gorge themselves on meat and wine: it was such eating habits that made them irresolute. The slumbering enemy, drunk on food and wine, was a commonplace of Roman historians. The legionary never gave himself up to pleasure until the war was over. If he slept or ate it was only to keep his body in good shape.

Army life lay at the root of the image of the soldier as the embodiment of 'civilized violence'. Mars was known as Mars the Cruel – etymologically, the 'god of spilt blood'. The soldier was cruel because he was unmoved by pain, or the spilling of human blood, whether his own or his enemy's; on the contrary, he might even find it exhilarating. But this was not merely blind, savage cruelty. The ideal Roman soldier was a prey to no passion and was susceptible to neither compassion nor vainglory. He submitted impassively to the enemy's insults and to the death of his comrades: he was a man of iron.

It is unlikely that Rome ever resorted to rituals of possession in order to put its soldiers into trances and so make bloodthirsty warriors of them. This Indo-European tradition, preserved by the Gauls, was incompatible with the civilized conception that the Romans had always cherished of warfare, even if traces of it may be uncovered in the memory of certain great families, such as the Horaces. It was the unbending discipline of the army that turned the Roman into a killing machine. The legionary was even more terrifying than the bloodthirsty Indo-European warrior, for his inhumanity was not that of the wild beast, but was fashioned of steel; it was not a throwback to the condition of savages, but the outcome of work undertaken upon himself, an education initiated in infancy.

DISCIPLINE

Roman soldiers were subject to rigid discipline. In the midst of battle, soldiers acted only on command. It was then up to the ensigns of each maniple (approximately one hundred men) to pass on orders. Nor was there any relaxation of discipline within the camp. There were no laws other than the commands of the general and the precedents of even harsher traditions. If, for instance, a soldier fell asleep during a night watch, he would be condemned to a camp beating. After the tribune gave the signal, each man who had been placed in danger by the man's negligence would take his turn to strike or cast a stone at him. Nobody wished him to escape with his life, for what would become of him if he did? He would be forbidden to return to his country, and certainly no member of his family would dare to welcome him home. Such discipline was based as much on a sense of honour as on violence. Roman soldiers could not bear shame.

Therefore the men in covering forces often face certain death, refusing to leave their ranks even when vastly outnumbered, owing to the dread of the punishment they would meet with; and again in the battle men who have lost a shield or sword or any other arm often throw themselves into the midst of the enemy, hoping either to recover the lost object or to escape by death from inevitable disgrace and the taunts of their relations.[81]

Punishment might be meted out to entire armies. Those defeated at Cannae, stigmatized and exiled to Sicily, were coldly sacrificed by Fabius Maximus during the Second Punic War:

Fabius schemed to draw Hannibal away from the neighbourhood, and therefore gave orders to the garrison at Rhegium to overrun Bruttium and take Caulonia by storm. This garrison numbered 8,000, most of them deserters, and the dregs of the soldiers that were sent home from Sicily in disgrace by Marcellus; they were men whose loss would least afflict and injure Rome. Fabius expected that by using these forces as bait, he would draw Hannibal away from Tarentum. And this was what actually happened.[82]

And so no more was heard of those defeated at Cannae.

Conversely, a soldier's courage might win him public praise and rewards. During a victorious battle against the Spaniards, the Roman cavalry demonstrated outstanding bravery. 'Before an assembly the next day, Gaius Calpurnius praised and decorated the cavalry with trappings for their horses and proclaimed publicly that the enemy had been defeated and his camp taken and captured mainly through their efforts. Quinctius, the other praetor, decorated his cavalry with chains and clasps.'[83]

Roman soldiers liked to adorn themselves with jewellery that recalled their exploits. They wore gold chains, and decorated their hair and their maniple's ensign with bright trinkets. Generals were careful to reward their men. Glory was so essential to soldiers that if they deemed themselves unjustly deprived of praise, they might actually desert or turn traitor.

During the war against Hannibal, Fabius Maximus learnt of a very courageous allied soldier who was contemplating betrayal. Fabius

was not incensed with him but admitted frankly that he had been unduly neglected; so far, he said, this was the fault of the commanders, who distributed their honours by favour rather than for valour, but in the future it would be the man's own fault if he did not come to him and tell him when he wanted anything. These words were followed by the gift of a warhorse and by other signal rewards for bravery, and from that time on there was no more faithful and zealous man in the service.[84]

ARMY ORATORY

The army may have been subject to Mars but it was still composed of Romans, a people spurred into action by the spoken word, which is why there was eloquence in the camps. The military forum was not merely the place where exploits were glorified after battle. We can be forgiven if, on reading accounts of Roman wars, with all those speeches delivered by generals, we feel a sense of literary contrivance – as if war was simply part of the art of rhetoric! Yet even if the Roman consuls and dictators did not deliver all the fine speeches attributed to them by Livy, eloquence was indispensable to a general. He had to convince his men that his strategy was the right one and that victory would be theirs. Romans were free men, and discipline on its own could not turn them into victors if they set their face against victory. There was nothing a general could do with an unwilling Roman army especially if the men's lack of co-operation was the expression of their political disapproval of his leadership rather than the effect of war-weariness or faltering courage.

During the war against the Samnites, the dictator Lucius Papirius Crassus had upset the Roman soldiers by persecuting his cavalry master, who had ridden into battle and secured a victory without the dictator's prior authorization. Crassus was close to gaining a final victory in the war:

> So great, however, was the importance of one man, Lucius Papirius, that if the goodwill of the soldiers had seconded the measures taken by their general it was held as certain that the war with Samnium might that day have been brought to a successful termination, so skilfully did he dispose his army, so well secure it with every advantage of position and reserves, and with every military art. But the men were listless, and, on purpose to discredit their commander, threw away the victory. There were more Samnites killed, more Romans wounded. The experienced general perceived what stood in the way of his success: he must qualify his native disposition, and mingle geniality with his sternness. So, calling together his lieutenants, he made the round of his wounded soldiers in person, and, putting his head into their tents and

asking each how he was doing, he commended them by name to the care of the lieutenants, the tribunes, and the prefects. This of itself was a popular thing to do, and Papirius managed it with such tact that in healing their bodies he rapidly regained their affection; and indeed there was nothing that promoted their recovery more than the satisfaction with which they accepted these attentions.[85]

The army was soon back on its feet and the Samnites crushed. The general gave his men their well-earnt booty and won a triumph for himself.

Whereas by rebelling, or merely by displaying ill humour, the troops would have put the general's back to the wall, since his position made it impossible for him to accept any recriminations from the army, by voluntarily exposing themselves to injury, without compromising eventual victory, the soldiers had managed to force their commander to yield and to modify his conduct. Moreover, far from discrediting themselves through cowardice, the troops had in fact demonstrated an exceptional ability to withstand pain and fear. They had displayed a mastery of body and soul that proved that they were capable of just as much harshness towards themselves as Papirius could inflict. The excessive severity of their commander was legible on the bodies of his soldiers, as if he himself had struck them, and it was written in blood.

The dialogue between the general and his troops did not take the form, as in the political arena, of an oratorical duel between himself and a centurion, spokesman for the soldiers. The battlefield was within the *imperium*, where speech only operated in one direction: from the commander down to the soldiers, from the soul to the body. The body could, however, express itself in its own right and demonstrate to the soul the disastrous effects of its severity.

THE IMPOSSIBILITY OF DEFEAT

The Roman soldier could not return defeated. From the third century BC onwards, defeat was no longer an acceptable outcome. Rome had a way of waging war that was incomprehensible to other nations and which transformed its soldiers into conquerors; it no longer played the traditional war game.[86]

Until the end of the fourth century, Rome was just another Latin city fighting regular battles against its neighbours: 'Their anxiety was sharpened by the fact that they must fight against Latins, who were like themselves in language, customs, fashion of arms, and above all in military institutions; soldiers had mingled with soldiers, centurions with centurions, tribunes with tribunes, as equals and colleagues in the same garrisons and often in the same maniples.'[87]

It was in precisely this kind of war that the toughest discipline had to be observed. This was perfectly logical, given that the purpose of discipline was to turn the civilian into a soldier by making him forget every human feeling and in particular every social tie founded in neighbourhood, friendship or hospitality. It was harder to kill a Latin who, owing to the vagaries of previous alliances, had once been your comrade-at-arms, than a semi-savage Gaul with horns on his head who yelled and screamed as he charged towards you.

This archaic type of warfare could only be waged between similar peoples: it involved a relationship and a degree of competition between Rome and its neighbours. War complemented the treaties of friendship which from time to time combined cities in a league with the purpose of doing battle against another city and *its* allies. War was essential to free cities in that it provided them with a way of distinguishing themselves from neighbours with whom they shared the same culture. In the absence of war, the free play of friendships and alliances might have caused the cities to merge into one another: blood that could have united had to be spilt in order to separate. Besides, as the Latin word *pax* indicated, peace was never anything but a truce between two wars. The only free and autonomous people therefore was a people under arms. This ancient warring did not call into question the existence of each warlike city, or the extent of its territory or its political sovereignty.

Any excuse would do. If three cows had been stolen or a crop pillaged, a war would be launched to see that the chattels were returned to their rightful owners. War was declared following a minutely detailed ritual, similar on both sides. A priest specially ordained by the people who had undergone the offence would throw a javelin into the enemy's territory by way of provocation. Thirty days later, hostilities would commence. After several battles, fought in far-flung areas untouched by the plough or in remote regions where shepherds grazed their herds in summer, one of the parties would acknowledge defeat – having perhaps lost only one man more than the other side – and then everyone would go home. Obviously, for this system to function smoothly both sides had to play the game and accept defeat when the rules said it was their turn to do so.

Whether owing to the Gallic invasion or to some other cause, from the middle of the fourth century BC onwards the Romans became bad losers, refusing to give in when beaten and continuing to fight until they were victorious. They replaced good-natured tribal wars with the terrors of modern warfare – wars that knew no pity and at the end of which the vanquished lost their freedom and could never fight again. Defeated cities would disappear, assimilated into Rome. The Roman soldier was incapable of surrender. Other peoples might consider him treacherous, he thought himself a hero.

In 321 BC, the Romans won a victory over the Samnites. The Samnites admitted defeat and wished to make atonement for a war they felt they had prosecuted against the will of the gods. They made some reasonable proposals including an undertaking to hand over to the Romans both the spoils of war and those among their number who had fomented the hostilities. The Romans rejected the terms, citing a variety of pretexts: they were bent on continuing the war. The Samnites returned to arms.

As a result of Samnite tactics and the carelessness of the Roman consuls, the Roman army found itself trapped between two mountain passes that the Samnites had cut off, at a place known as the Caudine Forks. The Romans could neither advance nor retreat. They built themselves what was now a useless camp and waited on the enemy's pleasure. The Samnites were as embarrassed as the Romans, not knowing what to do with their prisoners. They consulted a sage who one day told them to massacre every last Roman and the next day to let them go and to make friends with them. His son, a Samnite leader, decided that the old man was senile, unable to remember what he had said the previous day, and that in any case neither of his proposals complied with the customs of warfare. The allegedly senile sage then explained himself more clearly. There was a straightforward alternative. Either the Samnites should form a permanent alliance with Rome, by placing themselves under their protection and ceasing to make war on them, thereby sacrificing a portion of their liberty; or, by massacring the entire Roman army, they might deprive Rome for several generations of any further chance of waging war and thereby obtain peace. Unfortunately, the old Samnite was not heeded and the Roman army was treated like any other traditional army.

In the meantime, the starving Romans made hopeless attempts to scale the steep surrounding slopes before finally resigning themselves to sueing for peace with the Samnites. The proposals that the Samnites put to the Roman ambassadors accorded with the customs of warfare between cities. They were perfectly equitable: the Romans would acknowledge their defeat; they would hand back those Samnite territories that they had annexed and on which they had set up colonies; each side would withdraw to within its former frontiers; the two peoples would then draw up a pact of alliance as between equals. Lastly, the Romans would have to submit to the ritual humiliation of the yoke: the men, stripped of all weapons, would have to pass under a yoke, bowing their heads before the Samnite army, thus displaying the reality of a defeat they could no longer deny. To pass under the yoke was to receive an indelible brand: their days of fighting wars would be over – until the following year. As a political guarantee, the Samnites demanded noble hostages, the officers and 600 Roman cavalry.

To save their army, the Roman consuls accepted the Samnite terms, passed under the yoke divested of their red coats, with their soldiers stripped to their tunics.

In a daze, they then sought refuge with their Capuan allies who gave them new arms and horses and resupplied their consuls with *fasces* and lictors. Yet it would take more than warm Capuan hospitality to rouse the Romans from their torpor. Crushed by sorrow, they could not raise their eyes from the ground. It seemed to the Capuans that the Samnites had inflicted an indelible defeat on the Romans and that the Romans' morale could never recover. It was in the following terms that their messenger described for the senate the sight of the humiliated soldiers quitting Rome:

> They seemed to be much more sorrowful and dejected than before: their column had marched along in almost complete silence. The old Roman spirit was quite dashed; they had lost their courage with their arms. When greeted they did not respond; not a man of them had been able to open his mouth for shame, as if they still bore on their necks the yoke under which they had been sent. The Samnites, they said, had won a lasting as well as a glorious victory, for they had conquered not only Rome – as the Gauls had done before them – but also, which demanded far greater prowess, Roman valour and spirit.[88]

This view betrayed a basic ignorance of the Romans. Listening to the messenger from Capua, some senators concluded that the Romans were possessed not by the spirit of defeat but by simmering anger. The venerable Offilius Calavius declared that: 'their obstinate silence, their eyes fixed on the ground, their ears deaf to every consolation, their reluctance to look at the light, were all signs of passionate resentment boiling within their breasts; either he knew nothing of the Roman character or that silence was destined to cause the Samnites to cry and groan with anguish.'[89]

The army returned home, a sorry sight. The soldiers arrived back in

Rome one evening with the look of prisoners-of-war. They hid themselves deep inside their houses. Not one of them showed his face at the forum or in any other public place, either on that day or any day that followed. The consuls relinquished their offices and appointed a dictator to replace them. No longer soldiers in war, they no longer deemed themselves citizens in peace.

Plate 5   Roman cavalryman, first century AD
*Reproduced by kind permission of the Ancient Art and Architecture Collection
(Ronald Sheridan)*

Such a situation could not last. Spurius Postumius, one of the defeated consuls, came up with a politico-religious trick for reviving the war. The imposed Samnite peace had not been formally approved by the Roman people – who had not in fact been consulted. Consequently, it was only the hostages who could be held accountable by the Samnites, whereas the Roman people were not under any sort of obligation. So why not deliver the two consuls to the Samnites and let the war recommence? The consuls would be perfectly willing to submit to the rage of the foe. The senators accepted the plan and gave orders for them to be conducted to Caudium, the Samnite capital, by the fetials, the priests of treaties.

Try as they might to refuse the hostages, the Samnites had been duped. The Romans had never interiorized the defeat, never felt the humiliation of the yoke as an act of surrender. An enemy could do nothing to them, except kill them. The war broke out again and the Samnites were defeated.

STIRRING DEEDS

The Romans never tired of relating wondrous tales of war. With its extra-tough men, iron discipline and disquieting rituals to summon the powers of destruction, war was a land of legends. The deeds of soldiers whose courage and whose indifference to pain made them admirable if somewhat disconcerting heroes were constantly rehearsed.

Scaeva,[90] for example, with one eye gone, his thigh and shoulder wounded and his shield pierced in 120 places, none the less continued to guard the gate of the fortress placed in his charge.

Then there was Acilius, an ordinary soldier who, during a naval battle outside Marseilles, grasped the stern of an enemy ship. When his right hand was lopped off, he boarded the ship and forced the enemy back with the boss of his shield.

Other terrible and edifying stories were told in which a father, a general, punished his son, an officer, for contravening discipline. Titus Manlius, for example, at the head of an army fighting the Latins, forbade his soldiers from fighting outside their ranks. His son Titus was sent with some horsemen on reconnaissance near the enemy camp, where he came upon a Latin horseman who challenged him to a duel. Titus yielded to the provocation and the duel commenced, with the other horsemen forming a circle around the combatants. Titus killed his opponent's horse and pinned to the ground the Latin who lay trapped beneath his mount. Young Titus then carried the body of his slain enemy straight to his father's tent. Titus Manlius averted his gaze and then before the assembled troopers gave the order for his son's execution. The lictor bound the young officer to the stake and cut his head off. The men looked on in horror but their obedience kept them silent.[91]

8

Living in Rome

AN ENIGMATIC CITY

For the Romans the place to live above all others was Rome itself, the city. 'Rome, planted in mountains and deep valleys, its garrets hanging up aloft, its roads far from good, merely narrow by-ways.'[92] 'The appearance of the city is as if the ground had been gradually appropriated as the need arose rather than divided up according to a planned design.'[93] This was how two first-century BC Romans viewed the capital of the world.

Rome could appear either formless or multiform: everything was jumbled together, gods and people, warehouses and temples, parks and dilapidated buildings, vast uninhabited areas with here and there a huge mass of people. Judges worked next door to butchers, nomads slept on the steps of the aristocratic temple of Castor and Pollux, dubious-looking shops rubbed shoulders with princely lodgings. Shrines were used as banks, and brothels sprang up under the colonnades that skirted public buildings. On one side there might be a caved-in building, the charred remains of a house or some monuments under construction, while on the other a newly restored and freshly roughcast temple or a noble palace that its wealthy owner was having roofed with slabs of marble.

Rome looked like nowhere else. No initial design or concerted attempt at town planning had ever managed to impose even the roughest pattern on the tangle of houses, people and commercial, political and religious activities. There was no main thoroughfare, no central square from which broad avenues might radiate. A combination of dense crowds and roadworks congested the few streets that remained passable: 'In hot haste rushes a contractor with mules and porters; a huge crane now hoists a stone and now a beam; mournful funerals jostle massive wagons; this way runs a mad dog: that way rushes a mud-bespattered sow.'[94]

Via Sacra, its continuation Via Triumphalia, which ran right to the foot of the Palatine, and the parallel Via Nova, were the only reasonably wide streets leading into the forum, though their width was very irregular, varying between four and seven metres.

To explain away the anarchic shapelessness of their city, the Romans would point to the fact that at the beginning of the fourth century BC the Gauls had burnt the old city down.[95] To speed the city's reconstruction, its inhabitants had been authorized to take stone from wherever they could find it on the condition that they got their buildings up within one year. In their rush, the builders paid no heed to any building lines and nobody bothered to inquire exactly where a neighbour's property ended and one's own began. Wherever there was a gap, something was built to fill it up. Plots of land encroached on each other, and houses spilled over into the streets.

It seems unlikely that this is the only reason for Rome's lack of planning. Rome was constantly being destroyed and rebuilt, right down to the days of the empire. There was, for example, little need for the Gauls to sack the city, since fires would devastate the higgledy-piggledy houses all year round. There were on average two major earthquakes each century, and the Tiber regularly flooded those quarters that lined its banks.

The shape – or indeed the shapelessness – of a town tells us something about its inhabitants. Greek cities followed a geometrical layout; Rome modelled its colonial towns on the military camp. Rome has been painstakingly searched for the two main axes intersecting one another at right-angles, like the *cardo* and the *decumanus* of the colonial towns, but in vain. This is hardly surprising, however. The city stands alone, and its seeming disorder is a reflection of one of the features of the Roman mindset: the tendency to proceed by a process of accumulation.

Rome was several towns rolled into one: the centres of religion, politics and commerce. Temples, people and riches were heaped together. Each Rome had its own structure, focal points and boundaries. The sacred ring, the *pomoerium* traced by Rome's founder, consisting of a strip of earth encircling the city on which all building was prohibited, did not coincide with the city wall erected by

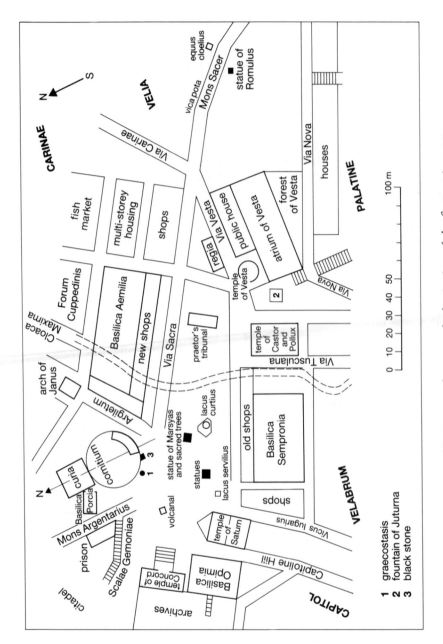

Figure 6 The Roman forum at the beginning of the first century BC

the ancient king Servius. The Aventine hill, to the south of Rome, was outside the *pomoerium* but inside the wall. The same was true of the banks of the Tiber and also of the northern part of the Esquiline hill, where the cemetery of the poor was situated.

THE FORUM

The one site that was common to all these towns that were superimposed on one another was the Forum Romanum, or simply the forum (see figure 6). This was a public square, 160 metres long by 75 metres wide, lined with stones and flagged. Lying at the foot of the Capitol, the forum is a depression encircled by hills: the steep slopes of the Palatine rising to the west; the small Velia to the south; and, to the east, the gently rising Viminal, Quirinal and Esquiline. To the west the forum opened on to a valley leading to the Tiber. Paradoxically for a centre, the derivation of the word 'forum' is 'enclosure, or door' and 'vestibule, or entrance'. Here one finds an echo of the structure of Roman houses: the centre of social life was located in the vestibule, for that was where the exterior and interior met.

The northern part of the forum boasted several of the high places of Roman political life: the rostra, or speaker's platform, the comitium, where the people assembled, and close at hand the curia, where the senate met. Opposite the curia stood the temple of Saturn, which housed the republican treasury, and between the two buildings, hiding the foot of the Capitol, towered the archive building, erected in more recent times. At the other end of the forum, to the south, stood several of Rome's most ancient and most hallowed sanctuaries: the regia, where the *rex sacrorum*, king of sacrifices, dwelt; opposite this, on the other side of the Via Sacra (which started at this point), stood the round temple of Vesta, the sacred hearth where the Vestals always kept a fire burning; and, adjoining the temple itself, the house of the Vestals. Alongside, the *atrium* of Vesta served as a residence for the *pontifex maximus*, the head of the Roman religion.

In the middle of the forum was the pinnacle of justice, the praetor's seat of judgement. But the forum also attracted business people: on its east and west sides, two rows of shops lined the square, some of which were decorated with a Samnite shield, announcing exchange facilities.

The forum was the hub of Roman politics, religion, justice, trade and social life. Business was carried on in the morning, and in the afternoon people would gather to gossip. It was at the forum that magistrates would harangue the assembly and there that citizens would flock to listen to the great lawyers who were also the stars of political life. And it was to the forum that citizens would spontaneously make their way whenever anything important happened. The forum was also the place where great families delivered funeral orations for their dead or put on gladiatorial combats.

URBAN SYMBOLISM

But the forum was not the only centre of the city. The Capitol looming over the forum was the hallowed seat of Roman domination. It was said that it derived its name from a head – *caput* – that had been found on its ground. It was up there that the gods of city life dwelt. Jupiter Optimus Maximus, Juno and Minerva formed a divine triad of wise and peaceful sovereigns, next to the temple of Juno the Adviser. Slightly lower down stood the temple of Concord, recalling the struggles between the orders and the need for solidarity between them. Often, at the most harrowing moments of political debate in the forum, all eyes would be lifted towards these elevated places.

Then there was the other city, the one that people actually lived in. The Palatine hill where the nobles resided was the seat of worldly power. The Aventine was the hill of the *plebs*, of Romulus' brother Remus, who had come second in the race to power. The Palatine and the Aventine confronted one another, as did the plebeians and the patricians. Likewise, the Capitoline triad was offset by the Aventine triad of Ceres, Liber and Libera.

Roman city-planning appears to have been organized according to principles more complex than could be set down on any straightforward two-dimensional map. The city was organized like Roman life: it was made up of conflicting sites that had to be reconciled by means of regular ritual ceremonies and routines.

If the contrast between the Aventine and the Palatine hills was an expression of political polarity, the circus, located between them, reunited every class in the great melting-pot of the games, during which all duels at the forum were suspended.

Rome's environs were organized in an equally subtle manner. On the other side of the river, the tranquil countryside provided a counterbalance to the dense urbanization of the left bank. The Tiber did not flow through the city, or even along its outer edge. Although there were two bridges that crossed the river, to the Romans the Tiber was like the sea, an abyss that separated them from another universe: the Etruscan shore. The right bank did in fact retain a rustic landscape with its fields, meadows, farms, gardens and woods. To cross the Tiber was to cut oneself off from Rome. One of the public rituals that brought in the new year, the festival of Anna Perenna in March, was held on this rustic bank. Romans would leave the city, cross the river and picnic in the huts that lined the river bank. In the evening they would return to the city as if from another world.

There were three ways of leaving Rome: going to the countryside; going off to war; or being laid in one's tomb. To the north of the city, outside the walls, at the foot of the Capitol, lay the field of Mars, a broad plain deliberately left fallow from the time it was first dedicated to the god Mars. It was forbidden either to farm it or to build on it. This was where the legions in arms and the assembly of the people marshalled in accordance with the *comitia centuriata* system would gather to vote. To the south, outside the walls, the Appian Way stretched into the distance across the city of the dead. From the gates of the city radiated a network of roads leading to the Roman countryside and the provinces beyond.

CITY PLANNING AND RELIGION

Rome seemed to hold itself together by balancing the different areas that constituted and bounded it. Every plan for urban renewal had to come to terms with this symbolic organization of space, and either preserve or reproduce it. The alternative was to turn everything upside-down and force through a cultural revolution. This is what Augustus cynically did, thereby ruining the symbolic system of liberty inscribed in the Roman soil. And it is precisely what Caesar wished to avoid when, just before his death, he drew up a plan to expand what was by then an overcrowded city.

By July 45 BC, Caesar had entrusted the technical side of his plan to a Greek architect. He intended to take personal charge of the religious side himself. Rome clearly needed to expand, but no one could decide in which direction. The easiest method would be to divide into plots a large plain on which no houses had yet been built and no land cultivated: the field of Mars. This would do away with the long and costly process of expropriation. Caesar well knew what that involved, having previously expropriated the land of the inhabitants of the centre of Rome, to the north of the forum, in order to create what had become the Forum Julium. Mars would, of course, have to be expelled, but that could be done; there were rituals tailor-made for that purpose. Eighty-eight plots had already been allocated in an area skirting the Capitol which had once belonged to the priests.

The difficulty was of a different order. Rome had to have a field of Mars. If this one was carved up, another one would have to be created. The field of Mars was the place where the five-yearly census was held, where the *comitia centuriata* voted, where the people's army gathered, where young soldiers drilled and – in the public farm – where the censors and foreign ambassadors lodged. In a word, it was on the field of Mars that Romans lived out every aspect of the aristocratic liberty that they had won in the revolution of 509 BC. This land, it was said, had belonged to the last king, Tarquinius Superbus, and had been confiscated by the people and consecrated to Mars.

Caesar determined therefore to rebuild a field of Mars on a nearby plain which, since it was situated on the right bank of the Tiber, had remained almost untouched by human habitation: the Vatican plain. The area could not remain as it was, however, for between the field of Mars and the Vatican plain flowed the Tiber. Indeed the Vatican plain was not in Latium at all but 'abroad', at a great symbolic distance from Rome. One might as well have told the people to go and vote on the banks of the Po. Caesar therefore planned to divert the course of the Tiber, by digging a canal to cut out the loop that the river described just before it reached Rome, rerouting it past the base of the Vatican hills.[96]

An explanation as to why he was prepared to undertake work on such a gigantic scale is offered by the definition of the field of Mars as a place situated 'between the Tiber and the city'. This definition is at once a description of the field of Mars as it had always been and, implicitly, a rule for what it should always remain. Since the field of Mars *was* between the Tiber and the city, that was where it *had to be*; not through timid conservatism but because this location made sense.

The Tiber, after all, was a frontier between Rome and a radically foreign place, the land of a non-Latin people, the Etruscans. The Etruscan shore, even if it had been subjected to Rome from quite an early date, continued to play a role as a foreign continent. Insolvent debtors who, after thirty days, or three markets, had not managed to find anyone to stand them bail, were at one time sold 'beyond the Tiber', as the law of the Twelve Tables stipulated that no citizen could be sold within the territory of Rome. When the time came to banish those Campanians who had failed to support Rome in the First Punic War, they were brought to Rome from the south of Italy and then despatched to the other side of the river.[97] The bed of the Tiber was itself an abyss, gobbling up everything that was thrown into it, spiriting it away from the world of humans. Everything that was *sacer*, destined for the infernal gods, was therefore cast into it: tyrants, patricides and hermaphrodites.[98]

From the outside, therefore, Rome was organized according to a polarity between the north-north-west and the south-south-east. To the south, the interior of the city contrasted with an exterior that was culturally similar to it – the Latin towns. To the north, it contrasted with one that was quite different – Etruscan – and from which the city was divided by the Tiber, an impassable barrier – unless, that is, a bridge was built. But the Tiber was not the only barrier; there was also the field of Mars. The city itself never touched the Tiber. The field of Mars, with its defensive associations, provided a symbolic echo of the natural barrier formed by the Tiber. Between Rome and Etruria there was no room for the god Terminus.

THE CITY AS LABYRINTH

Dwelling-houses clustered in quarters that were independent of one another. Unless you were born and brought up in a particular Roman neighbourhood it would seem like a labyrinth where it was impossible to find anyone you might be looking for. Even those who were familiar with a particular locality could easily lose their way. As soon as you strayed from the main thoroughfare, road names and house numbers vanished. The essential landmarks were public monuments, temples, colonnades and city gates:

> *Syrus*: You know that colonnade near the meat market, down that way?
> *Demea*: Of course I do.
> *S*: Go straight up the street past it. Then there's a turning going downhill; go straight down and you'll see a temple on this side and next to it that alley –
> *D*: Which one?
> *S*: Where there's a big fig-tree.
> *D*: I know.
> *S*: Go on through it.
> *D*: (after some thought) That alley hasn't got a way through.
> *S*: So it hasn't. What a fool I am. My mistake. Go back to the colonnade. Yes, this is a much shorter way and less chance of

going wrong. Do you know Cratinus' house, that rich
fellow's?

D: Yes.

S: (rapidly) Go past it, turn left, straight up the street, come to
the temple of Diana, then turn right and before you come to
the city gate just by the pond there's a small flour mill and a
workshop opposite . . . That's where he is.[99]

Neighbourhoods were meant to be lived in, rather than strolled
about in. The exception to this was the main street of each. A quarter
consisted of, in effect, a single street, and the Latin word *vicus* meant
both a quarter and a street. This central axis was never very wide,
although ancient Roman laws stipulated a minimum width of roughly
five metres. At each end of the main street there was a crossroads,
from which other road–quarters branched off, unless the street led on
to waste ground. The Via Tusculana, for example, began not far from
the forum, near the temple of the Dioscuri, where it crossed over the
Via Sacra, and it ended at the Forum Boarium (cattle market). These
central streets were the only ones that were really passable, even
though the entire quarter's trade would be concentrated in them, and
would spill out on to the road. It was the only part of the
neighbourhood into which strangers would dare to venture, the only
truly public area and the only clearly drawn and uninterrupted
thoroughfare.

Each quarter would specialize in a particular branch of business, all
the artisans and traders of a single neighbourhood working at the
same or at complementary crafts. Work in leather, for instance, was
the speciality of the Argiletum and of its adjacent streets. In the
Argiletum itself, books were manufactured and sold; nearby was the
street of the sandal-makers, then the street of the tanners, permanently
enveloped in the smell of the tannery. The stench of the Argiletum
would accompany anyone on their way up to the Suburra, a quarter
known for its low-life taverns and brothels. On the other side of the
forum, dipping towards the Tiber, the street of the Tuscans boasted
an array of luxury boutiques. There, where the smell of incense
mingled with that of purple dyes stewing in stale urine, one might find
beautiful papyrus scroll books and high-class prostitutes of both
sexes. Each quarter had its own special smell, which its inhabitants no
longer noticed but which would strike outsiders as a foul stench. The
more sophisticated men, such as the praetor Verres, would seek to
protect themselves with fragrant flowers when they went out on the
town. Women and effeminate men would carry in their hands a ball
of amber which from time to time they would rub and then sniff.

All the shops were in the main street, the rest of the quarter forming a maze of alleys, covered passages, culs-de-sac and steps in which any stranger would immediately get lost. Before long one might no longer be sure whether one was in a street where a fuller had hung his washing out to dry or if one had strayed into the backyard of his workshop. Overnight someone might close off what had been a public passage and build a house on it. From time to time, the aediles – magistrates in charge of the city – would order interloping buildings to be cleared; but others would soon spring up in their place. A broad flight of steps would come to a sudden halt at a terrace occupied by a portable stove, some washing hung out to dry and a tiny garden. A steep alleyway would narrow abruptly, weave a path between two houses, lead to an open door through which one might suddenly emerge into a small sun-drenched square dominated by the dilapidated temple of a rustic god whose half-forgotten name was barely decipherable, an abandoned garden with an enormous fig tree laden with sumptuous fruit, and a family of Syrian ragmen bivouacking with a whole brood of children in long coloured robes. Behind, standing out against the sky, one might see the tortured antefixes of the temple of Janus.

With luck, one might stumble through the backyards of one quarter and come out safe and sound on another shopping street. Otherwise, one might wander from backstreet to alleyway and from alleyway to meandering steps, eventually emerging on a track running past a line of gardens and petering out amid the scraps of waste ground that covered an entire area to the east and north-east of the city, just inside the Servian wall. Here were found first rubbish dumps and then the Esquiline cemetery for the poor, where corpses were heaved into pits with just a few shovelfuls of earth scattered on top. A foul stench hung in the air and carrion crows wheeled over the pits which witches would raid for fresh morsels of flesh.

A quarter was not bounded by other streets which formed a clear perimeter; it was defined by a central axis from which sprouted a profusion of offshoots. The only clearcut boundaries of the quarter were the crossroads at either end, at which gods stood watch. These crossroads *lares* were shared by the people of the quarters that met at a particular crossroads. The Compitalia, the crossroads festivities held in January, brought all the inhabitants of the various quarters, slaves included, on to these crossroad-squares, helping to weld the quarters together.

The *lares* were guarantor-gods for the permanent settlement of people on soil that was hence deemed to be definitively cultivated.

NOBLE RESIDENCES

Although all the quarters were structured according to the same principle, they were not all home to the same types of people or the same styles of house. In the countryside, the fact that nearly everyone shared the same harsh lifestyle meant that there were no fundamental differences – apart from their size – between the houses of the poor and those of the rich.

In the city, things were different. One had to display one's wealth there; a city house was a social façade, a place where one worked and where one received guests. In the countryside, space cost nothing; at Rome it was exorbitantly expensive, at least in the centre. And everybody wanted to live close to the forum, the only way of keeping abreast of the very latest news and the best venue for a pleasant afternoon's saunter. Air too was worth its weight in gold. Up in the hills you could breathe, but down in the hollows you suffocated. Around the forum, therefore, social hierarchy was reproduced vertically.

High on the hills, on the Palatine, the Velia and, in remote times, on the Capitoline, stood the noblest residences. Each of these hills was scaled by a winding track or two, a *clivus*, that carriages could climb. The Palatine, the most aristocratic of all the hills, was linked to the city below via the Palatine track and the Victory track which in some places were eight metres wide. The nobles dominated the forum with their power, displaying their wealth in architectural refinements. Crassus, nicknamed the Venus of the Palatine, consul in 95 BC, was the first to decorate his residence with Greek marble. He later sold it at a very high price to Cicero who, after his consulship in 64 BC, was longing to leave his house in the Carinae, at the foot of the Velia, to the south of the forum, so that he could show off his new-found glory.

The house was a representation of the man. A house built on a hill, dominating the people in the lower part of town, was a sign of excessive pride. Valerius Publicola had to demolish his residence to evade the accusation of tyranny, several years after the downfall of the kings:

'This Valerius,' they said, 'in concentrating all power upon himself, is not a successor to the consulate of Brutus, to which he has no right, but to the tyranny of Tarquin. Why should he extol Brutus in words, while in deeds he imitates Tarquin, descending to the forum alone, escorted by all the rods and axes together, from a house no less stately than the royal house which he demolished?' For Valerius was living in a magnificent house on the Velia. It hung high over the forum, commanding a view of all that passed there, and was surrounded by steep slopes so that access to it was difficult. His descent from this regal dwelling formed a lofty spectacle, and the pomp of his procession was worthy of a king. What Valerius did when he was made aware by his friends of the people's disapproval of his way of life shows how good it is for powerful men of high station to have ears that are open to frankness and truth instead of flattery. For he immediately got together a large force of workmen, and while it was still night had the house razed to the ground. In the morning, the Romans saw what had happened, and flocked together. They were moved to love and admiration by the man's magnanimity, but mourned, as if for a human being, for the destruction of the house's stately beauty, which their envy had provoked. They were also distressed for their ruler, who, homeless, was now sharing the homes of others. For Valerius was received into the houses of his friends until the people gave him a site and built him a house of more modest dimensions than the one he had lived in before.[100]

Publicola's strategy was thoroughly Roman. Instead of wrestling with public opinion, he adapted his behaviour to suit his political project which was to win the favour of the *plebs*. He carried off a public relations coup. His house was demolished overnight and Publicola himself – a man bearing the highest insignia – was reduced to vagrancy. Thus did he overturn public opinion, turning jealousy to compassion. He anticipated the traditional political sequence of events, when the people would condemn a citizen to be driven from the city, confiscate his goods and demolish his house. This was what generally happened to traitors. Often the site of the former residence would be left derelict to testify to the infamy of the man who had owned it. On the Palatine, for example, there was a piece of waste ground called the meadows of Vaccus in memory of the act of treachery committed by Vitruvius Vaccus in 331 BC.[101] So the people wanted to provide Valerius with a new home but without conceding that the jealousy aroused by his lofty residence had been groundless. They therefore built him a more modest house at the foot of the Velia. Valerius had sacrificed his patrician pride to a particular political image of himself that he wished to project. The people had recognized this sacrifice for what it was and had granted him a residence that corresponded to this image. It was said that his door remained thereafter permanently open to visitors, even the most humble.

Conversely, by making a present of an aristocratically situated house, the people could ennoble or confirm the nobility of a particular citizen. The brother of Publius, Marcus Valerius Publicola, after crushing the Sabines – he had caused 13,000 of them to perish without the loss of a single one of his own men – obtained the triumph and the gift of a house on the Palatine, constructed at the state's expense. Moreover, although at Rome, unlike Greece, doors normally opened inwards, it was decided that the doors of Marcus' house should open outwards. To Romans, the symbolism of this privilege was evident: the city had chosen to join in paying constant homage to the magistrate. Precedence was granted to those who were leaving his house, and those citizens who happened to be passing would be obliged to step aside to make way for them.[102]

A house on the Palatine might even spark off a serious political crisis and lead to revolution. The struggles between Cicero and Clodius, the tribune of the *plebs*, the practical outcome of which was that Pompey gained full powers in 52 BC, centred essentially on Cicero's house on the Palatine. Clodius, the ruined descendant of a very old and very aristocratic family, whose own residence was also on the Palatine, wished to drive the orator away. His scheme was to rid Caesar and Pompey, for whom he worked, of a man who was a mainstay of the senatorial party while at the same time satisfying an old personal grudge.

Several years earlier, Clodius had been accused of holding an amorous meeting with Caesar's wife at the festivities of the Good Goddess, in the residence of the *pontifex maximus*, her husband, where the feast was being celebrated. Clodius is supposed to have got into the residence disguised as a woman, taking advantage of the fact that on that day no males were allowed into the house. At the trial, Cicero had exploded Clodius' alibi. Later, to exact vengeance, Clodius forced the orator into exile. He also ordered the demolition of Cicero's house on the Palatine, scattered his statues and furniture, and annexed part of Cicero's land. This he used to enlarge his own house which, as it happened, stood next to Cicero's. On the remaining land Clodius had a temple built to Liberty.

But thanks to Pompey and to his friend Milo, who loosed his gladiators on Clodius' gangs, Cicero was able to return from exile, and his goods were restored to him. He tore down the temple of Liberty and started to rebuild his house. Work on the building, however, was continually held up by the incursions of Clodius' men, who attacked Cicero's workmen and even set fire to the site. Beside himself with rage, Cicero dispatched Milo and his henchmen to the

Capitol to smash the bronze tables bearing the inscriptions of Clodius' laws. In the end, Cicero managed to keep his house. In the meantime, however, Milo killed Clodius and was himself convicted for the crime and banished to Massilia.

CITY GARDENS

By the first century BC leading citizens were beginning to desert the centre of Rome. While Clodius and Cicero did battle over a quarter-acre site on the Palatine, masters of war, great military leaders who had subjugated the barbarous peoples of East and West, and such idle members of the nobility as Pompey, Caesar, Lucullus, Atticus and Clodia, withdrew to their vast gardens on the hills surrounding Rome, in some cases on the far side of the Tiber. To keep one's distance from the forum was also to stand aloof from a kind of popular political life that was vanishing. A master of war no longer needed personally to stand guard over everything that went on between the Capitol and the temple of Vesta. Instead he could station his paid men wherever he needed them: he was rich enough to buy off any of the ever-baying senators. Caesar even bribed Cicero to secure permission to expropriate land where he had a mind to build a new forum. Cato the Younger, who would swear to his own unassailable integrity, was unable to resist the pecuniary charms of an assignment that took him to Cyprus to recover an outstanding debt to the Roman state.

For glory and power, the masters of war now looked to their troops rather than to the Roman people in the forum. During the first few centuries of the republic, the forum had gradually gnawed away at the powers of the people of the field of Mars, overriding their vote on most laws. But at the end of the republic, the military raised its voice once again, though in the absence of any legal framework, and carried its generals to power. Subsequently, Pompey marched his troops into Rome, after the senate had passed an exceptional decree, and Caesar with his army of Gauls crossed the Rubicon.

So it came as no surprise that these new nobles began to abandon the political and social centre of the city in order to enjoy a privilege inaccessible to the vast majority – space. The mansions on the slopes of the Palatine were built on small plots of ground, and their back gardens were tiny. Cicero, who doubtless owned the largest of these properties – he had six giant elms that waved their canopies of foliage high over the other houses – was exaggerating somewhat when he boasted that he enjoyed all the pleasures of a park right in the centre of Rome. The grounds of his house measured less than 900 square metres, so the size of the others can easily be imagined. Small houses were in any case the rule in town centres. In Pompeii not a single house had grounds of more than 300 square metres.

A new type of residence began to appear on unoccupied land on the outskirts of Rome, many of them inside the Servian wall. The house would be situated in a park of at least one hectare and the rooms would open out on to the garden. Atticus, Cicero's banker friend, had inherited from an aunt some plots of land on the Velia which he had laid out as 'gardens', as such residences were called at Rome. Most of these gardens were high up on the Quirinal or Viminal hills, or even further away on the Caelian hill and beyond the walls on the Pincian hill, which indeed came to be known as the 'hill of the gardens'. Pompey built his gardens above the field of Mars, Sallust also had a vast property not far away. Evergreens – pines, cypresses, laurels and ivy – ringed the houses with walls of vegetation.

THE LOWER CITY

In contrast to the aristocratic quarters nestling in the hills, the two depressions on either side of the forum – the Velabrum towards the Tiber, and the Argiletum and Suburra threading their way between the Quirinal and the Viminal (the trading port between the Tiber, which was not lined with docks, and the cattle market), accounted for the most populous neighbourhoods. One hill, the Aventine, had always been home to plebeians, but since it was some distance from the forum it escaped the overpopulation of the city centre.

These quarters were crammed with an unbelievable number of inhabitants. The best-known attempt to tackle this overcrowding took the form of high-rise *insulae*. Designed for letting, these blocks of flats made their first appearance in the second century BC and mushroomed in the first. *Insulae* contrasted sharply with traditional Roman houses, which were never more than two storeys high. These tower blocks, with façades of between six and twelve metres in width, would have five or six floors and some might reach a height of over twenty metres. Flimsily built using light materials, cob and wattle, these constructions only stayed upright by leaning on each other, and even then they would regularly collapse. There were no modern comforts. A staircase climbed to the upper floors; on each floor there were two windows with a grille made of baked clay, which looked out on to a narrow street. If the absence of heating and lighting scarcely inconvenienced the Romans, who were accustomed to it, the lack of water and drains would have forced them to live in a foul-smelling squalor that they can hardly have found agreeable. These buildings were in fact temporary refuges rather than real homes and their inhabitants were people passing through: solitary freedmen; young people who had come to the city to launch their career; people on the margins of society. A real home had to be planted fairly and squarely on the ground, with a household shrine and gods: only thus could a family be decently accommodated. This is why those who lived in the *insulae* would make no attempt at home improvements, but would seek, as soon as they had a bit of money, to move to a real house. The one effort they would make was to put some pots of flowers in the windows: a Roman always had to have his little patch of garden. The *insulae* would be packed with people from the attics down to the damp basements. In 164 BC, Ptolemy Philomector, the Egyptian prince, at that time a refugee at Rome, was given shelter by a landscape painter in his shack built on a flat roof. Others, even more destitute, would set up lodgings in the nooks and crannies of public buildings, around the shrine to Vesta, the Porcia and Emilia basilicas near the forum, not far from their baskets which they would leave chained to a column. They would eat in the taverns and wash at the public baths. If a Roman was not the centre of a social unit – a family, or a network of clients – he had little need of a lodging.

On the other hand, even the poorest craftsman with a wife and children would live in a real house, however tiny. Such poor dwellings might be on the ground floor of an *insula* or form part of a nobleman's mansion. Rents were exorbitant and a single room would have to serve as shop and workroom by day, and after closing, when the heavy wooden shutters had been put up, as kitchen and shared living space. For a bedroom, everyone would have to make do with a single low-ceilinged mezzanine. But every Roman would aim to have a real house of his own, with a bit of garden where he could grow vegetables and a salting-tub where he could each year prepare his bacon and hams.

Butchers were available to sell pork to those city-dwellers who for whatever reason could not keep their own pigs. There were, of course, exceptions: pigs were known to wander round the streets of Rome, tripping up any passers-by that got in their way.

THE CITY AND ITS WATER SUPPLY

To judge by what the ancients said, a town was always a dangerous place for one's health. Lack of sleep and overcrowding brought on diseases and fevers, especially during the summer and autumn months. The corruption of the spirit through luxury and indulgence led to the corruption of the body. This was why the Romans never founded towns on sea coasts where the humidity would further aggravate the debilitating atmosphere that characterized urban areas: in their view ports were places of moral and physical perdition.

Yet Rome was a clean city; it streamed with water day and night and was washed by the running water of the fountains whose murmuring could be heard wherever one went.[103] Jupiter had decreed that all human and animal waste, like corpses, was to be cast outside the *pomoerium*. Water that was dirty, stagnant or putrid filled the god with horror. Before approaching the gods, whether by stepping into a shrine or tending the household fire, a Roman had to purify himself with water and sweep the ground where he was to officiate. Following a blood sacrifice, sawdust was scattered on the paving to absorb any blood, wine, water or milk that might have been spilled, and the floor was then purified with water. Sweeping was to the floor of a house what ploughing was to the earth: both served to expel those more or less infernal and savage deities that roamed about in fallow land and rubbish.

This was why from the earliest days Rome had a system for disposing of dirty water: it was essential for the shrines built first at the forum and later on the Capitol. Tarquin the Elder is thought to have had the Cloaca Maxima built in the sixth century BC. This was a large drain that ran from the foot of the Quirinal hill, crossed the northern part of the forum, followed the Velabrum and emptied into the Tiber. Originally it was both an open sewer and a drainage channel not only collecting liquid waste but also helping to drain the basin of the forum where rainwater from the surrounding hills had previously tended to collect, turning it into a quagmire. Later, the sewer was covered with a vault high enough to make it possible to travel along it in a small boat. With the construction of further shrines and housing, a network of secondary drains was developed that served the entire city.

The drains sometimes passed underground, with manholes outside each house so that dirty water and sewage could be tipped into them. The drains might then reappear as small muddy channels running along the street. Aediles, responsible for the city's temples and public buildings, were charged with the upkeep of the drains and made sure that they were cleaned and flushed out regularly. The aediles also oversaw refuse collection, which was put out to private contractors whose teams of slaves went round the city with large wagons which they used for taking rubbish from markets and public buildings out of the city. They also swept the main streets, which were gradually cobbled. Individual householders had to keep the patch of street in front of their houses clean and tidy and their rainwater drains free. They were prohibited from throwing bodies or carcasses into the roadway: these had to be taken to the mass grave at the Esquiline.

Each house had its manhole and its equally essential fountain. At Rome there was water everywhere one turned. Temples and squares had their own springs of pure gushing water. The numerous hillside springs, arranged as fountains, like the fountain of Juturna, near the temple of Castor and Pollux at the foot of the Palatine, fed round basins supported by columns. At Rome running water was associated with pleasure and repose. In private gardens and on public esplanades, fountains gushed forth from the depths of artificial grottoes, overgrown with moss and ivy, and from tritons and nymphs. When Pompey, in the middle of the first century BC, provided the Roman people with a special area on the field of Mars where they could walk and relax, he gave orders for a fountain to be built, which gushed from a crouching satyr in the midst of the trees. Water towers, built on hilltops, were excuses for decorative architectural work. They were given a Greek name: nymphs. The water tower in the gardens of Lucullus, on the Pincian, towered thirty metres above the field of Mars. And the one in Sallust's gardens was crowned with a dome and decorated with eight niches containing statues.

Before long Rome's springs were no longer able to meet the demand for water. The Romans therefore built aqueducts, four in all during the republic, the first of which was built at the end of the fourth century. A network of lead pipes carried this water throughout the entire city.

Streets were unlit and houses were unheated but Romans did have baths, mains drainage and plentiful clean water. Water was not supplied, however, in order to render life comfortable. 'Comfort' had no meaning in Latin. Comfort occupies a position between pleasure and austerity and presupposes a house closed in on itself, a huddled family and the cosiness of privacy. At Rome no such thing existed and the gentle pleasures of family life were confined to the countryside and remained simple and austere. Any domestic refinements were reserved for the city house, a residence dedicated essentially to social life, where luxury was required only for the purposes of ostentation or pleasure. Civilizations that have developed domestic comfort deem it innocent and legitimate; at Rome, ostentatious luxury and pleasure were never innocent.

COMMUNITIES WITHIN THE CITY

Rome soon ceased to be a community of people who all knew each another. The anonymity and the freedom of the great town were also a Roman phenomenon. There was no place for solitude, however: each man, each woman, whether free, emancipated or slave, was part of a close-knit and supportive social network. A helping hand was extended even to strangers from the provinces who arrived in Rome with nothing but a determination to make their way in the world.

This was the situation in which dramatic poets found themselves. Young people new to the city, wishing to sell their future works to the impresarios but without any acquaintances among the nobility, had only one course open to them: to go to the Aventine. This hill had always played a special role. South of Rome, overlooking the Tiber and separated from the Palatine by the depression of the Circus Maximus, the Aventine was outside the holy wall and enjoyed a certain aloofness. Ever since the fifth century, when the Aventine had been parcelled out into building lots for allocation to the fathers of plebeian families, it had been the traditional home of the Roman *plebs*. In fact, all kinds of people lived there, at one remove from politics: foreigners, widows, actors, courtesans, wholesalers whose warehouses stood a few metres lower down, along the banks of the river, and of course poets.

In the third century, the temple of Minerva, standing at the top of the Aventine, accommodated the corporation, *collegium*, of scribes and *histriones* – dramatic authors and actors – as well as their archives. Consequently, many performing artists lodged nearby. Similarly, at the top of the Aventine was a community of poets who helped one another. Ennius, the great author of tragedies and epics, who later came to believe himself to be the reincarnation of Homer and the equal of Euripides, achieved his debut thanks to the support of the neighbourhood. Ennius was a southern Italian. Demobilized from the Roman army in 204 BC, he arrived in Rome from Sardinia. This half-Greek settled on the Aventine, and appears to have been given shelter by a comic poet of his own age, Caecilius Statius. There was nothing to link the two men either socially or in terms of geographical origin – Caecilius was a freedman of Gallic origin – except Ennius' determination to be a poet. Caecilius looked after Ennius, introducing him to his neighbour, Sulpicius Galba, who later became praetor in 187 BC. Thus was Ennius launched. Galba, who was not yet in need of a poet – he had only just set out on his political career – presented Ennius to a number of influential people, such as Marcus Fulvius Nobilior and Scipio Nasica, for whom Ennius thenceforth worked.

Several years later, in 164 BC, when the young Publius Terentius Afer, known simply as Terence, wished to launch himself as a dramatic poet, he naturally made his way to the Aventine. There he too met Caecilius, who by this time was a very old man. Terence read him his first comedy, *The Girl from Andros*. Caecilius liked it, and recommended Terence to the aediles who then purchased the play.

Here one can see the effects of the mutual support provided by a corporation of artists living and working in the same area, forming an effective but closed community. Its members guarded their independence jealously and when the nobleman Julius Caesar Strabo, an amateur poet, sought admission on the grounds of his rank to the poets' sanctuary (at that time on the Palatine), Accius, the current president of the corporation, refused his application. The worlds of poetry and politics should not be confused.

There was in fact little communication between the various different communities within Roman society. Communities, which could take the form of social and professional groupings – poets, flute-players, thespians, scribes – as well as of great families in which free men and slaves lived together, might come and go between the country and the city, their members never meeting anyone outside a narrow circle of noble relatives and noble relatives' slaves. This was why the government lived in dread of conspiracy, of the formation of an underground counter-society that might elude their watchful gaze and whose night-time gatherings might undo the work accomplished by the daytime assemblies of the Roman people. This city of the night belonged to fantasies associated with the city: it was a town turned upside-down, where effort yielded to pleasure, virtue to vice; a city of banqueters, fallen women and young effeminates.[104] Curiously, Roman society, in which everyone lived out of doors, permanently on display, forever exposed to public scrutiny, and where information was all-powerful, was not transparent. There were hidden recesses of time and space that remained inaccessible to the gaze of the institutions. No one could quite know what might be going on at night in the lonely groves on the banks of the Tiber or by the city wall.

Rome was splintered into communities that often knew nothing of one another. It was only relations between neighbours that occasionally revealed a more transparent society.

One particular case that caused a great stir in Rome in the second century BC was in fact uncovered thanks to the close neighbourhood life on the Aventine. This was the scandal of the Bacchanalia, the celebration of the mysteries of Bacchus, which by a senate decree passed in 186 BC were finally prohibited at Rome and throughout the whole of Italy.

The affair had started when a Greek from Etruria claiming to be a priest had founded a sect of initiates devoted to the celebration of the cult of Bacchus. Strange rituals were enacted to the accompaniment of music performed on drums and cymbals. At the outset only women were admitted; they alone could be priests and they initiated others, in the daytime, three times a year. The sect, however, soon degenerated. On the instigation of a lady from Capua, young men were allowed to join, and the meetings came to be held at night-time five times a month. Orgiastic banquets were given and the presence of men led to an unleashing of sexuality, especially homosexuality. A powerful subculture came into existence: a twilight world peopled with fanatics drugged by priests with wine and sexual excess and taught systematically to overturn common morality. Absolute secrecy was imposed on the members of the sect on pain of death:

> Men, writhing about as if insane, would utter prophecies. Matrons in the dress of Bacchantes, with dishevelled hair and carrying torches, would run down to the Tiber, plunge their torches in to the water and, because these contained sulphur mixed with calcium, would bring them out still burning. Those who refused to aid and abet or join in the crimes were alleged to have been carried off by the gods, bound to some sort of engine, and borne away out of sight to hidden caves.[105]

The sect became a fearful instrument in the hands of its members. They assassinated their rivals or wealthy relatives, falsified wills, obtained false evidence and sought to disgrace sons from well-to-do families the better to manipulate them. Still nothing about these goings-on leaked out.

But at this point a young man living on the Aventine, a certain Publius Aebutius, the son of a knight, comes into the story. On the death of Aebutius' father, his mother had remarried a certain Titus

Sempronius Rutilus. Since Aebutius was still a minor, his stepfather had become the boy's guardian. Aebutius, however, was already fifteen or sixteen years old and growing up fast. Sempronius had no desire to be called to account for his dishonest guardianship when his stepson eventually donned the toga of manhood, and he began to wonder how to do away with his stepson or gain power over him. He could see only one way of achieving this: by initiating him into the mysteries of the Bacchanalia. The boy was sure to suffer either death or disgrace. So Duronia, Aebutius' mother, took her son to one side and told him that once when he had been very ill she had promised the gods that if he recovered she would have him initiated into the cult of Bacchus and that this vow had now to be carried out. The young man could see no harm in this and, not being particularly anti-religious, gave his consent. His mother told him that for ten days he would have to abstain totally from sex, that he should then purify himself with water and she would take him to the shrine.

But young Aebutius had a mistress who lived in the house next door, a kind-hearted courtesan named Hispala. Hispala, who in her youth had been a slave and a prostitute – her name indicates that she must have been a Spaniard from the region of Seville – had been obliged to continue in her former profession after her enfranchisement in order to survive. Having become a renowned courtesan, she had fallen in love with Aebutius from whom she asked no fee, Aebutius would in any case have found it hard to pay for his mistress' favours since his stepfather gave him no money. Because Hispala's patron was dead, she had obtained from the praetor a guardian so that she could make out a will and leave all her goods to Aebutius.

The young man had no secrets from the courtesan and he accordingly told her that he would be sleeping alone for several days because he was going to be initiated into the mysteries of the Bacchanalia. On learning of this, Hispala became distraught. She had herself been initiated in the company of her former mistress and she perceived that the intentions of Aebutius' mother were suspect. She made the boy promise to refuse to submit to the initiation. Returning home, Aebutius obediently announced to his mother that he would not be going with her to the mysteries. His mother and stepfather consequently threw Aebutius out of the house along with four slaves. The young man sought refuge at the house of his paternal aunt, Aebutia, who also lived on the Aventine. His aunt advised him to go and tell the whole story to the consul, including the circumstances under which he had been thrown out of home.

After listening to Aebutius' uncorroborated account, the consul decided to set up a discreet inquiry. Since it was a matter that concerned women, and in particular women who lived on the Aventine, a world that was quite foreign to him, he would need an informer – a female informer. As luck would have it, his mother-in-law, Sulpicia, was just the person for this task. Sulpicia was an elderly and infinitely respectable woman, who knew all the mothers in the district. The consul questioned her about Aebutia. Sulpicia assured her son-in-law that Aebutia was above any suspicion and quite incapable of calumny or lies. He could have absolute trust in her as a witness. To avoid acting in his official capacity, the consul asked his mother-in-law to invite Aebutia around in a neighbourly fashion, which she agreed to do. As if by chance, while Aebutia was at Sulpicia's house Postumius, the consul, dropped in. Striking up a conversation with them, again quite casually, he led the conversation round to young Aebutius. At this point his aunt dissolved into tears and told the consul how she had had to take her nephew in after he had been thrown out of home for refusing to be initiated into the mysteries of the Bacchanalia.

The consul then asked Sulpicia to arrange for Hispala to visit her house. Sulpicia could not actually invite Hispala to her house, since the two women could not under any circumstances be seen together, so Hispala was therefore summoned to appear before the great lady. This worried Hispala, who had never before entered the house of such a distinguished person. When in the vestibule she saw first the lictors, then the consul's retinue and finally the consul himself, she nearly swooned. Until that moment she had only ever caught sight of the great magistrates of the republic from a distance during religious ceremonies. Postumius led her to the inner part of the house, reserved for private family matters, where Sulpicia was waiting. Hispala was somewhat reassured by the old lady's presence. When, however, Postumius began to question her about the Bacchanalia, torn between the dread of divine anger and the holy fright that the consul inspired in her she began to tremble so violently that for a long while she was unable to speak a single word. She tried to deny everything, but the anger this aroused in the consul overwhelmed her. She then admitted everything, relating details of the orgies and the crimes committed by the initiates. The consul and his mother-in-law took charge of the two witnesses, Aebutius and Hispala, placing them under the protection of their clan. Hispala was concealed at Sulpicia's house, in a bedroom on the first floor, the exterior staircase to which was inaccessible. Aebutius was sent to the house of one of Postumius' clients.[106]

The Roman people generously rewarded Aebutius and Hispala,

each of whom received 100,000 *as* from the public treasury. Hispala was provided with a good dowry and granted the right to marry without the marriage bringing dishonour on her husband. As for Aebutius, his name was to be entered in the lists of those citizens who had fulfilled their military obligations. He was free not to serve unless he so desired and was considered thenceforth already to have come of age. This doubtless put a stop to the love affair between the two witnesses. The courtesan had become an honourable woman and the young man an adult. No doubt they both left the Aventine, each going off to begin their lives in another district of Rome where no one had heard of them.

The great size and huge population of Rome had served to conceal the goings-on of the sect. At night if a Roman had heard the music and shouting of the Bacchantes they had probably assumed that it was just a group of banqueters who had had a little too much to drink, or youths, their blood excited by wine, who were having a fight, or even some outlandish cult celebrated by strangers and customarily tolerated. To break through the divisions and partitions of the city, the consul had had to make his way through a quarter whose everyday life had remained that of a village.

9

Political life in the city

To those who chose it as their home, Rome was a city to experience day in day out, not just on feast days and holidays. With a social life quite unlike that of the army or the countryside, Rome was the city of non-stop politics.

PLACES AND POLITICS

There were only a few places in which it was possible to take part in political life, and all of them were in Rome. Political Rome, the centre of power, the place where assemblies and elections were held and magistrates religiously enthroned, was tiny. The inhabitants of Rome crowded round the forum because that was where everything happened, in a circle comprising the forum, the Capitol and the field of Mars. Sometimes politics might spill out as far as the Via Sacra or even reach the gates of Rome, but only rarely.

In Roman politics there were players and spectators. Only senators, nobles and a handful of knights could ever gain entry to the superior magistracies. But those who did not belong to this tiny political class – numbering a few hundred in all – could find other ways of participating. Once they had voted, elected their magistrates or ratified a law, Roman citizens became spectator politicians. But spectators were not condemned to passivity. Power was a non-stop show that could not be staged without an audience; indeed, it was often the audience who decided how the show should end. On the spur of the moment, a Roman citizen would walk out of his shop, market garden, bank, workshop, writer's den or house and rush off to the forum.

Magistrates and senators would travel round the city in the trappings of their office, preceded by their lictors or aides, *apparitores*. Dressed in white and red, they would drive a passage through the brown crowds. They published decrees, had citizens arrested and convicted, levied fines and convened assemblies. Since everything happened out of doors, magistrates were under the constant gaze of the citizenry. Public opinion was not always given a formal expression. Some magistrates were jostled, manhandled and their insignia of office torn from them, others prevented from doing their job.

Trials were held in the open, with judges sitting on platforms in the midst of a noisy crowd eager to say what it thought of the accused, the plaintiffs and the lawyers. Frequently, speakers could not make themselves heard above all the shouts and heckling. When the magistrates harangued the crowds from the rostra at the foot of the Capitoline hill, there was nothing to protect them from the mood of the populace. If, from his perch on a statue, some wit managed to direct a few well-aimed quips at a speaker, unleashing the laughter of the crowd, the speaker might be forced to beat a hasty retreat. Popular assemblies were trials of strength, all the more risky when it was by no means clear just who had right on their side. Magistrates, of course, had their *apparitores* to ensure that people treated them with respect. If there was only one ill-intentioned heckler, he could be unceremoniously ejected. But if an angry mob suddenly formed, try as they might, the *apparitores* would never gain the upper hand. Magistrates who set their face against the majority of an assembly would not last long: generally they caved in before a clear expression of public dissent.

There was a strong temptation to manipulate assemblies. In times of strife, the tribunes of the people, of varying political persuasions, convened meetings and counter-meetings. Each tribune would see to it that he was acclaimed by 'his' assembly. Sometimes, when an opponent was holding an assembly, a tribune might even send in armed gangs to clear the forum. When this happened, a few citizens were always left for dead. Since Rome had nothing resembling a police force, it was quite easy to resort to violence.

On their way to the curia from the Palatine or the Velian hills, senators had to cross the forum. On days when the senate had to reach a momentous decision, citizens would taken up position at 'their' comitium, on the edge of the forum. To reach the curia, the senators had to work their way through a murmuring scrum of citizens whose feelings did not require precise formulation in order to impress themselves upon the senators.

THE FORUM: WHERE THE PEOPLE MET

Whatever happened, Romans always met back at the forum. The forum was the centre of people power because it was there that people congregated.

Early in the morning, sometimes even before sunrise, citizens would make their way there in their togas, often in response to an official announcement. Perhaps a judgement was going to be read out or a magistrate or a tribune of the people might have called an assembly. A politician's clients would provide him with an escort from his house or arrange to meet him at the forum. The forum was a temple: everything took place under the gaze of the gods. Yet it belonged to no one god in particular, just as it belonged to no single citizen. It was neutral: everyone was equally exposed to everyone else's scrutiny. A man's rank and social standing were illustrated by the size and nobility of the crowd that milled around him.

In the afternoon, the forum was given over to one-to-one encounters, to gossiping and to a different form of social display. The afternoon crowd was a mass without form. Conversations overlapped in a confused buzzing and people moved to and fro between different groups, savouring the easy delights of good company. Talk would focus on everything and nothing. The main thing was the pleasure of conversation itself, and the need to make quite sure that everyone had the same catch-phrase with which to complain about the soaring cost of wheat, to exchange tittle-tattle about so-and-so's wedding or to argue about a certain tribune of the people. By swapping common-places, citizens strengthened their sense of belonging to a community. For those who strolled round the forum in the afternoon, the gossip and truisms that passed for news provided a way of restating their agreement on elementary shared values.

Roman satirists got many a laugh at the expense of the leech-like chatterboxes who even followed the unsuspecting over the Tiber and back.[107] The only way you could shake one off was to encounter another: courtesy demanded that strollers flit from one conversation to the next. The forum was the home of rumour. It was there that

anecdotes were peddled, there that Romans gained such nicknames as
'knock-knees', 'boss-eyes' or 'pet'. People would relay stories about a
certain miser, Avidienus, say, who would give his guests rancid oil[108]
and was nicknamed 'the dog', or about Caesar's friend Mamurra,
nicknamed 'the shaft' and accused of 'making a progress through the
beds of all'.[109] The forum was also the place to take an individual to
task. Everyone knew everything about everyone else's business, down
to the most intimate of details. The Romans were never alone, and
there was nothing that their slaves failed to see and relate. Rome was
tolerant of people's private foibles: as long as they remained private,
they provoked only indulgent laughter. However, if a man's political
ambition exposed him to public condemnation, any available
peccadillo would be thrown to the sniggering crowd.

Caesar's adolescent love affair with Nicomedes, the king of
Bithynia, which had allegedly flourished during a mission to that
country, when Caesar was nineteen, gave rise to countless jokes as
soon as his overarching ambition became apparent. People muttered
as he walked by, made sarcastic comments about him at the forum
and daubed graffiti on the walls of official buildings. They called him
a 'royal trollop', 'Nicomedes' pigsty' and the 'Bithynian brothel'. A
certain Octavius who, since people said he was crazy, got away with
all manner of insolence, one day publicly saluted Pompey as king and
Caesar as queen, at a time when the two men were sharing power.
Rumours, once they had taken root, soon emerged in official
assemblies. At the senate, when Caesar recalled the good deeds of
Nicomedes, Cicero replied: 'No more of that, pray, for it is well
known what he gave you, and what you gave him in turn.'[110]

But it was still possible to tackle public opinion head-on by
answering one joke with another:

> Of all the numerous provinces, he made the Gauls his choice, as
> the most likely to enrich him and furnish suitable material for
> triumphs . . . Transported with joy . . . he could not keep from boasting
> a few days later before a crowded house that, having gained his heart's
> desire to the grief and lamentation of his opponents, he would
> therefore from that time mount on their heads; and when someone
> insultingly remarked that that would be no easy matter for a woman,
> he replied in the same vein that Semiramis too had been queen in Syria,
> and the Amazons in days of old had held sway over a great part of
> Asia.[111]

Although such a reply might win the sniggerers to one's own side, it
was not really an effective riposte: its insolence was politically

suspect. Only those who aspired to tyrannical power deemed themselves above public opinion and the rumours of the forum.

THE FORUM: WHERE THE PEOPLE HELD SWAY

Sometimes the seething crowd at the forum would suddenly become a political community. There was nowhere else that this metamorphosis could take place. The forum made the voice of the masses sacred and turned them into a *populus*.

A fourth-century BC anecdote tells of a hideously skinny and filthy old man with long beard and hair who suddenly rushed into the forum. The citizens flocked round him and listened in silence to his terrible story. He related that he was a Roman citizen and peasant and that during the most recent war the Sabines had pillaged his harvests, set fire to his farm and stolen his herds. Consequently, to pay his taxes, he had had to borrow money. Then, unable to pay off his debts, he had been handed over to his creditors who had tortured him and thrown him into a dungeon. He bared his back to reveal the marks of a recent whipping.

This wretched creature, in legal terms a fugitive slave, made a ritual appeal to the pity of the Roman people. By wearing mourning clothes, he let it be understood that unless somebody came to his rescue he would allow himself to die. He entreated the citizens to consider his dignity as a man and railed against a misfortune that had in fact befallen him quite legally. He hoped that his conspicuous poverty would arouse the people's indignation and that he would manage to secure the repeal of the law that placed insolvent debtors at the mercy of their creditors. To achieve his purpose he had to win over the entire people: Rome would have to join in his mourning. An individual cause suddenly became a political issue: the law against debtors spelt disaster for the individual and therefore disaster for the entire people.

The idea snowballed. Other insolvent debtors, some of them in chains, started to appear in public entreating the citizens to come to their aid. A tide of outrage broke over the forum, pity giving way to indignation. After a growing number of citizens took to wearing mourning, the city split into two factions: the majority yelling out in sorrow and indignation, offset by a few senators standing aloof from the collective mourning. The crowd rushed the senators, and their lives were saved only by the timely intervention of the consuls, who stepped in to separate the factions and broke up the fight. The crowd then besieged the senate to force a repeal of the law. This was eventually accomplished.[112]

This kind of political ritual was a regular occurrence at Rome. It enabled society to confront the state without having to negotiate the usual institutional channels. Any individual could change the law provided he won a majority of the people over to his side. The most widely used ritual was collective mourning. There was no action anyone could take against an entire city in mourning that displayed a suicidal tendency.

A single citizen, acting alone, might on the other hand put an end to public mourning and thereby prevent society from paralysing the workings of the state.

After the battle of Cannae, in which the Carthaginians had massacred the Roman army, the entire city went into mourning. Fifty thousand Romans had lost their lives and 14,000 had been taken prisoner. Fabius Maximus, not a magistrate that year but merely a senator, displayed an extraordinary sang-froid. With Hannibal at the gates of Rome, Fabius Maximus walked calmly round the city, amiably greeting everyone he met, preventing the women from beating their breasts and dispersing the crowds of people that formed to vent their distress in public. He made it possible for political life to resume its course, persuaded the senate to reconvene and the magistrates to return to their work. He managed, singlehandedly, to prevent the citizens from abandoning the city.[113]

GREAT RECONCILIATIONS

As well as such spectacular moments, when the city split into two camps, there were equally dramatic scenes of reconciliation.

During the siege of Veii, sedition was smouldering at Rome. The tribunes of the people accused the senate of deliberately prolonging the war so as to keep young people out of political life. They also criticized them for forcing the soldiers to go on living in tents when it was freezing and snowing. Appius Claudius, a tribune with consular power, clashed with the tribunes of the people in lengthy debates before the citizens at the forum. Suddenly terrible news arrived. The besieging troops had built a terrace and brought a wooden tower almost up against the city walls. However, taking advantage of the inadequate guard that the Roman forces kept on the construction work after dark, the inhabitants of Veii had made a night-time sortie and had set fire to the Roman war machinery. Many soldiers had died in the fire and months of hard work had gone up in smoke. On hearing this, the senators at Rome were terrified that the peace party would gain strength from this turn of events and that the tribunes would triumph. But things turned out quite differently.

Suddenly,

> those who were of equestrian rating but had not received horses from the state, having first taken counsel together, came to the senate, and, being granted a hearing, volunteered to serve on their own horses. These men had received a vote of thanks from the senate, in the most honourable terms, and the report of it had spread to the forum and the city. Almost at once the plebeians ran together to the curia, and declared that it was now the turn of the foot-soldiers to proffer their services to the state, whether it would have them march to Veii, or anywhere else. If they should be led to Veii, they promised that they would not quit their ground until they had taken the enemy's city.
>
> Then the senate could control its joy no longer. They did not, as with the knights, issue an order to the magistrates to thank them, nor did they call them into the curia to receive an answer. The senate did not keep within the house, but each man cried out from above, to the multitude standing in the comitium, and by speech and gesture signified the general jubilation. Rome was blest, they said, and invincible and eternal, because of this noble harmony. They praised the knights, they praised the plebeians, they extolled the very day itself, and confessed that the courtesy and good-will of the senate had been surpassed. Fathers and commoners mingled their tears of joy . . .[114]

The public outpourings of emotion were a means of communication and a ritual. The *plebs* had made a gesture and challenged the senate to a duel of generosity. The senate had to respond. Back inside the curia, the senators therefore issued a decree, a *senatus consultum*. They made an official recommendation to the magistrates that the military tribunes should publicly declare to the assembled people their gratitude to the cavalry and infantry and assure them that the senate would never forget the patriotic spirit they had shown. Newly enlisting soldiers would receive a full year's pay and henceforth the cavalry would also receive payment. Finally, those responsible for supplying the besieging army at Veii would make sure that the troops would no longer want for anything.

Melodramas of this type were enacted regularly at Rome and were its life blood. Yet each time a civil conflict came to an end there was an enormous sense of relief – for nobody could ever be sure just how far such hostilities might go.

WHEN ROMANS ABANDONED ROME

Political clashes did sometimes tear huge holes in the fabric of Roman society. When the people of the forum were unable to impose their will but the magistrates still failed to regain the upper hand, crisis would ensue. Luckily, there was a social ritual that dramatized the conflict and thereby helped to prevent the outbreak of civil war. This ritual, known as 'secession', involved the people's literal physical departure from Rome.

In the middle of the fifth century BC, the decemvirs, ten magistrates appointed to draw up a law code, usurped power and reigned as tyrants. The senate went on strike and refused to hold session. Rome was under threat of foreign attack and much of the populace was under arms. It was at this juncture that a decemvir, Appius Claudius, fell in love with Virginia, a young plebeian. Intending to make her his concubine, he claimed that she was in fact the slave of Marcus Claudius, one of his clients, and made an attempt to kidnap her as she walked through the forum on her way to school. Virginia's father was in the army and therefore unable to defend her. Appius wanted to hold the girl at his house until the trial, and was legally entitled to do so, but Virginia's nurse cried out for help and a crowd of citizens gathered. It was not long before they discovered that the girl in question was Virginia, the daughter of Virginius and the fiancée of Icilius, both very popular and well-known men. Appius tried to disperse the crowd, but they refused to leave him alone. Virginia's fiancé Icilius and the girl's maternal uncle then arrived on the scene. The crowd was stirred by Icilius' words as he refused to retreat before Appius' lictors, who had orders to take the girl away. What was at stake, Icilius told the gathered citizenry, was no less than the recognition of the plebeians' right to marriage and family, indeed to civilization itself. He injected a political element into the indignation of the crowd. Appius gave in before the assembled crowd, but fixed the trial for the very next day. Icilius rushed off to fetch Virginius from the army camp.[115]

But in the city at break of day, as the citizens stood in the forum, agog with expectation, Virginius, dressed in mourning and leading his daughter, who was also clad in mourning garb and was attended by a number of matrons, came down into the market-place with a vast throng of supporters. He then began to go about canvassing people, not merely asking their aid as a favour, but claiming it as his due,

saying that he stood daily in the battle-line in defence of their children
and their wives.

Virginius reminded them of his bravery as a soldier and of his
services to the army, his complaints turning gradually into a
harangue. Icilius spoke to the crowd in a similar vein. The matrons
wept, unable to speak. It made a pathetic spectacle. But Appius,
taking up his post on his judge's platform, remained impassive. This,
comments Livy, was proof of his madness, for Appius was behaving
like a tyrant. He should have been moved by the feelings of this crowd
– the Roman people. He was setting his face against the entire city.
From his lofty tribunal, he declared his judgement that the young girl
was indeed the slave of Marcus Claudius.

The crowd was struck dumb with horror. Appius gave orders for
the sentence to be enforced and commanded one of his freedmen to
seize Virginia from the throng of matrons, who at once sent up a
piercing wail. The women and the champions of Virginius formed
a cordon around Virginia while Appius ordered his lictors to force
a path through the crowd. Respecting the political authority that
the lictors embodied, the crowd parted. Virginia now stood alone and
defenceless in the middle of the square. Adopting a conciliatory tone,
Virginius asked Appius to grant him one last talk with his daughter
and her nurse in order to discover whether she really was of servile
origin. He led Virginia away towards the new shops and there, seizing
a knife from a butcher's stall, he killed her to save her from
dishonour. He accompanied his deed with a curse. Turning towards
Appius, seated on his tribunal, he said: 'With this blood, Appius, I
curse your life.'

To Romans, infanticide was one of the worst possible crimes. It
defiled Virginius, making him untouchable, a figure of horror, even
more fearsome than Appius. Appius yelled out orders to arrest
Virginius, but to no avail. Virginius walked on in silence, his hand
gripping the bloodstained knife, the sight of which opened a path
before him wherever he went. The crowd followed in his wake and
gave him protection. He led them all to the gate of the city. The
women shouted and wept while the men of Virginius' family
displayed the young girl's corpse to the people. Meanwhile, other
citizens had arrived at the forum. The lictors no longer commanded
obedience, the people broke their *fasces*, thereby toppling Appius
from his position of authority. Pulling his toga up over his head,
Appius fled to his nearby house.

Then the plebeians deserted the city, the soldiers abandoning their camp, the civilians abandoning the city. They sought refuge on the Aventine, the hill of Remus, outside the walls of Rome, and from there made their way to the Sacred Mount, the traditional site for secessions.

'Now all Rome was desolate with an unwonted loneliness, and there was nobody in the forum but a few old men, and it appeared, particularly when the Fathers had been summoned to the senate-house, quite deserted.'[116] The fate of the decemvirs was sealed. Rome was a dead town. As if devastated by fire or plague, its citizens and soldiers had all vanished, its heart had bled dry. The decemvirs handed their resignation to the senators, merely asking that they be spared the people's vengeance.

A SCRIPT FOR JUSTICE

Virginius, newly elected as tribune of the people, now set out to prosecute Appius Claudius. And so the tale began again, this time in reverse. Appius went down to the forum with an escort of young noblemen. Virginius used his influence to have Appius imprisoned until his trial. Appius' family, dressed in mourning, then occupied the forum and begged every citizen to release the wretched Appius from his irons, since he was rotting in a dungeon surrounded by highway robbers and base scoundrels. Virginius too refused to leave the forum, where he never ceased to describe to anyone who cared to listen each of Appius' crimes as well as the circumstances of Virginia's death. Since Appius' family failed to win public opinion to their side or to obtain his release from prison, the former decemvir committed suicide.[117]

The death of Appius provides a clear picture of the way in which Roman justice operated. As in politics, it was essential never to be rejected by the community. On the southern side of the Capitol, above the comitium, the prison in which Appius languished was a deathly, dark and terrifying place. Surrounded by filth and deprived of any form of sustenance, prisoners in this *carcer* soon rotted away. The only ones to survive were those who received help from the community.

At Rome imprisonment was not a matter of punishment, it spelt death. The only people who escaped were those who had managed in the course of their lives to achieve a sufficient degree of recognition and dignity for a group of their supporters to press the magistrates and senate to set them free before the trial.

However, although abandonment by his group led an individual to certain death, his community might express its collective disapproval of a punishment and successfully oppose it. The general pattern was as follows. From his tribunal, a magistrate would deliver a speech justifying a conviction and then command his lictor to seize the condemned man.[118] The lictor would grab the convict by the throat and place a rope around his neck. This he would tighten until blood spurted from the man's eyes, ears and mouth. The convict was then dragged off to prison.

It was now up to the crowd to play its part. If the condemned man remained silent, everyone present, all his friends and relatives, appalled by his crime and terrorized by the machinery of power, would abandon him to his fate. His enemies would applaud with glee. Under a tyranny, the sound of suffocated wailing would rise from the crowd to show that their assent was forced.[119] However, if the man called out for help, the situation might be reversed. It mattered little whether his appeal took a precise legal form or remained informal: the condemned man would 'provoke' the surrounding crowd (the act of *provocatio*), the tribunes of the people and his friends, challenging them to come to his rescue. It was a question of standing up to coercion from the magistrates, engaging in a duel. Relatives or friends of the condemned man, or a social grouping such as the senate or a body of knights, would display their disagreement with the judgement. They would go into mourning, letting out loud wails as they walked with the prisoner to the prison. The crowd would then assemble at the prison gate and hold a round-the-clock vigil to alert the town and sap the magistrate's support. The magistrate would respond to the challenge, brandish his weapons and send in the lictors. The conflict would then spread and escalate until the senate would decide to act. An oratorical joust would bring the process to a close.

Whether on political or on legal grounds, it was always at the forum that the city enacted or embarked upon its ritual acts of splitting apart. Secession, *provocatio* and the deployment of tribunes were not flaws in the system: they had a practical function. The Romans made no sharp distinction between social rituals and political institutions. If Rome was a stranger to direct democracy, there was at least a kind of street legitimacy in operation. The Roman individual did not exist, had no power, no real rights. What counted was the ability to mobilize a good number of citizens, either as a social grouping (for example, knights) or as a family clan. The resulting 'party' could attack its adversaries with symbolic violence that might involve nothing worse than going into mourning and wailing a great deal. In this way, Roman citizens, most of whom were legally barred from exercising any power, managed none the less to take an active part in political life whenever they were in Rome.

POLITICS AND ITS MONUMENTS

The scenery and props of Roman political life were important. When an orator spoke at the comitium, the listeners saw the forum, the Capitol and the curia; when he spoke on the field of Mars, they saw the Capitol and the citadel. The decision of a tribunal or of an assembly might depend on its physical backdrop.

> Quintus Capitolinus was made dictator, and he cast Manlius into prison. Thereupon the people put on the garb of mourners, a thing done only in times of great public calamity, and the senate, cowed by the tumult, ordered that Manlius be released . . . When Manlius was brought to trial, the view from the place was a great obstacle in the way of his accusers. For the spot where Manlius had stood when he fought his night battle with the Gauls overlooked the forum from the Capitol, and moved the hearts of the spectators to pity. Manlius himself, too, stretched out his hands toward the spot, and wept as he called to men's remembrance his famous struggle there, so that the judges did not know what to do and again postponed the case. They were unwilling to acquit the prisoner of his crime when the proofs of it were so plain; yet they were unable to execute the law upon him when, owing to the place of trial, his saving exploit was, so to speak, in every eye. So Camillus, sensible of all this, transferred the court outside the city to the Peteline Grove, from where there is no view of the Capitol. There the prosecutor made his indictment, and the judges were able to forget the man's past services in their righteous anger at his present crimes. So then Manlius was convicted, carried to the Capitol, and thrust down the rock, thus making one and the same spot a monument of his most fortunate actions and of his greatest misfortunes. In addition, the Romans razed his house to the ground, and built there a temple to the goddess they call Moneta. They decreed also that in future no patrician should ever have a house on the Capitoline hill.[120]

The account of Manlius' sentencing is, among other things, a story about the power of different places. It was not possible to convict Manlius within sight of the Capitol, the site of his previous glorious exploits. Once convicted, however, it was there that Manlius faced execution, and his death banished all private dwellings from the hill. Thereafter, whenever a speaker, with a sweeping gesture, drew the

attention of his audience of judges to the Capitol, he would recall that
it was but a short distance from the temple of Jupiter to the Tarpeian
rock and that even the saviour of the fatherland was not above the
law.[121]

Anyone who spoke at the forum could see the statues of the city's
great men, Camillus near the rostra, Horatius Cocles on the
comitium. Year by year the town centre filled with statues, monuments
and memories. The temple of Concord on the Capitoline hill, built at
the time of the struggles between the plebeians and the patricians,
constantly reminded citizens of the vital need for political consensus.
By the end of the fourth century, most of the monuments were in
place. In 338, Maenius, conqueror of the Latins, hung the prows
(*rostra*) of warships captured from Antium at the tribune of the
harangues, which is why it was thereafter known as the rostra. At the
close of the century, the equestrian statues of the consuls who had
vanquished the Latins also took up their position in the forum. With
its exemplary history, the city gave gravity to the speeches and acts of
politicians. At Rome every speech, whether delivered at the curia or at
the forum, rested on this scenic backdrop. The blood of sacrificial
victims, the bronze of glory, the round silhouette of the temple of
Vesta and the dazzling roofs of the temples of Jupiter and of Concord
contributed more to the pathos of Roman speeches than any other
rhetorical device.

Political life was a never-ending, colourful, over-the-top, tragi-
comic play. The plot was fixed from the start and everyone played
their allotted role. There would be a stand-off between the senate and
the people, between consuls and praetors on one side and people's
tribunes on the other. Tension would mount to breaking-point and
then everyone would reunite in a grand melt-down of previous
differences. Rome was part of the show, and the north end of the
forum, with its view of the Capitol, supplied the scenery.

Any alteration to this physical backdrop had an effect on political
life, reshaping the collective memory and providing orators with new
points of reference for their speeches. Aware of this, many politicians
sought to leave their mark on such sites. The declared purpose of the
large-scale public buildings, basilicas and porticos that began to go up
in the second century BC was to provide people with shelter from the
sun or rain, thereby enabling them to carry on their business at the
forum whatever the weather. The Porcia basilica and the Emilia
basilica – large, closed and covered market halls – replaced the small
shops on the east and west sides of the forum. Porticos now lined the
principal streets, the Via Sacra, the road up to the Capitol and the

routes that ritual processions followed. This literal petrification of solemn routes and of places of mass assembly was no accident. It had the effect of turning rituals into institutions, of freezing particular places in a single function, of introducing a sharp separation between society and the state. This was what the empire was to accomplish. Eventually, the streets of Rome would just be places to go for a stroll and no longer a venue for the performance of political rituals.

Part III

Time and Action

10

Time and the Romans

TIME IS NOT A GOD

Perhaps, under the republic, there was no such thing as time at
Rome. It was certainly not a divine force. The only gods who had
anything to do with time were Janus, who was first and foremost the
god of a particular kind of place, the god of gates, and Juno, the
goddess of births. People did not experience time in its own right but
only in so far as it marked beginnings. At Rome time was not a
concept that people used in order to come to terms with the way in
which the world was ordered. Accordingly no god was required to
defend time or to act as its guarantor.

In the days of the republic, the Romans only knew of their own
experience of time. They did not fantasize about the beginnings of the
world or worry their heads over history. They believed neither in the
power of time to transform people and things nor in any history of
mankind. When, however, a notion of historical time did emerge at
the end of the republic, it applied only to a single city and a single
people and its effects were destructive. Roman historians associated
time with decadence, viewing it more as an incidental process of
moral decline than as historical necessity. According to the historians,
the arrogant and grasping Romans had conquered the world to
satisfy their thirst for gold and pleasure and to lord it over other
peoples. As a result, they had become victims of their own passions,
crushed by an empire that was too immense, corrupted by a life that
had grown too comfortable.

To Roman minds it was a truism that happy peoples had no history. The ideal world was a stable and unbroken order enjoyed by a civilized version of mankind – that is, the gods and the worship they received. When asked to define eternity, Horace said that it was not the bronze tables on which the law was engraved, nor was it the Pharaoh's pyramid; eternity would last 'so long as the Pontiff climbs the Capitol with the silent Vestal.'[122]

This explains why Romans organized their years and their days in accordance with their own direct experience of time, action, and the life of the body and spirit. Above all, time seemed to provide a framework for the alteration of occupation and leisure, effort and relaxation.

WINTER AND SUMMER

Rome knew nothing of divine or historical time; human time, cut into slices for action, was all that mattered. And it made no difference if such action were religious or profane.

The year was divided into two seasons: the war season (summer), from March to October, and the season when citizens normally returned home (winter), from October to March. Sometimes, of course, soldiers had to stay in their tents throughout the winter and undergo considerable hardship. This did not, however, involve any departure from tradition. Romans divided every action into two distinct phases. The beginning of an action was the decisive moment which set off a whole train of events, and it was therefore important to begin every undertaking under the best possible circumstances, using the most appropriate gestures and words. What happened after that was simply the inevitable result of a good or bad beginning. To declare war later than October would therefore be an infringement of a taboo, indeed a serious mistake, and the war would probably be lost as a result. But there was nothing to prevent Romans from prosecuting throughout the winter a war launched in the summer. On the other hand, although summer was the season for war, there did not have to be a war every single summer.

As a rule, summer was a time of exertion. As well as being the moment when the republic was liable to call upon its citizens to rally to the flag, it was then too that they would be busy with clearing the land, ploughing, irrigating and generally preparing the earth for cultivation. Summer was also the season for journeys, when ships were taken out of dry dock and fitted out for trade expeditions. Summer brought the Romans out of their villages.

In peacetime, even if a citizen worked every day on his land, he was still considered to be resting. After all, in comparison with army life and the pain and suffering of war, the exertions of rustic life were a form of relaxation. Any economic activity, inasmuch as it was private and based in the home, belonged to rest time, *otium*.

But the real season for resting was the winter. Not only were soldiers normally back from the war but there was less work in the fields and rain kept the peasant indoors. This was the time for entertaining and for throwing family parties.

This relative inactivity gave the peasant plenty of time to take part in city life – that is, politics. Elections, held each year in November, December or March, were an exciting event for the whole civic community. Candidates' canvassers would pour into the Roman countryside to organize meetings, parties and rallies in public squares. They would use the death of a relative as an excuse to put on gladiatorial combats and funeral games.

This busy politicking disrupted the peace and quiet that had reigned after the end of the wars. Roman *otium* thus gave way to its opposite, *negotium*, civic activity. While *negotium* only kept peasants, craftworkers and other ordinary citizens busy for a few days each month, it completely took over the lives of the political class. Even if they were not all magistrates with full workloads, Roman politicians would be lawyers, jurists, senators or candidates. They would act for their friends, provide their own defence before the courts, work as legal consultants, sit on commissions to draw up new laws and sort out all the private problems that their clients brought them, such as marrying off a daughter, securing a bank loan or setting up a conscripted son with a position on the consul's general staff. For such men, a trip into the country really did spell rest and repose.

MORNINGS AND EVENINGS

But whether they were in town or on their farms, Romans lived out their lives according to both the annual and the daily alternation of effort and rest. For the day too assumed this rhythm, the morning being set aside for action and the evening for relaxation.

In the morning, at first light, the Romans, who slept in their tunics, got up, pulled on their togas and, if they were in town, began work immediately. A citizen's clients would crowd into his *atrium*, and would be received all at once, everyone remaining standing. They would then make for the forum for the main business of the day, arriving there shortly after sunrise. By this time, unless the weather was particularly inclement, the peasants would be at work in the fields. This was the time for effort, *labor*. Everyone worked hard till noon, when the least zealous would break off. One by one, as the afternoon progressed, everyone would stop working, depending on their strength and enthusiasm for the task. By the middle of the afternoon everyone would have returned home or repaired to the baths. The law courts were deserted, the money-changers' shops closed.

The evening then got under way, a time for pleasure and banqueting, a time to unwind physically, freeing the spirit which, with the help of a little wine, forgot all the worries of the day. The

Plate 6   Roman matrons spreading cloth
Reproduced by kind permission of the Ancient Art and Architecture Collection (Ronald Sheridan)

forum would again fill with people, but the evening crowd was more friendly than the morning one. Instead of togas, people wore brilliant and colourful tunics and huge hooded coats. Everyone would wander and mingle: men, women, citizens, slaves, courtesans in their togas, male prostitutes, their body hair removed and their faces disguised under heavy make-up. Freedwomen, lacking any matronly restraint, would eye the young men and chuckle with their servants. Strolling hawkers sold honey cakes, sausages and hot drinks. There were jugglers, story-tellers, prophets and impersonators: the squares and streets displayed all the pleasures the town could offer. The day ended with the only real daily meal, the *cena*, taken either at home with one's family or at the house of a friend who was throwing a banquet. This was the best moment of each day. It was what resting was all about: lying down, sipping wine, eating tender and delicate foods and recovering from the toils of the morning.

THE DREAD OF BEGINNINGS

It was when they had to embark upon something that the Romans came face to face with time. They were terrified by beginnings: this dread was one of the sicknesses of Roman culture. Since the success of an enterprise was determined by the way it began, it was thought wise to obtain as many guarantees as possible before starting anything. And the gods supplied the best guarantees.

This is why half the Roman religion was devoted to the quest for and interpretation of portents (the other half was liturgical). Unlike the Greeks, Rome did not use soothsayers, prophets or oracles. At Rome portents took the form of natural signs. There were three kinds of portent: those requested of Jupiter, known as auspices; those that were observed but unsought; and extraordinary phenomena, known as prodigies, that forced themselves on people's attention.

A magistrate was first and foremost someone who was empowered to consult the auspices on the republic's behalf. When Rome was about to undertake something that concerned all its people – the enactment of a law, say, or the declaration of hostilities – the consul or superior magistrate responsible for calling the meeting would consult the gods by means of the auspices. This involved an examination of signs in the sky: thunder, lightning, birds. The term *auspice* literally means 'bird observation'. The sky was Jupiter's domain and it was Jupiter whom the magistrate was really questioning.

Reading the auspices was not an attempt to obtain a prediction,

nor was it an entreaty for a successful outcome: it was more a matter
of checking that all was as it should be with the gods. The magistrates
were helped in their task by a college of priests known as augurs. To
'inaugurate' a place, a meeting or an individual involved asking
Jupiter: is this the right place, the right moment, the right individual?
A strict code governed the ritual, and the augurs spelled out in
advance what signs they were expecting to see and in which part of
the sky. The following is a description of how to 'inaugurate' a man.

After the death of Romulus, the Romans asked a Sabine, Numa
Pompilius, to become king.

> On being summoned to Rome he commanded that, just as Romulus
> had obeyed the augural omens in building his city and assuming regal
> power, so too in his own case the gods should be consulted.
> Accordingly an augur . . . conducted him to the citadel and made him
> sit down on a stone, facing south. The augur seated himself on Numa's
> left. His head was covered, and in his right hand he held the crooked
> staff without a knot which they call a *lituus*. Then, looking out over the
> city and the country beyond, he prayed to the gods, and, fixing his eye
> on a distant landmark, marked off the heavens with a line from east to
> west, designating as 'right' the regions to the south, and 'left' those to
> the north. Then, shifting the crook to his left hand and placing his right
> hand on Numa's head, he uttered the following prayer: 'Father Jupiter,
> if it is heaven's will that this man Numa Pompilius, whose head I am
> touching, be king in Rome, do thou exhibit to us unmistakable signs
> within those limits which I have set.' He then specified the auspices
> which he desired should be sent, and upon their appearance Numa
> was declared king, and so descended from the augural station.[123]

Inaugurations always followed this pattern, and the science of
augury made it possible to achieve a perfect mastery of events. The
auspices could either allow or prohibit a magistrate to act. If it was
later observed that some procedural mistake had been committed, the
auspices could be annulled:

> Tiberius Sempronius Gracchus had already arrived in his province
> when, leafing through various books concerning public religion, he
> realized that an error had been made during the consultation of the
> auspices for the consular meetings over which he had presided. He at
> once wrote to the college of augurs who made a report to the senate.
> The senate then issued an order recalling consuls Gaius Figulus and
> Scipio Nasica back to Rome, the former from Gaul and the latter from
> Corsica. On arrival in Rome, both consuls abdicated the consulship.[124]

Nobody was fooled by Tiberius Gracchus' ploy. The Sempronii and the Cornelii Scipiones were political opponents. The mistake, however, was genuine, and the elections therefore had to be invalidated.

THE EMPIRE OF SIGNS

As well as the auspices requested of Jupiter there was a throng of unsolicited signs that assailed one from all quarters. Things made themselves manifest; the gods sent signs. Birds flying past, a storm rumbling in the distance, a snake falling in through the *impluvium*, a cock crowing in the dead of night, a word carelessly let slip: it was not always obvious what to examine and what to ignore. Such occurrences were by no means extraordinary and yet they might hide a sign of vital importance for the future of Rome or for one's own personal future.

Magistrates' lives would have been insupportable if the science and practitioners of augury had not come to their rescue. The augurs had classified and foretold everything: the various bird species; those whose flight one had to observe; those whose song alone was significant; the favourable and the unfavourable birds. They knew how to interpret the height and manner of flight, the type of perch chosen, the way a bird walked on touching down. Signs possessed their own arithmetic. If a woodpecker gave a sign but an eagle then arrived to take its place, the sign given by the eagle would cancel out that of the woodpecker. For military campaigns, the augurs had elaborated a special system for examining the auspices, which involved sacred chickens. On the morning of battle, they looked to see if the chickens were eating properly, letting food drop from their beaks. If they were, then the auspices were deemed favourable. If they were not, it was best to avoid engaging in combat. During the First Punic War, the chickens of Publius Claudius Pulcher, commander of the fleet, had no appetite – perhaps they did not like being at sea. In his fury, the commander threw them overboard, yelling, 'If they won't eat, let them drink!' After losing the battle, the people condemned him. It was felt that his impiety had brought about the death of many citizens.[125]

Words spoken inadvertently, what the Romans called *omen*, were the most awesome of signs. Augury was of no help here: it was up to each person to grasp and accept the portent in the instant that it appeared. It was conceivable, of course, to ignore the signs – to insist on seeing and hearing nothing, stop one's ears and go about in a closed litter. But the careful observance of portents was part and parcel of political science. After the Gauls had taken Rome, an unexpected portent decided its future. The senate was meeting to decide whether the Romans ought to rebuild the city now that the Gauls had completely destroyed and desecrated it, or whether they should all emigrate to nearby Veii, which they had recently captured from the Etruscans and whose buildings were still standing. A centurion, returning with his men from guard duty (Rome, its buildings and even ramparts reduced to rubble, had become a kind of military camp) stopped in front of the comitium, close to the senate, and shouted out the following order: 'Standard-bearers, fix your ensign; here will be our best place to remain.' The senators heard this phrase, rushed outside and declared: 'We accept this presage!' The *plebs*, waiting at the door of the curia, shouted their approval.[126]

Portents were just as ubiquitous in private as in public life. Each morning in their houses, Romans would consult the auspices, and each time a sign was encountered, would seek to interpret it as best they could. Even in the most intimate aspects of their lives, Roman men and women resorted to portents.

In around 132 BC, Caecilia, Metellus' wife, found a husband for her niece in the following way:

> Caecilia had a niece, her sister's daughter, who was of marriageable age. She relied on an ancient custom to obtain presages during the first half of the night. Caecilia went with her niece to a small shrine and sat there for a while without hearing anything relating to her plans. The young girl, who had to stand, began to feel weary and so asked her maternal aunt to make room for her so that she too might sit down. Caecilia replied: 'I am perfectly happy to let you take my place.' These words, a simple expression of Caecilia's generosity, proved later to be prophetic. For Caecilia died and Metellus was soon to marry his wife's niece, the subject of this account.[127]

This story provides a rare and precious insight into the life of women and their procedures for divining the future. One cannot help but note the existence of a kinship that follows women's lines of descent, the young girl being the daughter of Caecilia's sister; and the existence of religious practices in which women take the initiative. The passage also reveals the existence of shrines, and hence of deities, that oversaw women's interests in matters of marriage. Perhaps the deity in question was Aurora, the goddess of maternal aunts.

Nor can one overlook the clear procedure involved in divining the future. One had to await the oracle sitting down, and the shrine, it appears, contained a divining seat. In line with tradition, Caecilia was to expect the portents in the first half of the night. The phrases spoken by her niece and herself, therefore, possessed oracular value. This was why, when waiting for portents, it was best to keep absolutely silent.

Just as magistrates used the many signs that appeared to them to further their political interests, citizens in their private life would use and abuse religious pretexts whenever it seemed expedient to do so. It was thus possible to delay forever an unwelcome marriage even if one had committed oneself to it:

> *Antipho*: But why should he delay? What reason will he give?
> *Geta*: Well, if you must know, he could say: 'I've had so many warnings since then . . . a strange black dog came into my house, a snake fell from the tiles through the skylight, a hen crowed, a soothsayer spoke against it and a diviner forbade it. Fancy starting on anything new before the shortest day!' That's the best kind of excuse; and that's the sort of thing he'll say.[128]

PRODIGIES AND EXPIATION

Then there were *monstra*, prodigies, or monsters, miraculous events that revealed that all was not well with the world and foreshadowed yet more serious disorders, such as foreign wars or internal revolutions. For example, in 102 BC, among other wondrous occurrences, blood rained from sky on the Anio river (Teverone), at Aricia a young boy was enveloped in flames without being burnt, a swarm of bees settled on a temple at the cattle market and the temple of Jupiter was struck by lightning. None of this was surprising given that the Cimbri and the Teutones had descended the valley of the Rhone and were threatening the Narbonnaise area.

To keep such prodigies at bay and to rid them of their malefic nature, the Romans used rituals of expiation and consulted Etruscan priests known as haruspices who read the woes of the world in the entrails of sacrificial victims and interpreted lightning according to the part of the sky in which it was seen. The republic asked them merely to perform expiation rituals and not to interpret such signs; it was the Roman people that entreated the haruspices to tell them more and to prophesy. And so the haruspices ended up waiting in the street for passing custom, getting varicose veins while they stood around between the baker's and the butcher's.[129]

When the haruspices' science proved to be inadequate to the job, the senate requested that the Sibylline books be consulted. The priests who undertook this service would find out from them which rituals needed to be performed. The entire people would then take part. A great quantity of animals would be sacrificed; crowds of women would go to entreat the female deities; *lectisternia*, sacrificial banquets to which the male gods were invited, and *sellisternia*, to which goddesses were invited, were held.

At times a leaden collective fear would grip Rome: a dread of the end of the world, the death of the city or its desertion by the gods. This panic would reach its height at times of civil war and paved the way to power for providential men capable of curing the people of their apocalyptic terrors. These terrors would return each time that Rome was struck by a defeat, civil strife or plague – all of which involved the same fundamental process: the disintegration of the body of civil society. Thus it was that in 364 BC, the first scenic games were introduced to put an end to that most terrible of prodigies, the plague.

Plague had broken out in around 367 BC, claiming the lives of high magistrate and ordinary citizen alike. A *lectisternium* was offered and games were performed, but to no avail: the plague dragged on for two further years. The authorities decided to try out a new kind of entertainment that was imported from Etruria: a kind of early theatre, or stage games. For the first time, a stage and a scenery wall were erected, in front of which dancers performed pantomimes to the accompaniment of flutes. The Romans greeted this spectacle with enthusiasm and theatre gained a foothold in Rome. But the plague persisted.

> However, the plays, first introduced to appease divine anger, neither freed men's minds of religious fears nor their bodies of disease. Indeed, it fell out quite otherwise. The games were in full swing when an inundation of the Tiber flooded the circus and put a stop to them, an accident which, suggesting as it did that the gods had already turned away, rejecting the proffered appeasement, filled the people with fear. Then the elders recollected that in the days when Gnaeus Genucius and Lucius Aemilius Mamercinus (for the second time) were consuls, and men's minds were more troubled by the search for means of propition than were their bodies by disease, it is said that a pestilence had once been allayed by the driving in of a nail by the dictator.[130]

A dictator was selected and a nail driven into the temple of Jupiter on the Capitol. At this point someone recalled an ancient custom that had been allowed to fall into disuse. It involved the praetor hammering in a nail each year on the Ides of September. This must be what they had neglected to do. The plague came to an end. It was decided to conserve the stage games and to hammer in nails regularly.

Innovation and tradition were the two possible responses to the fear that the world was coming to an end. Rome held on to all the ancient prescriptions and welcomed every new formula as it arrived. Anything that might one day serve to stave off catastrophe was entered in a huge register. Roman peasants too kept these vast books, handed down from father to son from the earliest times, at the back of their houses and each new generation would add its own experiences and findings. This store of knowledge was expected to help the city face the unforeseen: a drought; a sickness; a prodigious harvest or monstrous offspring. The books would contain prayers and medicinal prescriptions; farming techniques; 'tricks' for healing plants, animals and people; rituals to keep illnesses and calamities at bay and to placate ghosts; and moral maxims. A Roman's knowledge was empirical, founded on tradition and experience. Everything in these books had been tried and tested: they were the best defence against time's little surprises.

II

Measuring time

THE SOLAR DAY

In Greece, there were two ways of measuring time: counting it by means of a clepsydra (water-clock), or using shadows to tell the hour with a sundial. Neither of these two objects was in traditional use in Rome. The Romans did not have the same pressing need as the Greeks, especially the Athenians, to measure out the trickle of time. Each Greek litigant had the same amount of time at his disposal. In Rome there was no limit to the time one could take to set forth a case, perhaps because lawyers did not read out their speeches and each plea was a performance in its own right. It was only in the army that the Romans counted time: the night was divided into four watches and the guard was changed at the end of each watch. It seems that calibrated candles were used.

The only need a Roman had to know the time of day was if he had a law-suit pressing; in this case he would need to know when it was midday, since judges demanded that citizens who had been summoned to appear before the courts should arrive before that time. Generally speaking, both public and private law-suits had to be started in the first half of the day. A consular *apparitor* would stand at the top of the steps of the old curia from where he could keep a watchful eye on the course of the sun as it moved between the rostra and the graecostasis, the platform where ambassadors waited for an audience with the senators. When the sun was properly aligned – that is, due south – it was deemed to be midday and the *apparitor* would give orders for the trumpets to be sounded.

For the rest of the day, the Romans trusted to the sun. Both public and private business began at sunrise, in summer and winter alike. Most activities ceased when the sun began to decline, in the middle of the afternoon – the exact time would vary slightly, depending on the individual and his or her occupation, though this was more a matter of custom than a rule. The senate alone, which generally managed to elude constraints imposed by the time of day or the calendar, might work in the afternoon if it so wished. But not even the senate could hold session after sunset.

The Romans did not feel any need to cut the day into tiny slices. They did not require a unit of time. Indeed, in ancient times, Latin had nothing equivalent to the term *hora*, which it later borrowed from the Greek. Yet borrowing a word does not necessarily involve importing whatever the word originally referred to. The Romans in fact created their own definition of an hour: it was considered to be one-twelfth of the day or the night. The Roman hour therefore varied slightly every day, and daytime hours were only the same length as night-time hours at the equinoxes. The daytime hour ranged in length from about three-quarters of a modern hour in midwinter to about an hour and a quarter in midsummer. The only fixed point was midday, since midnight could never be exactly pinpointed. Clocks, both sundials and the imitation-Greek water-clocks manufactured at Rome from the second century BC onwards, were extremely complicated machines. Roman clepsydras used a head of water that changed every day – decreasing in the summer and increasing in the winter. Sundials had different gradations corresponding to the different seasons and only gave an average time.

Any notion that the Romans chose this seemingly complicated way of measuring and telling the time because of some presumed technological clumsiness may be discarded. In the Roman method of telling the time the proportions remain invariable from one day to the next. The ninth hour, when political and judicial business was generally concluded for the day, always fell in the middle of the afternoon, even if towards the summer solstice our modern clocks might show the time to be a quarter to four, and near the winter solstice, a quarter past two. What was important to the Romans was to set aside the same relative portions of each day for effort and for relaxation. If they had used our modern system of twenty-four equal hours to the day, all year round, they would have felt as though they were getting up and stopping work at a different 'time' each day.

Historians have had many a laugh at the Romans' expense over the fact that in 263 BC they brought back from Catania a solar dial but then 'failed' to recalibrate it to take account of the position of the sun at Rome. For a whole century, they are supposed to have gazed in doltish admiration at an object that gave them the wrong time. In fact, of course, there was no point in calibrating in the Greek manner a solar dial which would then have given them the exact but equinoctial time. They had no use for it.[131]

The variable Roman hour embodied a relationship with time that had nothing to do with stars and mathematics, and everything to do with people. In Mediterranean countries, you can feel the ninth hour of the day on your skin. Suddenly the slanting sun no longer warms you in the same way. In the summer, a sudden gentleness softens the atmosphere; in the winter, the air has a chilly edge. It was time to bathe when, in summer, one felt the need to refresh oneself, removing the last trace of the day's sweat, and, in winter, one wanted to warm oneself, heating up one's body to face the cold of the evening in a barely heated house.

THE LUNAR MONTH

While the sun regulated the time of day, the moon measured out the months. The month and the moon were tied together so closely that it was hard to tell whether the month was a 'lunar month' or the moon a 'measuring star'. The latter, however, appears more etymologically probable.

Since the moon takes roughly twenty-nine and a half days to circle the earth, daily solar time and monthly lunar time cannot possibly coincide. If one insists none the less on starting the month at the beginning of a day, the resulting month is not precisely lunar. The Roman month, an attempt to reconcile the sun and the moon, therefore had no fixed number of days, but varied between twenty-nine and thirty.

The first day of the Roman month, known as the Kalends, coincided with the new moon. When the watches, sent to their look-out stations by the priests, had seen the last crescent of the waning moon disappear, they proclaimed the Kalends: the word for this day in fact derives from a root signifying 'to proclaim with a loud voice'. This proclamation was both a statement of fact and a decree. If, owing to mist, the priests got it wrong, it was too late, the Kalends had none the less arrived. On the same day, they would announce how many days it would be before the Nones, the day of the first quarter. The *rex sacrorum* thus fixed an appointment with the people, for it was on the Nones that the religious calendar of the month was published.

The Kalends were dedicated to Janus, the god of passages and openings, and above all to Juno, the goddess of birth. On each Kalends, the wife of the *rex sacrorum* would sacrifice to Juno either a sow or a she-lamb.

Seven or so days after the Kalends came the Nones, the ninth day of the month. On the Nones, the *rex sacrorum* and a higher magistrate announced the month's festivities and set a day for the Ides, which marked the full moon. The Ides, the midpoint of the month, always marked a festival in honour of Jupiter, the god of apogees. The moon then declined towards the Kalends of the following month.

The month thus consisted of two parts of unequal length. Between the Kalends and the Nones there were no festivities. After the Nones, there was a series of festivities, varying in number from month to month, but always falling on odd days. Odd numbers were considered perfect, even ones imperfect, and only things that were perfect could be dedicated to the gods. To give a particular day in the month a numbered date, Romans counted back from the Nones, the Ides or the Kalends immediately following the day in question. This means of dating was used for official deeds, especially by the clerks of law courts and assemblies. It is impossible to provide a precise equivalent to the Roman system of dates, because we cannot tell on which day of our calendar the Kalends, Nones and Ides fell from one month to the next. It was only with Julius Caesar's reform of the calendar in 46 BC that the dates of the Nones and the Ides were fixed for each month. But since the Kalends no longer marked the new moon, the months of the Julian calendar were no more than fictitious lunar months, as indeed are ours. (For the sake of convenience, this book dates events according to the Julian calendar, but it should not be forgotten that these dates are mere approximations.)

When it came to publishing laws, there was another and wholly independent way to measure time, using a solar rather than a lunar unit. Every eight days (nine by Roman inclusive reckoning), starting on the first day of January, a market, known as the *nundinae*, that is the ninth day, was held at Rome. These market-days were used to spread political information. Peasants came to market in throngs to sell and sometimes to buy goods above all to hear about the latest laws. Everyone made this journey, at least one market-day out of every three. Every law or public decision was published on three consecutive *nundinae*, after which ignorance of the new provision was deemed no excuse. The *nundinae* were more than market-days: they were the essential meeting-place at the heart of every citizen's social and political existence. The *nundinae* were accordingly dedicated to Jupiter, the god of urban social life. On the *nundinae*, Jupiter's *flamen* always sacrificed a ram to the god.

THE ELASTIC YEAR

If days were solar and months lunar, one might well wonder which heavenly body controlled the passage of Roman years. The lunar year, consisting of twelve lunar months, could account for only 354 days, eleven and a quarter days short of a solar year, which itself was not a precise number of days: there was that quarter day hanging over.

Until Julius Caesar introduced his reform, the Romans organized their year as follows: the year began neither at an equinox nor at a solstice but in March, to be precise at the Kalends of the third month following the winter solstice. The year then extended over ten months, each consisting of twenty-nine or thirty days alternately. This brought one to December – as its name indicates, the tenth month. The year then took two more months, January and February, to finish and begin again. In a sense, however, the new year began before the old one ended, for January, the month of Janus, the god of passages and openings, preceded February, a month for purifications the purpose of which was to get rid of the old year. As January had thirty days and February only twenty-eight, the Roman year was still distinctly incomplete at 353 days. As a result, once every two years, an intercalary month was added to the end of the year, slipped in between February and March, to make up the difference. Five days were lopped off February and an intercalary month of twenty-seven or sometimes twenty-eight days would begin on the twenty-third day of February.

This system would have worked quite smoothly, had the Romans used these intercalary months according to specifications. The decision on this matter, however, rested with the priests. Since these intercalary months were free of any kind of religious constraint and allowed for uninterrupted political or judicial business, it was tempting to delay or suppress them in order to paralyse an unwelcome political law-suit, prosecuted, say, by one's arch-opponent. By 46 BC, when Caesar decided to grapple with this situation, the

Roman year had fallen so far behind the course of the sun that three intercalary months were needed to ensure that Roman peasants resumed harvesting in the summer and picking grapes in the autumn. Contemporaries noted that people were praying to the gods for a break in the scorching heatwave while their teeth chattered with cold, and offering up sacrifices for rain while the snow piled up outside the door.

The Julian calendar, the principles of which we have inherited, introduced a purely solar year and the rhythm of the passing months lost its religious significance. Now that January ushered in the new year, the festivities at the beginning of March had little meaning.

THE ENIGMATIC CENTURY

At Rome, pinpointing a particular year in the past was a tricky matter. The Romans dated an event by mentioning the names of the two consuls then in office. To locate a particular year within this chronological system, you had to have at your fingertips the complete list of consuls, or *fasti consulares*, stretching back through the years. This was not, however, as simple as it might appear. Pairs of consuls did not always correspond to a full year. To make matters worse, the political year sometimes began in January, sometimes in August and sometimes in neither. In some years, no elections could be held and therefore no consuls were appointed.

Evidently, chronological dating was of no interest to the Romans, nor had they any notion of there being a point at which time began. At Rome the present was always the starting-point. To count the years that separated an event in the past from the moment at which one was speaking, one simply used the consular *fasti* and counted back through the pairs of consuls. Towards the end of the republic, imitating the Greeks, the Romans gave historical time a point of departure: the foundation of Rome itself, which they set at a date which we would identify as 21 April 753 BC. This move, however, failed to fit in with any habit of Roman thought whatsoever, and the old system for identifying dates by counting consuls survived.

The difficulties we encounter in transcribing Roman dates also derive from the fact that the Romans had no chronological conception of the past. Their past was divided into two.

First of all there was the recent past, the family-based past of the *memoria*, going back through six generations of relatives. Of this past there remained direct witnesses, or people who had heard accounts from direct witnesses. The structure of kinship gave time its depth. Beyond this stretched the remote past, without memory or depth, composed of handed-down family anecdotes, the past of the ancestors, the *majores*, lacking any clear chronology (see p. 104). Noble families did of course preserve the memory of ancestors more ancient than the *parentes*: the ancestral masks in the *atrium* cabinets, linking to form family trees, might extend right back to the kings. But these genealogies often skipped a generation or more, since they preserved the memory only of those men who had occupied a superior magistracy. The young men who had died in war did not figure in the record; nor did the political failures, whose sons consequently appeared to be the sons of their grandfathers. Then there were the adopted children who might well be great-nephews, grandsons or cousins and who were thus detached from their own generation. These genealogies manufactured a fictional time, a family immortality that varied from one family to the next but never had anything to do with historical chronology. There was the time of the family and the time of the state, and the two remained distinct.

A longer unit of time, the century, or *saeculum*, did, however, emerge. The Romans celebrated the end of a century with solemn 'secular' games, which recurred at intervals that varied between approximately 100 and 120 years, perhaps modelled on the over-lapping lifespan of six generations of *parentes* and designed to celebrate a renewal of the *memoria*. It may be that no new games were held until the last person who had taken part in the previous ones had passed away. What is known is that secular games were held in 249 BC, that Augustus celebrated them in 17 BC and that they continued to be held under the empire. Varro wrote that in his time, at the end of the first century BC, the eighth *saeculum* was under way. Be that as it may, the Roman 'century' was not a unit of time in a larger system of dates. Its significance was purely religious.

The Roman calendar and festivities

A POLITICAL CALENDAR

At Rome no one could be ignorant of the calendar. It organized citizens' time and actions, indicating the religious and political character of every day that dawned. Calendars were posted on temple walls and loudly proclaimed on the Nones of each month – that is, at the first quarter of the moon.

The annual calendar was above all political and legal: it established when law courts might sit and popular assemblies meet. It also fixed the *nundinae*, the days for the regular markets held every eight days. The calendar was divided into twelve columns, corresponding to the twelve months, and each day was marked with a large capital F, C or N. On days marked F (*fastus*), people could go about their business, with the approval of the gods. Courts would sit, business people would draw up contracts, peasants would embark on new work: ploughing, harvesting or sowing. Of these lucky days, those marked with a C (*comitialis*) were particularly blessed and it was then that popular assemblies would meet. On days marked N (*nefastus*), on the other hand, the gods looked askance at work and exertion. This did not automatically condemn people to inaction. One might, for example, continue with work already started. On such days, however, it was certainly best to avoid planting a tree – it would be sure at some later date to fall on your head.[132]

Certain days were part lucky and part unlucky: 24 March, 24 May and 15 June, the day the house of the Vestals was subjected to thorough cleaning, were *nefasti* in the morning and *fasti* in their middle. Even more complicated, there were eight days that were unlucky in the morning and evening, but lucky in the afternoon. In general, about two-thirds of the days in any year were lucky and one-third unlucky. A republican calendar known as the calendar of Antium, after the place where it was discovered, counts 109 *nefasti* days, 235 *fasti*, 192 *comitiali* and eleven days that were mixed.

Certain days were deemed so unlucky that not only human action but also any form of religious observance was out of the question. These 'black days' included every day immediately after the Kalends, Nones or Ides, every day that saw the return of the dead, and the anniversaries of major national catastrophes – like the Ides of July, which commemorated the defeat the Romans had suffered at the Allia at the hands of the Gauls, after already having marked the death of the 300 men of the Fabian *gens*, an entire family whom the Etruscans had cut to pieces.[133] On such days, life would come to a complete halt. Tragic anniversaries such as these bore witness to an empirical understanding of time: events had demonstrated that that particular day was disastrous, so it was best to watch out.

The Roman calendar was not binding; it simply provided people with an idea of their chances or of the risks they would be running if they took any action on a particular day. Such hints were as valid for private as for public matters. If, when engaging on some public action, a magistrate overlooked the advice of the calendar, the people would notice. If the action then failed, they would indignantly protest and might even take him to court. If, however, his action was crowned with success, his oversight would be forgotten.

This calendar did not establish the political year; it only provided it with a religious framework. The dates of elections, of the inauguration of magistrates and of assembly sessions were extremely variable. The political year could begin in January or in August; elections might be held in March or in November. Furthermore, since assemblies could not meet until the auspices had been consulted, no calendar could ever provide an advance schedule for them.

FEAST DAYS

Against certain days in the Roman calendar, alongside the capital letters, one could read, in smaller capitals, the name of a feast. These were public holidays celebrated by the entire *populus*.

To the distinction between lucky and unlucky days – *dies fastus* and *dies nefastus* – the calendar added a distinction between feast day and working day – *dies festus* and *dies profestus*. A feast day celebrated the cult of a particular god. Prayers and sacrifices were made to entice the god to mingle with the worshippers. Generally, no work was done on feast days, since all feast days were unlucky (*nefasti*), even if not all unlucky days were feast days.

Apart from the public festivities marked on the calendar, the Romans celebrated private family feasts, such as birthdays, and feasts that involved a particular district or profession. These feasts recurred on fixed dates.

But the priests and magistrates who compiled the calendar also announced each month a number of movable feasts, whose dates were often not fixed until the last moment. Many of these were agricultural feasts which thus escaped the haphazard nature of the Roman year. Lastly, there were unforeseen one-off feasts. These were usually ceremonies of expiation, proclaimed by priests in charge of dealing with wonders and prodigies.

The calendar was constantly swelling with new public feast days as new gods and consequently new temples made their appearance. Such feast days were fixed on the anniversary of the relevant temple's consecration and often involved games. Little by little, as foreign conquests piled up, the life of the Roman people became a dizzy round of feast days.

THE CULTURAL CALENDAR

At first glance, the calendar of Roman feasts gives an impression of total randomness. Certain months, for example September and November, were almost completely *fasti*, with very few feast days; whereas two-thirds of February and half of April were *nefasti*.

There was no trace of the solar year in the way that the Roman republican calendar was organized. No public festivity marked the equinoxes or the summer solstice. Only the winter solstice was marked by the festivity of a minor deity, Bruma, which meant 'the shortest'.

Nor was it a farming calendar whose festivities followed the rhythm of work on the land, emphasizing ploughing, sowing and harvesting. Although there were several feast days that had to do with work in the fields, they did not determine the year's structure and do not conform to our image of an agrarian religion. In the autumn we might expect there to be a festivity featuring wine-presses and grape-pickers crowned with vine branches invoking Liber, the god of wine, as they trod the grapes. Instead we find that the feast to celebrate cutting the first grapes is dedicated to Jupiter. In July we might expect to see a blonde Ceres, crowned with ears of corn, venerated by young harvest-girls, their arms bearing the first fruits. At harvest-time, the Romans in fact celebrated Neptune, god of irrigation canals, and a certain Furrina, goddess of wells and water towers.

The Roman calendar of festivities reflected Roman culture in the way it continually led people from place to place: from the fields to war; from war to the city; from the city back to the fields. The feasts did not serve to celebrate nature or natural forces, such as water, sun and sky, but rather human culture in all its forms. It was not water or fire that the Romans worshipped but the gods who kept an eye on irrigation and watched out for scrub fires. Even celebrations of Faunus, the god of the wild, Silvanus, the god of uncultivated fields and forests, and Feronia, the goddess of wild life, always had a strong cultural dimension. Silvanus' woods were pasture for flocks of sheep, and shepherds would sacrifice to him a goat, considered to be the wildest of all domestic beasts. As for Feronia, ever since primitive times, it had been her vocation to integrate and 'cultivate' people of savage origins. This was why, like the Greek goddess Artemis, she was involved in children's education and was also the goddess of enfranchisements. Slaves went to her temple, sat down on a stone seat and when they stood up again, wearing the *pilleus*, a Phrygian hat signifying their emancipation, they were free. Feronia was the goddess of everything that was green and virgin. She also presided over informal human encounters at which political distinctions were forgotten. Her festivals took place on the edges of different territories, in no man's land.

The Roman year was thus divided into holiday cycles, each celebrating one of the essential Roman activities. There were three cycles concerning living people – war, work on the land and politics; a cycle around February concerning the dead; and a cycle concerning women around June.

Some holiday cycles were a succession of feasts, often in three-day bursts. They might also involve an opening ritual, followed by a long interval without any festivities relating to the cycle, and then a closing ritual. Holiday cycles were clearly separated by long empty periods.

MARCH AND OCTOBER: THE CYCLE OF WAR

March, the first month of the year, the month of Mars, was dedicated to war. The military season began in March and ended in October. October, studded with military festivities, brought to a close a sequence that March initiated. Festivities were held on 14, 17, 19 and 23 March. The most striking of the rituals was the dance of the Salii, which was followed by a feast of the cavalry and the purification of trumpets and shields. On the Kalends, the Salii 'dancers', a Roman priesthood, dressed as ancient warriors, fetched the sacred shields from the regia – where the priest known as the *rex sacrorum* lived – and brandished them as they danced through the town. Not until October did they bring the shields back to the regia. The Salii formed two groups, embodying the two aspects of the god: a furious Mars and a tranquil Mars, an attacking and a defending army. The Mars of the Salii dancers was not the god of the offensive or the lancer charge. Indeed, when they danced through the town brandishing the shields, they struck them not with weapons but with simple sticks.

Between March and October the only festivity celebrating war was the parade of young cavalrymen on the Ides of July. This followed a route from the Capena Gate to the forum, where sacrifices were made at the temple of Castor and Pollux. According to the ancients, this was a magnificent spectacle.

When the army returned to Rome in October, a ritual known as the 'sister's beam', held on the Kalends, turned the warriors back into civilians. Then, on 19 October, the soldiers' weapons were ritually purified, as in March. Armed soldiers offered up sacrifices and carried the sacred shields through the town and deposited them at the regia. Together, these two feasts cleansed the soldiers of the taint of the murders committed during the war and of their 'cruelty', their indifference to violence, their taste for bloodshed. But the most extraordinary festivity of the whole war cycle was the 'October horse', which involved two Roman districts.

The 'October horse' took place on 15 October, the Ides of the month, and involved a *biga* (two-horse chariot) race on the field of Mars. In Roman eyes, horses were *the* animals of war. After the race, the right-hand horse of the winning chariot was killed by javelin and sacrificed to Mars. The horse's head and tail were then cut off. A runner would take the tail as fast as he could to the regia, just to the south of the forum, so that the blood would still be dripping from it when he got there. He would then let some drops of the blood fall on the floor so that the regia took part in the sacrifice. Meanwhile, the horse's head was decorated with loaves of bread, and a match began between the inhabitants of two districts of Rome – the Via Sacra area and the Suburra valley, rising from the forum between the hills to the north. The two sides would fight for possession of the head. If the Via Sacra team won, they would fix their trophy on the wall of the regia; if the Suburra side won, they would place it on the Mamilia tower.

The Romans wondered, just as we might, about the meaning of this ritual. We know that Mars protects civilized life and defends Roman stores of grain from pillagers, and both these features are displayed here, but the rest remains obscure. This is typical of Roman rituals, however, which seem better suited to performance than to authoritative interpretation.

A single month might contain several festive cycles. Mars, the opening month of the war-waging season, was also the first month of the year and as such was dedicated to Juno, the goddess of childbirth. The Kalends of March was a feast day for women, the Matronalia, or 'feast of the matrons', and women visited the temple of Juno the Giver of Life on the Esquiline. Husbands stayed at home for the day to pray and gave their wives presents and money.

As far as Jupiter was concerned, though, the year only really began with the Ides of March. The Romans dedicated this day to Anna Perenna, the goddess of the returning year. This feast was extremely popular and was celebrated both publicly and in private. As part of the festivities, Romans crossed the Tiber, thereby going 'abroad' 'into the Etruscan countryside' – that is, to the opposite bank of the river, where they would picnic in huts made of branches or flimsy tents. They drank heavily for it was said that you would live as many years as the number of cups you quaffed. Ovid relates that everyone, both men and women, drank enough to attain the age of Nestor or the Sibyl, miracles of longevity.[134] When they could drink no more, the celebrants staggered back over the bridge, their happiness a delight to behold.

On 15 March, during the ritual purification of weapons, a rather more plebeian festival was celebrated at the sanctuary of Minerva. This was a guild festival, assembling all the trades of Minerva: weavers, fullers, dyers, cobblers, doctors, schoolteachers, sculptors and painters.

THE RUSTIC CYCLE

April ushered in a series of agricultural and pastoral festivities relating to growth, flowers, fruit and reproduction, on the one hand, and to the making of preserves and the laying-in of stores on the other. Other kinds of agricultural work were also celebrated, for example irrigation work and land clearance for cultivation. These feast days peppered the months from April to December, when the food reserves were opened.

On 12 April, the Romans celebrated the feast of Ceres the corn-goddess, though this was a private religious occasion. There followed a spate of public feast days: on 15 April, the Fordicidia, the 'death of the pregnant cow'; on the 19 April, the feasts of Ceres; on 21 April the Parilia, the feasts of Pales, the goddess of herds, held again on 7 July; on 23 April, the festival of wine; on 25 April, the Robigalia, intended to protect the corn from blight; on 29 April, the feast to celebrate the flowering of cereals. These festivities formed ritual sequences, following on from one another after a gap of three days. Thus, the feasts of Ceres, the Robigalia and the flowering of cereals belonged in one cycle; and the Fordicidia and Parilia in another. These last two feasts were linked in the following way.

The Fordicidia provided an opportunity for sacred butchery in thirty different places in Rome, both on the Capitol and in privately owned fields. A pregnant cow was sacrificed to the earth, which was itself pregnant with sown seed. The embryo was torn from the cow's belly and taken to Rome to the Grand Vesta. The priestess then burnt the embryo on Vesta's fire, the fire of the earth, and kept the ashes, which were subsequently used at the Parilia. The ritual performed at the Parilia took place near the sheepfolds or cattle pens: in April the feast was devoted to small livestock, mainly ewes and rams; in July, to larger beasts, especially cows and calves.[135]

The shepherd would sweep out the sheepfolds, and burn sulphur to purify the bleating sheep. Then, at dusk, he would sprinkle water over the animals. Garlands and greenery were hung on the sheepfolds, fires were lit and on them were thrown olives, the ashes of the embryos burnt at the Fordicidia, the blood of horses and beanstalks without their pods. Both men and beasts would then leap three times over these fires. The shepherd would offer non-blood sacrifices consisting of grain and cake millet and warm milk. He would then address a prayer to Pales. Mid-April was the breeding season for sheep as July was for cattle. The Parilia had to do with the renewal of the herd and with the general safety of both animals and shepherds. It protected them against sickness, wolves, desiccated grass and dried-up springs.

There were no agricultural festivals in May, June or the beginning of July. Nothing in the public calendar related to Ceres or harvesting: this was the time for private rituals.[136]

On the other hand, at the end of July and throughout the whole of August, there was a series of feast days that related to the upkeep of the countryside. On 19 and 21 July were held the Lucaria, or feasts of clearings. *Lucus* was the Latin term for a clearing ringed with trees. When land was cleared for farming, not every tree and bush was uprooted; lines of trees were left like hedges surrounding the new fields. Religious respect and ecological concern combined to protect the land and its fauna and helped to ensure the prosperity and beauty of the Italian countryside. These tree-hedges supplied firewood, soaked up surface water, provided cool shade and were home to throngs of birds.

The Romans celebrated two different clearings feasts, since there were two techniques for preparing land for agriculture. Weeds and scrub could simply be cut, burnt and the land ploughed. If, however, the land was wooded, the trees had to be felled and their stumps pulled up.

Hard on the heels of these feasts of the countryside came others relating to water. The feast of Neptune was held on 23 July, two days after the second Lucaria feast, and the Furrinalia, associated with the male god of the source, was celebrated on 25 July. Neptune became god of the sea only at a later stage, after his identification with the Greek Poseidon. For religious purposes, he was quite clearly the god of irrigation. He provided protection against both flooding and drought by encouraging the correct treatment of surface waters, lakes prone to overflowing and unpredictable rivers.

Whereas the feast of Neptune celebrated the building of diversion canals, the feast of the Furrinalia and the source celebrated the work of water-diviners and well-diggers, their search for and harnessing of elusive underground water supplies. With the development of technology, these gods became the protectors of the water towers that supplied the town fountains. These water feasts culminated with the feast of the source on 13 October, a time of year when the springs began to fill and to flow again.

Just as April had protected the flowering corn, the festivals held in August were intended to protect fruit trees and vines from the scorching sun. On 19 August, the feast of the vine addressed a plea to Jupiter, the master of the sky, not to send any storms, hail or heavy rain to ruin the grapes before they could be harvested. The Vulcanalia, festival of Vulcan, the god of fires, was held on 23 August to mark both the devastating and the useful effects of fire. Vulcan threatened full barns at harvest-time but also came in handy for clearing meadows of excess brushwood: the grass would spring up again after the first autumn showers. Three days later, on 27 August, the Volturnia feasts protected ripening grapes and other fruit from the scorching south-east winds that, like a breath of fire, could shrivel them where they hung.

On 11 October, with the armies returning to Rome and the grape harvest in full swing, the feast of the medicaments was held. Addressed to Jupiter, the god of wine, this feast ensured that the delicate process of pressing the grapes to produce the *mustum*, fresh grape juice, went smoothly. The juice generally had to be boiled down to reduce its initial volume by one-quarter or even one-third: left untreated, the *mustum* might ferment and turn sour. If, owing to a lack of sunshine while the grapes were ripening, the juice was too light, good-quality wine from the previous year, boiled down to one-third of its original volume, would be added. This was how new wine was 'cured', with old wine serving as the 'medicament'. Since the entire grape harvest was at stake, exactly the right measurements had to be used and the needs of the *mustum* had to be gauged with precision. This was well worth a feast to Jupiter.

Alternating with these fire festivals, there were two feasts marking the creation of food stores: on 21 August, the feast of Consus, the god of the granary; and on 25 August, the feast of the plentiful stores.

BRIMMING WHEATLOFTS AND THE PLEASURES OF SOCIAL LIFE

September, November and December were set aside for social life, either in its civic aspect, with the feasts of Jupiter Capitolinus, god of sovereignty and of citizens' assembly, or in its domestic aspect, with the Saturnalia. Both these feasts entailed sharing out the pleasures of plenty, the consumption of war plunder and the opening of the wheatlofts.

In September and November, few days were set aside for public feasts: Jupiter had an unchallenged monopoly. The Ides, devoted every month to Jupiter, were celebrated more sumptuously in September and November, when a ritual banquet was given to the god; 13 September was the anniversary of the temple of Jupiter on the

Plate 7   *Roman harvesting machine; the donkey pushes the scoop into the corn*
Reproduced by kind permission of the Ancient Art and Architecture Collection (Ronald Sheridan)

Capitol. But the most important events in these two months were the Roman games starting on 13 September and the plebeian games starting on 13 November. Both games were in honour of Jupiter and from the mid-fourth century onwards, would go on for several days. The games were a high point of the year, when people could assemble in joy and freedom to celebrate the town as a place of peace and pleasure. In September they came from the army camps, in November from the fields; in September they were the soldiers of Mars, in November the peasants of the god Quirinus. But in either case, they flocked to Rome to pay tribute to Jupiter, the god of wine and of cultivated city life.

At this time of year, the best-known – and least-understood – festival was the Saturnalia, held on 17 December. Under the empire, this festival assumed a new importance and lasted a whole week. It became a kind of carnival.

On 15 December, the opening of the granaries was celebrated with a festival to Consus, the god of the granary; on 19 December, the festival of abundance was held: these two feast-days echoed those of 21 and 25 August. Between these two feasts, the festival of Saturn, the good king of the golden age, was celebrated on 19 December with a public sacrifice followed by a meal. On that one day, slaves ate at their masters' table and every household distinction between free men and slaves was suspended: everyone wore the *pilleus*, the cap of the free man, and no one wore the toga. Slaves ordered others to wait upon them and addressed their masters without the usual respect.[137] Cicero, to avoid this ritual, always fled to the countryside for the day. Not that everyone was set free for one day: rather, everyone was enslaved. It was a festival of licence and transgression, not of freedom.

As a festival of shared abundance, the Saturnalia included a *lectisternium* to the gods in the morning. But it was also a festival of chance and the one day in the year when slaves were allowed to gamble with dice. The Saturnalia was also a festival of deceptive appearance: people would give each other worthless gifts, *trompe-l'oeil* sweetmeats made of clay and paste. For one day, nothing was as it seemed: neither the relationships between people nor the presents that changed hands. Order would return on the following day. Anarchy, chance, deceptive appearance: the Saturnalia was the flip-side of the true life of Roman citizens.

The Lupercalia, held in February, had the same purpose as the Saturnalia: the Lupercalia restored civic order at the beginning of each year, just as the Saturnalia did at each year's end. The Luperci

were a college of priests, young men of good family, who, in this
ritual, ran up and down through the city naked but for a goatskin
loincloth, and whose shrine was a grotto on the Palatine, known as
the Lupercal. They embodied wolf-men, companions of the wild god
Faunus, and represented a sort of proto-society held together by
violence, like a wolf pack.[138] This explains why the Luperci were
associated with Mars, the god of the warrior community. The ritual
would begin with a sacrifice of goats and a dog, with whose blood the
officiating priests would then smear the foreheads of two noble
youths. The blood was wiped off with wool dipped in milk, while the
youths laughed. The Luperci would then don the blood-soaked skins
of the sacrificial victims and eat and drink heartily. They would then
run several times around the Palatine hill to purify the Lupercal
grotto, from where the race started. As they ran, they would brandish
long strips of skin cut from the sacrificial goats and lash out at women
who, eager to remedy their barrenness, had placed themselves in their
path.

The significance of this ritual is clear, especially if one bears in
mind the relevant accounts of Romulus and Remus. The twins, sons
of Mars, were presented as the first Luperci. As savages, shepherds
and hunters, ignorant of agriculture and without either house or
children, they were doomed to vanish without trace. To survive,
Romulus and Remus had to abandon the savagery of the shepherds,
found a city and capture women. But if they failed to respect the
distinction between different areas, thereby obstructing the creation
of a city, they would be doomed. And so, because Remus, by jumping
over the beginnings of the future city wall, scorned the sacred furrow
of Jupiter, he had to die. Romulus, after founding his town and
marking out Jupiter's realm, had to make sure that the citizens were
provided with women who could create families and fill their houses
with children. This was why the Romans seized the Sabine women.

Much has been made of the licentiousness that surrounded the
Saturnalia but the Lupercalia also gave free rein to sexual fantasies. In
Roman society, where the main erotic temptation was homosexuality,
beardless youths had to be prohibited from taking part in the
Saturnalia in order to protect their virtue. Although certainly not
ritualistic in nature, Roman homosexuality was a significant form of
deviancy. It represented a society of wolf-men without women.
However, a society that consisted only of the sons of Mars was as
impossible in its way as one that was made up solely of the children of
Saturn. Each year the Saturnalia and Lupercalia reasserted that men
could only be men if they lived in a city, under the political

sovereignty of Jupiter. The children of Saturn were subject to a king, the wolf-men of Mars were ignorant of any constraint: neither group were true men or citizens, neither formed a viable society. The merrymakers at the Saturnalia were a mere façade, and the savages at the Lupercalia were childless. Jupiter alone could give men the political dimension they needed in order to exist and to reproduce themselves.

THE GREAT FESTIVAL OF GAMES

The festival to end all festivals, the social melting-pot – bringing the whole world together in the town – was the games, presided over by Jupiter, the god of civilized community.

Various annual games were instituted during the last three centuries of the republic but the oldest, providing a model for all later games, were the great games or Roman games, held at the end of the summer, during the first fortnight of September.

The Roman games, or *ludi Romani*, were part of that sequence of rituals that brought the military season to a close. Returning from the territories of Mars, the combatant was absorbed back into Jupiter's city of peace; the soldier became a civilian once again and the legionary shook off the bonds of military discipline. The first day of the games was devoted to untying the bond, thanks to Jupiter Capitolinus who for that one day reigned supreme over the city. Jupiter's priest, the *flamen dialis*, could not support any chain in his house, knot in his clothing, ring on his fingers, nor the sight of any form of violence, constraint or death. The games celebrated these values of non-violence, freedom and life in dance, music and theatrical performance. Jupiter, their embodiment, was god of the theatre.

Under the republic, the amount of time devoted to the Roman games steadily increased. By the first century BC, they lasted a fortnight, from 4 to 19 September, with a banquet to Jupiter Capitolinus on the Ides to mark the anniversary of the god's temple. Feasting was suspended for one day only, 14 September, since the day following the Ides was by tradition a 'black day'.

The ritual began early in the morning of the first day with a long procession through the town, from the field of Mars, up to the Capitol, back down to the forum and then across to the Circus Maximus, between the Palatine and the Aventine.[139] Subsequent mornings were given over to shows in the circus and especially to theatre.

It was this procession that established the characteristic 'ludic' atmosphere of the games – a climate of unreality and good humour, where worries were forgotten and a thirst for dance and music took over. On the previous day they had been at war, and in a fortnight's time they would be at work in the fields: now was the time to party.

The procession was led by the magistrate in charge of the festival – a consul, praetor or aedile – wearing the victor's tunic under his own great embroidered cloak of office.[140] (When games were organized privately, the host wore a similar costume.) Behind the magistrate, came a group consisting of the sons – still pre-pubescent but already able to play at soldiers – of all those citizens eligible for military service. Those who, owing to their fathers' ranking, would one day serve in the cavalry, rode past on horseback, the others walked or ran. Together they formed a children's army complete with centuries and cavalry platoons.

Behind the children came the performers in the circus: the charioteers on their chariots, the horsemen on their horses; the boxers and wrestlers ready for action, naked but for their loincloths.

Next came the dancers, known as *ludiones*. Along with the flute-players, these were the most important festival-goers. If any *ludio* or flute-player stopped dancing or playing, the ritual would be halted and everything would have to start again from scratch. The *ludiones* were divided into three groups: men of military age; adolescents; and children. They all wore soldiers' scarlet tunics, with a bronze belt, and wielded a sword and short spear. The men also wore a bronze helmet topped with a feather. Everyone jigged non-stop to music played on flutes and lyres. Each group of *ludiones* was led by a dance-conductor who demonstrated the steps and figures they all had to follow. The dances were warlike and mimed the fighting of the battlefield.

Behind the *ludiones* came bands of clowns, in flowery cloaks with goatskin belts, their hair standing stiffly upright on their heads. They aped the *ludiones* and made everyone shriek with laughter.

Bringing up the rear was a rabble of flute-players, lyre-players and incense-bearers, clouds of smoke rising from their thuribles. Behind them came citizens, bearing statues of the gods.

After the procession but before the circus got under way, a great number of cattle were sacrificed.

The procession provided a playful representation of warfare, while the reality of war was exorcised by mockery. Those not yet old enough for the real thing played at war, with children mimicking their fathers. In Latin, this mixture of apprenticeship and imitation was also called a game, *ludus* (see p. 225). War was a ballet danced by *ludiones*. The horsemen, charioteers, wrestlers and boxers were there to mime the pursuit of the enemy and the hand-to-hand fighting of the battlefield.

One last time before the onset of winter, the violence of war was invoked, only to be expelled from the city – until the following year. Since play and mockery alone could banish war, nothing serious or weighty was allowed to cloud the games. For two weeks all appearances were false, all warriors fake; everything was song and somersaults. Imitation took over, with the *ludiones* mimicking soldiers and the clowns mimicking the *ludiones*. Images were all that mattered and endless ludic laughter rang out: nobody and nothing was as it seemed.

CIRCUS AND THEATRE

After the sacrifice, the audience would flock to see the circus show or – more often – the theatrical entertainment, performed with the same playful scorn for reality that was apparent during the procession. The various performing arts combined to create a festival of sham, non-violence and good clean fun.

The circus shows only lasted one day, usually the final one, but they could draw between 250,000 and 300,000 spectators to the Circus Maximus – men, women and children all jostling together. Slaves, at first barred entrance, were later admitted on condition that they stayed in their allotted place, right at the back.

The Circus Maximus was a hippodrome shaped like an elongated U, with a low wall running down the centre, dividing it into two runs (see figure 7). At both ends of this wall was a stone marker, which the chariot teams had to drive round on each of their fourteen laps (seven in each direction) of the hippodrome. Under the republic, two stables competed in this race, both of which fielded several chariots. The Romans called these stables 'factions'; one used green as its colour and was known as the Greens or the Leeks; the other used blue, and was known as the Blues or the Venetians. The two factions also had different political colours: the Greens stood for the popular party, the Blues for the conservatives. A Roman who bet at these races did so according to his political opinions and not because of any merit that a particular team or charioteer might possess. The two factions laid out vast sums of gold to secure the best teams and the best charioteers. The charioteers, if they came out of the race alive, might end up extremely wealthy – riches compensating somewhat for the lowliness of their social position.

At the races passions ran high. Tens of thousands of spectators held their breath, waiting for the starter's signal. Then, from his platform, the praetor threw down his handkerchief, and they were off, into 'the headlong speed of the chariot race when the chariots hurtle forth from their stalls! . . . the charioteers shake the waving reins wildly over their dashing steeds, bending forward with the lash! Then applause and shouts, and the zealous cries of partisans, fill the air.'[141]

The most thrilling moment was when the chariots circled the markers. The chariots had to run very close to them without actually touching the stones. If they went too fast, their centrifugal force would make them swerve dangerously and they might even tip over. As the winner crossed the finishing line, the crowd would erupt in a great roar, and the whole of Rome would be able to tell whether or not the Greens had carried the day. Then, after a short pause, the next race would begin.

Theatrical performances drew smaller crowds, usually of about 20,000, but were held more frequently. The Romans were keen theatre-goers. Successful actors, like charioteers, became sought-after stars, though their status remained low. Roman theatre was a forum for musicians and actors more than for writers. Often a script would serve as nothing more than a springboard for songs and dances.

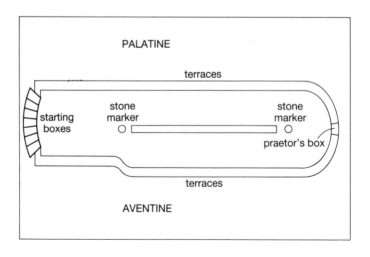

Figure 7   The Circus Maximus

Latin drama was entirely playful, imbued with a sense of unreality. The theatres themselves were makeshift structures: there was no permanent theatre in Rome until 55 BC. Plays were performed in front of an enormous and ornately decorated stage wall, painted in *trompe-l'oeil*, and there were wooden terraces to create the necessary acoustics. From this façade would issue forth a variety of peculiar, frightening or grotesque characters.

In tragic drama, everything was deliciously unreal and fearsome. The Greek mythological heroes, clothed in gold and scarlet, would turn into monsters and commit blood-curdling crimes to an accompaniment of flutes. Thyestes would eat his children for dinner, Medea would kill hers, Oedipus would slay his father and sleep with his mother; and all of them would sing about their pain and fury in resounding emotional arias. The black, white and red make-up, the high wigs and flowing robes, and the coded gestures banished all realism from the performance of actors who, in any case, were interested only in effect. In singing and dancing passages, a single role would be played by two actors at once: one would sing, the other would dance, while the musician, also on the stage, would play flute and foot-drum at the same time. Machinery, trap-doors, imitation thunder: no effort was spared to put on a good show. Gods would flicker across the skies and blood-smeared ghosts, screeching with hatred, would erupt out of Hell. It was all so appalling that the tragedy had at once to be followed by a knock-about farce designed to put everyone back in a good mood. A band of clowns would improvise the comic interlude in front of a half-raised curtain. Each actor would impersonate a stock character, rather as in the Commedia dell'Arte. There was Pappus the ridiculous old dodderer, Maccus the nincompoop, and so on. Leaping around and cracking jokes, the clowns would put on *Maccus the Maiden* or *Pappus Loses the Elections*. Since their only aim was to restore the audience's sense of humour, as soon as the spectators could be seen belly-laughing, the actors would make one last joke and wind up the farce, tripping and waddling from the stage in their huge flat shoes.

Comedy drew on the same aesthetic resources as tragedy – dance, music and unreality – except that instead of mythological crimes, comedies would present Romans with fabulous, fanciful and melodramatic stories staged for their entertainment. Tales were told of newborn babies kidnapped by pirates, maidens abducted by slave-traders or set upon and raped by a stranger one moonless night, or a son lost in a theatre fire. All kinds of happy and unexpected endings could be engineered, concluding with: 'Oh! father of mine!', 'Ah!

sister dearest!', 'I recognize the ring!' or 'Where have those baby clothes come from?' But before the denouement could be arrived at, the stage would witness a procession of all the ridiculous characters that made up comic society: cantankerous old skinflints, whining and penniless young lovers, slaves running themselves ragged to get for their young masters the woman they loved and the money they needed to wine and dine both her and their friends. In the process, the slaves would spin a tissue of lies, assume a gallery of disguises and weave the most tortuous of plots.

Everyone sang and danced according to the demands of their role. The old men would follow sonorous bass parts and a plodding rhythm, while the young would screech and squawk and jack-knife in pain or sorrow. The slaves, thick-calved and red-faced, would improvise, invent, imitate: they were capable of anything. A prostitute might appear, dressed up to the nines, wiggling her behind and throwing glances of passionate promise in the direction of anyone likely to foot the bill. Pimps and bankers, obese and snarling, would be met with the joyful loathing of the audience. A lone, pasty-faced parasite, skinny as a beanpole, ever on the look-out for a banquet to gate-crash, would bay at the moon in shrill falsetto. The audience would shriek with laughter at his woes and questionable appearance.

The show would end with a dancing free-for-all. The young man would get his maid and the money to celebrate with; the pimp would be robbed, thrashed and thrown out on his ear; the father would give in and pay up; the slave would drink his fill; and the parasite would receive an invitation to the young things' junket. The audience would applaud and go off to their own banquets.

THE POLITICAL FUNCTION OF PLAYFULNESS

From the second century onwards, the number of days given over to games increased rapidly. There were annual public games, games dedicated to a god during the course of a war, funeral games: Rome had at least fifty days of games each year. Those who put on games sought to outdo the lavishness and thrills offered at the previous games. The result was spiralling one-upmanship, justified by the loot of conquest.[142]

When the games took place the Romans could enjoy the spectacle of seeing their city transformed into a place of unreality, an ephemeral city of licence, mockery and pleasure, decked out especially for the occasion; a *trompe-l'oeil* city. Once the games were over, everything was torn down – not just theatres but even colonnades and basilicas that had been used as temporary exhibition sites or mass dining-halls for the banquets thrown by generous hosts.[143]

This collective merrymaking strengthened the bonds that linked citizen to citizen as well as those between citizens and the gods, and smoothed over class and political divisions between the popular party and the conservatives. The underlying purpose of games, celebrated by way of atonement during outbreaks of the plague – in other words, when the political body was threatened with disintegration – was to 'maintain the stability of the republic'.[144] The sharing of pleasures during the games had a religious, political and social rationale. The Saturnalia created too broad a society which, since it even included slaves, gave all the members of that society a servile outlook. The Lupercalia, on the other hand, was an example of an excessively narrow society which, since it excluded women, was doomed. The games alone reflected the true nature of the civic community. But a community of playfulness was no more viable than a kingdom of slaves or a pack of wolf-men. It was incapable of taking action; it was not a political people, regimented and marshalled by the census. The Circus Maximus society of play could not be dissociated, however, from the census-registered people of the field of Mars. Yet, once the field of Mars had disappeared along with its census and republican freedoms and permanent theatres had been founded in Rome – all of which happened under the empire – the society of play became a civic society and the *homo civilis* was no longer a *homo spectator*.

But perhaps the games, the Lupercalia and the Saturnalia were also a ritual way of working out abstract categories and principles which, once they had been formulated, could serve as a model of the city.

THE FESTIVAL EXPERIENCE

We can attempt no more than a rough reconstruction of Roman rituals, and look on as mere bystanders as the crowds gather, make sacrifices, drink, dance, shout, laugh, take fright and so on. To know how the Romans actually experienced the religious ceremonies that punctuated their lives is another matter. Luckily, however, there is at least some evidence in Horace's *Odes*. Although he lived a life of leisure, flitting between his place in the country and Rome, and although he was a bachelor and even considered himself something of an Epicurean, Horace took care to celebrate those public and private feasts that directly concerned him. He even compiled his own personal religious calendar. For Horace, a religious feast remained very much a feast. He made no distinction between the joy of feeling himself the recipient of the gods' favour and the sensual pleasures afforded by the celebration of the feast itself.

Horace's *Odes* tell us a great deal about Roman religion, a religion of few words and no theory that lived through its rituals alone. Yet, if these rituals were free of dogma, they were no mere mechanical gestures. From their earliest infancy, religious rituals became second nature to the Romans so that, whether joyous or serious, they became associated with the atmosphere of each day. It was not so much a matter of putting their faith in some form of spirituality but rather having faith in the Roman way of doing things.

For the Kalends of March, the first day of the year and also the festival of matrons, a bachelor like Horace might have to rack his brain to find a dignified and fitting form of celebration. Horace seized on a personal accident – he had almost been knocked out by a tree on his own estate – as a pretext to make it a celebratory day. Each year he set up a portable altar outdoors and offered flowers and incense to the god who, on the Kalends of March in a previous year, had saved him from the tree. He also sacrificed a white male goat and made offerings of some cakes. He then went back indoors, opened an amphora of vintage smoked wine and, with the help of a friend, spent the night gradually draining it.[145]

In April, the month of Venus, on the feast of the Ides, which also happened to be the birthday of his friend Maecenas, Horace threw a banquet to which he always invited a young female friend. Before the banquet, with the help of a team of slave boys and girls from his household, he sacrificed a lamb on an altar decorated with foliage.[146]

For celebrating the feast of Neptune in July, Horace preferred wine to water. He left all cares about matters such as irrigation channels to his farmer, and fetched an ancient amphora from his cellar. He would start to drink its contents at the beginning of the afternoon. With Lyde, he then addressed his songs to Neptune, but once night fell Horace devoted himself exclusively to venerating Venus.[147]

For the feast of the source in October, Horace observed the cult of his own household spring with a sacrifice and a song that made the Bandusia fountain one of the most famous in literature:

O Fount Bandusia, brighter than crystal, worthy of sweet wine and flowers, tomorrow shalt thou be honoured with a firstling of the flock whose brow, with horns just budding, foretokens love and strife. Alas! in vain; for this offspring of the sportive flock shall dye the cool waters with its own red blood. Thee the fierce season of the blazing dog-star cannot touch; to bullocks wearied of the ploughshare and to the roaming flock thou dost offer gracious coolness. Thou too shalt be numbered among the far-famed fountains, through the song I sing of the oak planted o'er the grotto whence thy bubbling waters leap.[148]

Horace did not merely adapt his personal calendar to the annual round of public festivities. Like Cato, he saw to it that the farmer's wife on his estate performed the rites regularly. He reminded her that on the Kalends, at the beginning of each month, she must make a sacrifice to Juno on the altar to the *lares*. Juno would then keep a watchful eye on the birth of all the 'fruits' of the farm: grapes, corn, and the human and animal offspring that the poet tenderly described as 'sweet nurslings', *dulces alumni*. She was enjoined to sacrifice to the god, if at all possible, a sow and incense. Otherwise she should bedeck the altar with myrtle leaves and rosemary and offer the god meal and crackling salt. Horace mentioned that while Phidyle, the farmer's wife, officiated at the altar to the *lares*, the pontiffs in Rome were busy axing and sacrificing much larger victims on the public altars. Religion brought city and countryside closer together through simultaneous household and public worship.[149]

Every December Horace took part in a local cult, a village feast in honour of Faunus that resembled the Lupercalia and Saturnalia. He sacrificed a great deal of produce, especially wine and incense, and a goat kid was slaughtered – it was, after all, the season of plenty. The poet would then go into the uncultivated fields and dance with the working people, surrounded by untethered cattle.[150]

In addition to public festivals and friends' birthdays, Horace was also bound by vows to observe certain annual festivals linking him personally to a particular deity. Wishing to ensure the health of a young pine tree he was planting, Horace made the following vow to Diana: 'O maiden goddess, guardian of hill and grove, thou that, thrice invoked, givest ear to young mothers when in travail and rescuest them from death, goddess of the triple form, thine be the pine that overhangs my dwelling, that gladly through the passing years I may offer to it the blood of a boar practising its first side-long thrusts!'[151] This poem is easier to understand if one recalls that pine trees in Latin are feminine.

For Horace, every happy event was an opportunity for what other religions call thanksgiving. Often the feasts that Horace kept were the result of vows taken at a time of worry or uncertainty. For example, after his old schoolfriend Numida had left to fight in Spain, Horace had made a vow. The two men had taken the *toga virilis* in the same year – a ceremony that created a particularly strong bond. When Numida eventually returned uninjured from the war, his friends gathered to greet him. Lamia, Bassus, Horace and Damalis, an extrovert and passionate young woman, were all there. Horace had promised the gods a calf, incense and a song. So, on the strength of Horace's vow, the friends organized a feast. Wine was brought from the cellar, the guests donned crowns of roses and lilies, and they all danced till they dropped. And that night Damalis granted Numida her favours.[152]

RELIGIOUS LIFE

In Rome religious life, whether public or private, was never a matter of theological dogma or individual spirituality: it was, rather, an integral part of Roman culture. Roman religion was a tissue of daily, monthly and yearly rituals, and it was often hard to distinguish the social ones from the religious. Roman banquets fell into both categories.

Religious experience did, however, exist in its own right, at the moment of sacrifice. In the silence that then reigned, whoever was officiating belonged to a world apart, isolated by the surrounding circle of worshippers. The pungent smell of the sacrificial animals, the shrill piping of the flutes, the ritual objects that were handled, the prayers that were intoned all increased the sense of separation from everyday life. As the incense ascended to the attendant gods, the priest himself would become a god. For a fleeting instant, he would be one of the forces of nature, doing exactly what had been ordained. Strength and assurance would flow through him. He would often have seen others performing the same actions, and would automatically know what to do without thinking about it. The act of sacrifice would come quite naturally. Plunging the knife into the animal's throat, feeling the sticky warm blood gush over his hands, he would feel close to the dying beast: they would perform the act together. He would experience all the drama of the young life that was being sacrificed but see that it was necessary. And then the feast would erupt, death would be drained of its mystery, leaving the pleasures of meat, wine and dance. After all, sacrifices were for mortals too.

Plate 8   Sacrifice, first century AD
Reproduced by kind permission of the Ancient Art and Architecture Collection (Ronald Sheridan)

Only in the observance of such rituals could any sense of religious feeling emerge. It was not that the rituals themselves had no spiritual meaning for the Romans, rather that they knew how to use rituals as a means of expression, without having to provide them with a running theological commentary.

Caesar, who was not much of a theologian, even if he did become first Jupiter's *flamen* and later *pontifex maximus*, was a past master in the art of drawing rhetoric from religion. We have already witnessed his mastery of urban symbols (see pp. 141–2), but he was equally skilled at playing on the ritual of the Lupercalia.[153]

By 44 BC, Caesar had begun to entertain regal ambitions. He was afraid, however, that once crowned he would become the object of the Romans' ancestral hatred of tyranny, which dated back to the fall of the Tarquins. At the Lupercalia in February 44, Caesar tried a little experiment. He attended the celebrations, seated on the rostra and dressed in triumphal clothes. Mark Antony, then a consul, was one of the runners in the sacred race. He ran into the forum, holding in his hands a diadem ringed with a laurel wreath, thus combining the emblem of the Roman *triumphator* with that of Oriental kings. As he held out the diadem to Caesar, faint applause could be heard among the people, where Caesar had placed some of his men. When Caesar rejected the proffered diadem, the entire crowd applauded. Antony repeated his gesture and again muted applause was heard. But when Caesar again pushed the wreath away, the crowd roared out its approval. The test was conclusive. Caesar would be ill-advised to style himself king.

Mark Antony's gesture was made at the moment when Rome was enacting the social spectacle of the Lupercalia and preparing for a new round of political and civic activity. Antony was proposing a transfer of sovereignty from the *comitia centuriata* to Caesar, the king of triumphs. Normally the *comitia centuriata* elected two consuls, who also became victorious generals. Caesar had in effect nominated himself to become the people's sole and lifelong general on the grounds that he was the perpetual conqueror – as the *triumphator*'s garb indicated, the incarnation of Jupiter himself.

Caesar's murderers, by choosing to do the deed on the Ides of March, the first feast of Jupiter in the new year, after the February purifications were all over, displayed a keen sense of humour.

13

The ages of man

CHILDHOOD, ADULTHOOD AND OLD AGE

Children learn, grown-ups act and the elderly pass on what life has taught them. Yet there is nothing natural or inevitable about these three stages. At Rome it was not thought to be nature's job to raise children and turn them into adults. Children, they reasoned, were not born human; they came into the world as unformed and savage creatures, with neither the physical nor the moral attributes of grown men or women. Upbringing alone could turn children into grown-ups, draw them into a culture. Nature's gifts were not enough.

Childhood and old age were each divided into two parts. Before becoming a child and beginning to learn, a baby was an infant (*infans* – 'without speech'), as dumb as the animals, incapable of articulate expression. He would spend the first three years of his life gradually becoming a human being.

Old age too came in two parts. At first the elderly remained in full possession of all their faculties; then, quite suddenly, the body began to fall apart and this disintegration proceeded steadily until death intervened.

Between childhood and old age, there was what Latin speakers referred to as 'youth'. Roman youth comprised all those men in their prime who took part in attacks on the enemies of Rome and of their families.

INFANCY: MOULDING THE BODY

Within moments of coming into the world, a Roman child had to be
chosen to be the child of the family. Merely to be born into a Roman
family was not enough. First, the father of the family had to accept
the baby as a nursling. As soon as the child was born, the midwife
would take the baby and place it on the floor of the house, in front of
the father. If the father decided to keep it, he would, if it were a boy,
lift it into his arms. By so doing, he showed that he recognized the
baby as the offspring of his legitimate wife and undertook to feed it,
while at the same time he established his rights over the child. If, on
the other hand, the baby were a girl, the father would merely give
orders that she be fed. In either case, the mother or the wet-nurse
would then give the son or daughter their first feed.[154]

If the father did not want the child, the baby would be left out on
the street, suffocated or refused food. This would happen if it were
sickly, deformed or seemed in any way retarded. Any physical
malformation was thought to signal an animal nature. A child would
be left to die if it was androgynous or if it had an elephantine head,
since it could never become a person. Such births, moreover, were
interpreted as prodigies requiring expiation. Sometimes, however,
perfectly normal babies were abandoned at birth because their family
was too poor to bring then up or because the father did not want his
already meagre estate to be divided on his death between an even
greater number of sons. Illegitimate children were not automatically
abandoned: they might be brought up by their mother's father, whose
name they would then take, though instead of being called Gaius or
Titus they would be known as Spurius – that is, 'Illegitimate'.

Abandoned babies were generally picked up by slave-traders,
though the original family might claim the child back at a later date.
Melissus, a slave of Maecenas who had been abandoned at Spoleto,
was finally traced by his mother when he was already grown-up and
employed as a librarian. Since working for Maecenas was an enviable
job, Melissus refused to follow his mother into freedom and poverty.
Maecenas later enfranchised Melissus who then became head
librarian of the library in the Portico of Octavia.

At Rome babies were weaned at the age of three. From this
moment on, the baby's natural father would take responsibility for
his upbringing. If, however, the child was an orphan or illegitimate,
the grandfather would step in to play this role. As a rule, the head of

the household would act as foster father to all the slave children born under his roof.

Feeding a baby boy was not enough to turn him into a man, however; babies were not thought to assume a human form naturally as they grew. At their birth, they were soft and formless: they therefore had to be hardened and moulded. For the first few months, they were imprisoned in their cradle, wrapped in swaddling bands tied particularly tight around elbows, wrists, knees, hips and ankles. Their hands were kept open, and splints were used to keep their legs straight. Their arms were strapped straight against their bodies. After two months of this regime, the bands were loosened a little and the right hand was freed to ensure the child grew up right-handed. The baby would be bathed each day in cold water, since warmth was believed to have a softening effect. Bathtime provided a further opportunity for moulding the child's body. The nurse would knead the child's skull in an attempt to make it as round as possible and try to fashion his jaw, nose and buttocks. She would also pull and stretch his foreskin. One obvious result of this was that babies loathed baths.[155]

Nothing was done to make newborn babies' lives easier – quite the reverse. Any demonstration of affection was avoided for fear that the baby might grow attached to it. Rich families would even change the baby's wet-nurse several times prior to weaning. This tough regime was not prompted by any lack of love; parents simply felt that it was essential so as to turn the unformed savage into a human being. Fathers were as involved as mothers in such babycare: 'After the birth of his son, no business could be so urgent, unless it had a public character, as to prevent [Cato] from being present when his wife bathed and swaddled the babe. For the mother nursed it herself, and often gave suck also to the infants of her slaves, so that they might come to cherish a brotherly affection for her son.'[156]

Cato's preoccupation with the day-to-day care of his son, his baths and his swaddling, reveal the importance that was attached to the way the baby's body was handled during the first few months. By ordering his wife to breast-feed not only their own son but also the slave babies born in his household, Cato sought to ensure the loyalty of his son's future slaves and freedmen.

This harsh treatment meant that Roman babies, after undergoing an initial process of selection at birth, were immediately subjected to a second weeding-out. Shackled and fettered, pummelled and kneaded, abandoned to their cradles, plunged into cold water and handled with systematic harshness, only two out of every three babies survived their first year. Then, once weaned, they had the hurdle of infant disease to overcome. Less than fifty per cent of children reached the age of puberty. One is reminded of Cornelia, the mother of the Gracchi: only three of the twelve children she brought into the world arrived at adulthood.

But to a Roman the important thing was not simply that his children should survive – even if he might grieve terribly over their deaths – but that they should begin to take on the shape of civilized beings, eating, walking and speaking like grown-ups. To help the Roman baby turn from crawling and wailing worm into bread-eating and Latin-speaking biped, a whole host of deities were called upon to intervene, from the moment his father raised him from the ground to the day he took his first step. Vitumnus gave him the breath of life, Sentinus his senses; Opis welcomed him on the ground; Vaticanus opened his mouth for his first scream; Levana lifted him from the ground; Cunina watched over his cradle and Ruminus over his breast-feeding; Paventia allayed his fears; Potina and Educa taught him how to drink and eat; Stativus showed him how to stand upright; and Adeona and Abeona helped him to walk to and fro.

Infants lived under constant threat from all kinds of afflictions. The main terror of nurses was an illness that would 'empty the child's flesh' (infantile dysentery?), believed to be the work of evil Harpies known as Strigae, who came in through the bedroom window: 'They sucked his infant breast with greedy tongues, and the poor child squalled and craved help. Alarmed by the cry of her fosterling, the nurse ran to him and found his cheeks scored by their rigid claws. What was she to do? The colour of the child's face was like that of late leaves nipped by an early frost.'[157]

To keep such evil at bay it was thought wise to place a sprig of hawthorn close to all bedroom windows, which needed to be as narrow as possible. And each June sacrifices were to be made to the goddess Carna who afforded protection against all illnesses affecting the belly.

CHILDHOOD: THE YEARS OF APPRENTICESHIP

By the time a baby boy learnt how to speak, eat and walk, he had survived his infancy and become a child, a *puer*. He was not yet a free man but like a slave child he was already a human being. The lengthy apprenticeship that would lead to moral freedom had begun.

He would, of course, have to face the dangers of the outside world. His parents would worry constantly about how to protect him from the corruption of the adult world. To elude evil spells, he would wear around his neck an amulet, or *bulla*, of either leather or gold, depending on the wealth of his family. This was a round capsule that contained charms. The Roman boy donned the *toga praetexta*, a light-coloured toga decorated with a purple border that signalled that he was free-born and therefore untouchable. Corruption might take one of two forms: seduction, which threatened both boys and girls from infancy onwards, and the habit of pleasure. Children were thought to be like modelling clay – still soft and liable to lose their shape if allowed to sag. This was why children were forbidden to take warm baths or to eat lying down. According to Varro, children should sleep and eat little for otherwise they might become stupid and sloppy and never grow up: their growth would also be stunted.[158]

The first thing that every Roman child had to learn, whether boy or girl, was how to read and write. For the Romans grew up in a civilization based on the book and the register, and no one, either free man or slave, could afford to be illiterate – unless they were mere tenders of herds in some far-flung corner of Apulia. The written word was all around them, in both public and private life: laws, calendars, regulations at shrines and funeral epitaphs were engraved in stone or bronze. The republic amassed huge archives of reports on every aspect of public life. Praetors and magistrates kept records of every judgement that was handed down, and this mountain of material formed the cornerstone of Roman jurisprudence. The very nature of Roman memory, dwelling as it did on accidental occurrences, on the one-off, the freakish, relied on written records. At home too, writing was important. Families, noble families at least, had their own archives, including in particular the funeral orations delivered at the burials of those ancestors who, after their deaths, were entitled to have a funeral mask, an *imago*, in the *atrium* of the family home. But whether or not they had distinguished ancestors, all families, noble or humble, kept books of farming tips, prayers and remedies. Writing played a vital role in business too: contracts of sale, hire, association and estate management were all recorded on tablets and registers. Then there were the innumerable letters that Romans travelling far from home sent back to their friends in the city. Whenever a Roman politician was unable to be at the forum, he would wait nervously for news about events at the centre of the world. Rich families kept teams of slaves whose only function was to rush on foot or on horseback across Italy carrying their master's correspondence and bringing back the replies. The state had its own postal system for corresponding with provincial governors and generals. Writing was also a leisure activity: the nobility amused itself by composing verses, encyclopaedias or philosophical essays. Romans who 'wrote' made many rough copies and revisions: writing was not merely a means of giving a fixity to something that had already been composed orally, but involved the handling of tablets and engraving tools.

The Romans did not read in the same way that we do. Words in Roman texts were not usually separated, and there was no punctuation to guide the reader or show where a sentence might end. The text was not divided into paragraphs or sections. It was impossible to skip or skim-read a passage: it would have to be read aloud, or at least muttered under the breath, to make it intelligible. Reading meant decipherment. So when a Roman wanted to read for pleasure, he would use the services of a slave reader.

Unlike either the Greeks or numerous other Italian peoples, the Romans did not pool the education of their children.[159] Whereas the Greeks wanted their children to feel that they belonged to a particular city as soon as possible, the Romans raised their children within the family, keen to instil family values before anything else. While these values were, of course, those of the city, each family placed a paramount stress on one particular set of virtues rather than another: each family therefore presented a slightly different civic profile. Since Rome cultivated diversity, children's education was left entirely up to their father, who was considered to be the natural teacher of his offspring. The father would decide whether to teach his children himself, to purchase a slave teacher or to send them away to school. Even if he chose the third course, he would still keep a very careful watch over his child's education. Since children had to learn Greek as well as Latin, Greek being the *lingua franca* of the whole Eastern Mediterranean, southern Italy as well as that of many cities in Gaul, these slave teachers were often of Greek origin. Livius Salinator had Andronicus, a young captive from Tarentum, specially trained so that he could later act as his son's teacher.

Cato the Elder, on the other hand, preferred to take personal charge of teaching his son everything he needed to know.

> As soon as the boy showed signs of understanding, his father took him under his own charge and taught him to read, although he had an accomplished slave, Chilo by name, who was a schoolteacher, and taught many boys. Still, Cato thought it not right, as he tells us himself, that his son should be scolded by a slave, or have his ears tweaked

when he was slow to learn, still less that he should be indebted to his slave for such a priceless thing as education. Cato himself was therefore not only the boy's reading-teacher, but also his tutor in law and his athletic coach, and he taught his son not merely how to hurl the javelin, fight in armour and ride a horse, but also how to box, to endure heat and cold and to swim lustily through the eddies and billows of the Tiber. Cato tells us that he wrote out his *History of Rome* with his own hand in large characters so that his son might have in his own home an aid to acquaintance with his country's ancient traditions.[160]

This extract gives us a good idea of the Roman boy's course of study: reading and writing; law; morality; and physical training to prepare him for his later role as a soldier. All other subjects, viewed as merely technical, were set aside for slaves. If the free Roman were taught basic arithmetic, it rarely went beyond addition and subtraction. It has to be said that the Roman counting system, which did not use zeros, made doing sums a very complicated business: an abacus had to be used. Arithmetic was therefore only taught to slaves marked out as future stewards, accountants or cashiers. Top families, however, under the influence of the Greeks, trained their children in the fine arts, as if they were nobles of the Hellenic world. This is the course that Aemilius Paullus followed with his sons, while remaining a model Roman father. He trained them

> not only in the native and ancestral discipline in which he himself had been trained, but also, and with greater ardour, in that of the Greeks. The Greeks were not just teachers of grammar, philosophy and rhetoric; the sculptors and painters, overseers of horses and dogs and teachers of the art of hunting, by whom the young men were surrounded, were also Greek. And the boys' father, unless some public business prevented him, would always be present at their studies and exercises, for he had now become the fondest parent in Rome.[161]

Roman children were taught how to imitate their masters. The word *ludus*, which meant 'game', denoted this kind of apprenticeship and also meant 'school'. Learning was a matter of imitation and repetition. The Roman child, once he could recognize the letters of the alphabet, would learn to read by repeating aloud and tracing against his text what the master was reading. To learn how to write, the schoolboy would copy out either the Twelve Tables, the Romans' most ancient code of justice, or one of the imitation-Greek epics written in Latin by Livius Andronicus or Ennius. Every time he made a mistake, the teacher would beat him with a cane. Eventually, by dint of imitation and beatings, the child would learn to read and write as well as his master. The young Roman learnt how to fence in the same way, by aping every movement the fencer made, while wielding a wooden sabre. This was how he would interiorize the choreography of fencing. Gladiator training schools, also called *ludi*, proceeded in the same way. Roman teaching methods had no use for empirical learning, for trial and error or step-by-step improvement. A child could achieve nothing until he had totally assimilated the right set of gestures and the proper behaviour. As soon as his education was complete and childhood was behind him, the Roman's first public performance had to display complete mastery of the skills he had learnt. He had entered upon the serious business of life; playtime was over. Learning was a game, *ludus*, because children merely went through the motions: they only imitated action.

If a Roman father had no teacher at home and was unwilling or unable personally to oversee his child's education, he would send his son or daughter to one of the schools near the forum. The journeys to and from school were dangerous, however, since the child might have unsavoury encounters. A son would therefore be accompanied by his teacher and a daughter by her nurse, and sometimes by other slaves too. But even teachers were not entirely beyond suspicion, and slaves might easily be bribed to act as someone's go-between. Horace's father was so wary that he preferred to take his son to school himself: 'He himself, a guardian true and tried, went with me among all my teachers. Need I say more? He kept me chaste – and that is virtue's first grace – free not only from every deed of shame, but from all scandal.'[162]

Horace was virtually alone in this. As long as they were still beardless, Roman boys were pursued relentlessly by adult men. Girls too were much sought after, but since they went out less and tended to be surrounded by women, there was less risk of them being seduced. Few Roman boys escaped unscathed – by rumour at any rate. They seemed easy prey; it would only take a gift or two to seduce them. The act itself was considered less serious than what it revealed about the boys who were seduced: they were seen as inclined to softness and submissiveness. What was normal for a slave was a source of corruption for a free-born child. Even if his body had grown straight and firm, a child's soul might still be soft. He was not yet a free man and if his soul received bad impressions, and assumed a bad shape, he might never attain that moral freedom that was the very essence of citizenship.

If children were constantly molested, it was because Roman adults

Plate 9 *Teacher with pupils, Romano-German period*
Reproduced by kind permission of the Ancient Art and Architecture Collection
(Ronald Sheridan)

found that the deepest-rooted passion and the one that was hardest to overcome was sexual desire for very young boys and girls. Luckily, there were slaves and child prostitutes in the Suburra district to placate the most pressing of urges. There were also the young children of the poorer class of enfranchised Romans, people who were free but without honour and who were easily conscripted into low-life vice. Since these little boys and girls engaged in prostitution quite openly, their clients could not be charged with rape, *stuprum*, which was defined as 'sexual practices with a free male or female partner, outside marriage'.

It was therefore easy for young freedmen with appealing figures and dainty dancers' bodies, like Roscius the comedian, to enjoy a glittering career among city nobles. Their protectors would give them a literary and artistic education and make sure they learnt Greek, poetry, music and dance. When puberty caught up with them, they would become actors, singers or dramatic poets. Many of the heroes of Latin republican literature were former gigolos who had made good: Livius Andronicus, the founder of Latin theatre; Terence, the comic poet; Publilius Syrus, the most illustrious of all mime-writers.

Consequently Roman fathers were tempted to pack their children off to the countryside, away from the moral turpitude of the towns. Yet it was vital that a son lived close to his father and did not spend his time in the company of slaves and peasants, because it was through contact with his father that he would be initiated into city life. The Roman child, in his *toga praetexta*, trotted along behind his father, following him everywhere, to the forum, to the sacrifices, perhaps even to the senate. By carefully observing his father there was much that he could learn: how to behave in society; how to speak; how to offer up sacrifices.[163] For a long time this was how young Romans developed eloquence. It was not until the second century BC that Roman children were sent to rhetoric teachers as soon as they could read and write. So as the Roman boy grew up, his father would summon him back to town with increasing frequency, though he would also make sure that the boy's time in the countryside was usefully spent in hard work on the land to make him physically tough. Fathers would survey their sons with care, considering their various aptitudes and worrying about whether they would make fit successors. There was still time for one last selection procedure. Any son who proved mentally dull or physically frail, who had a speech impediment or was lazy, would be left in the country. If none of his sons struck a father as capable of pursuing an honourable political career, the father would look out for a gifted son-in-law or would adopt a brilliant boy from a respectable family.

ADOLESCENCE AND THE TOGA OF MANHOOD

The end of childhood was marked by a ceremony that, whether held in public or in private, was of great importance: the assumption of the *toga virilis*, the toga of manhood. The young Roman thus entered adulthood by a kind of social decree at the age of sixteen or seventeen, though he might be married legally at fourteen. The change in dress was of symbolic importance: he no longer required the special protection signalled by the toga's purple border: he was now old enough to protect himself against the evil eye or seduction. He had become a fully fledged citizen, though he remained subject to his father's authority.

The ceremony took place at the festival of Liber, on 17 March. First of all, before leaving the house and in the presence of his father, the boy would dedicate to the *lares* the outward trappings of his childhood: the *bulla* he had worn round his neck and his *toga praetexta*. He would then offer a sacrifice to the household gods. Then the youth, his father, his entire family, and friends and clients of his father would all proceed to the Capitol. The choice of place was significant: Jupiter, the god of the civic community, was about to receive the young man. On that day the whole city would be busy celebrating, family processions would criss-cross Rome, escorting the young men whose big day had come. In the streets, old women sold special cakes made with honey. A fragment of each cake that was sold was offered up to Liber on a small portable fireplace installed especially for that purpose.

School-time was at an end, the Roman boy was now a young man, a *juvenis*, and could become soldier, orator, lover, even priest. Caesar was only sixteen when he became a *flamen* of Jupiter. The time for imitation was past; the young men were ready for serious action and their first feat was eagerly awaited, as it would provide a foretaste of their future career. The first exploit of a young nobleman was often an attempt to avenge his father by dragging one of his enemies through the courts. The more distinguished and formidable the adversary, the more dazzling was the effect. Marcus Cotta, on the same day he assumed the *toga virilis*, instituted proceedings against Gnaeus Carbo, who had had Marcus' father convicted. Marcus won the case and saw Carbo convicted, and this triumph augured well for his character and future career.[164]

Early adulthood, or *adulescentia*, was a dangerous stage in any youth's development. It lasted until about the age of thirty, the age when men took on their first magisterial responsibilities, and it was during this time that they would discover the pleasures of banquets, female company and nocturnal forays with their companions into the night-clubs of Suburra. They were vulnerable to pleasure and to the 'pleasure nerve' – money. The more ambitious among them would enlist in the army to make a start on the ten campaigns that had to be chalked up before a political career could be launched. If they decided to stay in Rome and their fathers proved unforthcoming, they could soon find other men willing to provide them with the means to live in proper Roman luxury.

Cicero gave the following account of Mark Antony's adolescence:

> You assumed a man's gown and at once turned it into a harlot's. At first you were a common prostitute; the fee – by no means a small one – for your infamies was fixed. Curio quickly turned up, however, and took you away from your meretricious traffic. You were as firmly wedded to Curio as if he had given you a matron's robe. No boy ever bought for libidinous purposes was ever so much in the power of his master as you were in Curio's. How many times did his father throw you out of his house? How many times did he set watchmen to make sure that you did not cross his threshold? And yet, under cover of night, at the bidding of lust and the prompting of the money you received, you were let in through the roof tiles. The house could no longer bear such infamies. I know what I am talking about. Do you remember that time when Curio's father, sick at heart, was lying on his bed. His son, throwing himself at my feet, with tears commended you to me. He implored me to defend you against his own father for fear that he should sue you for six million; for this, he said, was the amount for which he had become your surety. In the ardour of his passion he assured me that he was willing to go into exile rather than endure the sorrow of being parted from you.[165]

In the end Cicero persuaded Curio's father to pay off his son's debts. In return, he ordered his son to break off all relations with Mark Antony.

To prevent this kind of depravity, some fathers kept their sons in the countryside long after they had assumed the *toga virilis*. This, however, prevented the youths from pursuing their careers as citizens. Indeed, this shackling of a son was just the kind of misdeed with which a man on trial might be reproached. In 462 BC a tribune publicly accused Lucius Manlius Torquatus of imprisoning his grown-up son on a farm and of befuddling him with mindless drudgery, thereby depriving the state of the services of a talented young man.

The story had a stormy ending, for when Manlius' son heard of the accusation against his father he went straight to Rome and gained access to the tribune's home just as day was breaking. Convinced that his visitor had come to bear witness against the father who held him captive in the countryside, the tribune led the young man into a separate room. Manlius' son then produced a dagger and threatened to slit the tribune's throat unless he swore to withdraw the allegation. The tribune wisely complied.[166]

Some fathers had the good fortune to see their sons overcome every obstacle and pitfall that childhood and adolescence could place in their way. They eluded death and seduction, grew into neither halfwits nor weaklings, took refuge in neither madness nor hysteria. They did not go lame or boss-eyed, did not mistake themselves for good king Saturn, avoided sinking into Epicureanism or developing too great a passion for Greek vases or intoxicating liquor. So far so good. Yet they would not necessarily bring honour to the family. To become an eminent citizen was, after all, no mean achievement.

So Cato worked at the task of moulding and fashioning his son to virtue, finding his zeal blameless and his spirit answering to his good natural parts. But because his body was rather too delicate to endure much hardship, he relaxed somewhat in his favour the excessive rigidity and austerity of his own mode of life. His son, although delicate, made a sturdy soldier, however, and fought brilliantly under Aemilius Paullus in the battle against Perseus. On that occasion his sword either was smitten from his hand or slipped from his moist grasp. Distressed at this mishap, he turned to some of his companions for aid and, supported by them, rushed again into the ranks of the enemy. After a long and furious struggle, he succeeded in clearing the place, and found the sword at last among the many heaps of arms and dead bodies where friend and foe alike lay piled upon one another.[167]

This anecdote reveals the pitiful lengths to which these young men would go to avoid being shown up in situations that were really beyond them. Mediocre offspring of exceptional fathers, the strict education they had received could never make them equal to the challenge they faced. Whatever they did, they could never measure up to their fathers. How could anyone be the son of Scipio Africanus? Glory often skipped a generation, returning to adorn a great man's grandson. Scipio Aemilianus, the grandson of Africanus Major, razed Carthage to the ground and thereby in his turn earnt the title Africanus. This perhaps also explains why those who had been left fatherless tended to enjoy more successful careers.

VENERABLE OLD AGE

Whereas there was a sharp break between childhood and adulthood, marked by the ritual assumption of the *toga virilis*, the passage from adulthood to old age was gradual and blurred. It is hard to say quite when Roman old age began. The army distinguished between younger men, *juniores*, from seventeen to forty-six, who could be called up, and older men, *seniores*, who could only be called up in extreme cases.[168] But just because the republic no longer mobilized a man did not mean that it had no further use for him. There was no upper age limit for magistrates: indeed, consuls had to be forty or over. Senators too, in earlier times, had to be at least forty, though in the last century of the republic they might be as young as thirty.

Old age, far from debarring a man from public office, was a necessary qualification for appointment to the highest magistracies. The Romans did not consider old age a handicap. Older people had a vital role to play: without them there could be no city.[169] Old men – that is, men over forty-six – possessed a wisdom born of experience: they understood tradition and had lost that feverish ambition that made younger men so dangerous. This gave them a special prestige and lent their views an authority that Romans called *gravitas*. Romans treated their elderly with respect: they made way for them in public; stood up in their presence; provided them with an escort; accompanied them back to their homes; and turned to them for advice. It was this prestige that gave the senate its power, for the very word 'senator' derived from *senex*, the Latin word for 'old man'. The elderly magistrates who formed the senate kept watch over the city and exercised a dual function: as mediators and as repositories of tradition.

At Rome young and old worked well together, combining their complementary qualities: the elderly contributed wisdom and reflection, the young daring and action – though this is not to say that the elderly were barred in any way from an active life. The only brake on a man's public activity was his own declining strength and the increasing weariness with political life that ageing men often register. Many used physical old age as an alibi when they just wanted peace and quiet. But the best remained active as long as there was breath within them.

Camillus was one such indefatigable old man. He became dictator for the fifth time at the age of eighty, albeit somewhat reluctantly. The Gauls were once again threatening Rome, thirteen years after he had rid the city of them. He agreed to go to war again and resolved to draw on his past experience. He was familiar with the Gauls' weaponry and knew that what made them dangerous was their massive heavy swords which, owing to their build and stature, they were able to bring crashing down on their enemy from a considerable height. Camillus decided therefore to re-equip his Roman soldiers. He gave orders that they be supplied with solid iron helmets, well polished so that the Gauls' swords would simply skid off them. He also had the legionaries' wooden shields edged with bronze. Lastly, Camillus trained the Romans in the use of wooden javelins to parry sword thrusts. Thus equipped, he led them into battle. The soldiers, brought up on tales of Camillus' great victories, trusted their old general, and crushed the Gauls at the river Anio. Camillus, at eighty, had conducted the military operations in person.

The old dictator returned to Rome eager to bring an end to dictatorship. The senate, however, in conflict with the *plebs* and fearful of elections, opposed any such move. Thanks to his venerable age, Camillus managed to reconcile the parties, after vowing on behalf of the state to raise a temple to Concord. Camillus then returned home, though he died the following year of the pestilence.[170]

The Romans had great admiration for men whom old age did not wither and who were convinced that they owed their prolonged vigour to a life of self-control and regular exercise.[171] Longevity was a sign of morality. Romans who lived to a ripe old age tended to be skinny: a flabby or puffy appearance was considered a sign of ill health and the outcome of a soft and lazy life. The obese died young and discredited.

It has been calculated that thirty per cent of Roman men and women reached the age of forty and thirteen per cent reached sixty. Bearing in mind that barely fifty per cent of children reached adulthood, the proportion that enjoyed old age appears quite high. Once they had survived the two main scourges of adulthood, war and childbearing, Romans tended to enjoy remarkable longevity. Each new census recorded a solid crop of centenarians and there were cases of individuals living to be 150 years old. Leaving to one side such prodigies of longevity, there were some famous 100-year-olds: Valerius Corvinus, born in 371 BC, who farmed his land until the very last; blind Appius Claudius Caecus who, when he had grown too weak to walk, gave orders that he be borne on a litter to the senate whenever he wanted to speak out against what he judged to be a bad policy. Cato the Elder, at eighty-six, instituted proceedings against Galba.[172] Women also sometimes lived until they were over 100. Clodia, wife of Ofilius and contemporary of Caesar, who had given birth to fifteen children, was 103 when she died. Terentia, Cicero's first wife, also lived to be 103. The actress Lucceia delivered a stage recitation at the age of 100.[173]

RETIREMENT

Although from time to time an aged nobleman might make a surprise appearance on the political stage, elderly citizens generally preferred to withdraw into private life and take it easy after many years of stress and hard work. Their sons would carry on their work, freeing them to enjoy their farm at their leisure. The time had come to take pleasure in life, just like the women and children whose relative physical weakness they now shared. After a life of austere discipline, an old Roman wished for nothing more than to contemplate his native countryside.[174] He could watch his vine put out shoots and grow, its tendrils winding themselves round the poplars. Delicately he would prune them to stop them producing luxuriant foliage at the expense of fruit. Basking in the spring sunshine, he would observe the little buttons that would soon swell to become clusters of grapes. Resting in the shade, by a cool spring, he would watch the fruit of his vine darkening each day in the August heat, protected by its leaves from the scorching rays.

Had the elderly Roman not lived such a long time in the city or in a distant province, he might not have had such a great appreciation of the beauty of the Roman countryside. In retirement, he was content to admire the sight of gardens and orchards, the animals grazing in the meadows, the bees and the flowers. Looking up, he could survey the patchwork of cultivated fields and woods, with the hills in the distance. He could work at his own pace, seeking the shade when the sun grew too fierce and warming himself in it on cooler days. He stopped driving himself too hard and punishing his body. He put away his toga and donned broad tunics, comfortable cloaks and hats to ward off sun and rain.

Like a child, he ate just enough to restore his strength, but not so much that he felt weighed down.[175] He would be served food that was easy to digest: vegetebles, barley porridge, dried fruit, cakes made with cheese and honey. Old men enjoyed banquets but not because of the food and drink on offer: 'Old age lacks the heavy banquet, the laden table and the oft-filled cup; therefore it also lacks drunkenness, indigestion and loss of sleep.'[176] What they liked was the chance to engage in open-ended conversation with other men of their generation. They would meet, contemporaries and neighbours, and chat half the night away. In the summer they would drink in the cool night air, and in the winter they would relax in the warm glow of the fire.

Old men were allowed to take only the gentlest of physical exercise, a little gardening or catch-ball. Intellectual exercise, on the other hand, was strongly recommended. The elderly formed the city's natural memory bank and were fond of erudition. Some became experts in private or pontifical law, others in Greek literature or the Etruscan language. They compiled huge scholarly tomes and wrote technical treatises for the instruction of their children and grand-children. They translated and adapted manuals on agronomy and philosophical dialogues from the Greek or Punic languages, wrote all kinds of encyclopaedias, anthologies of proverbial sayings, cookery recipes, political essays or astronomy books. Gaius Gallus, a friend of Aemilius Paullus, was one such serious-minded old man. He had been consul in 166 BC, but in his declining years his favourite pastime was to study the sun and moon. He learnt how to predict eclipses of either with startling precision.

Then, too old and tired for anything more strenuous, Romans would play knucklebones with their grandchildren.

Part IV

The Roman Body

14

The body: moral and physical aspects

THE BODY IS THE MAN

The Roman citizen consisted of a name and a body. When Cato got up to speak to the senate, in his close-fitting toga, his beard unshaven, his gestures sober, his physical appearance would make those present anticipate the gravity of his words even before he opened his mouth. As far as the Romans were concerned, bodies could not lie or dissemble: they were not, as certain Greek philosophers might argue, the tombs of the soul. The truth about a man was engraved in his body for all to read.

This was why nothing and nobody could replace the physical presence of a citizen. To take an action, a citizen must be present in person. The general had to be at the head of his troops, the governor tour his province, the trader go to sea with his goods, the land-owner pay regular visits to all his estates. So the more important a Roman citizen became, the more he would have to rush hither and thither, travelling across the empire, trapesing round town, proceeded and protected, if he was a politician, by his lictors. To be rushed off one's feet was evidence of political or financial activity.

When he took on a case, a lawyer did not act merely in his client's name and on his behalf; he threw his entire personal authority into the balance. A magistrate did not just 'represent', or stand in for, his electors or the Roman republic; he gave himself to them body and soul. At Rome representation was unknown in either justice or politics.

No citizen could represent another because the Romans made no distinction between an action, be it the delivery of a speech or the casting of a vote, and the person who took that action. It was inconceivable that the practice, common in Greece, whereby an accused man would read out in court a defence speech written by someone else, could ever take hold in Rome. It would be guaranteed to fail. The defendant would be nothing but an actor reeling off someone else's lines, and the audience would instinctively sense the fraud and dismiss the defence plea out of hand. A speaker might dramatize and amplify his own feelings, but he would never get away with turning them into a performance.

One's body could not lie: the image communicated to others was an expression of one's character. Roman culture was without inwardness: a Roman's awareness of himself came from the way that others looked at him. His virtues and vices were an open book: they were printed in his movements, style of dress, voice. The Romans were forever on stage but they played themselves. They used their hands, face and gestures as well as words to express themselves. Everything was loudly expressive: even sobriety could be outspoken and flashy. *Gravitas*, the senatorial virtue *par excellence*, meant a careful step, a close-fitting toga, a ponderous delivery, few gestures. Cato's physical appearance was the outward sign of his convictions, and seemed to advertise his political programme: austerity and 'puritanism'.

CIVILIZING THE BODY

The body of a citizen was the man himself, the 'embodiment' of the truth about him, but only as long as there was nothing animal-like about his body. The body that the citizen put on display should be clothed, scrubbed and under control. Nature – that is, anything to do with procreation or defecation – had to be concealed. Both processes had to take place in secret, in special hidden places, and neither were considered fit matter for conversation. It was not in itself shameful to perform such functions, but to speak of them or to do them in front of others would be disgraceful. This sense of shame was assumed to be part and parcel of human nature.[177]

This was why Roman citizens always kept their genitals covered, even when otherwise naked. It was also why citizens had to take care of their bodies. This care, referred to as *cultus*, involved washing, keeping hair and beard properly trimmed, and eating adequately. If a man let himself go, abandoning this minimum of *cultus*, he became repugnant, despicable, sordid, bestial and savage. He became a stinking tramp and could no longer regard himself as a citizen or a man. In Roman eyes, there was no such thing as a 'natural man'. To repeat the old adage: it was natural for a man to be part of a culture; if he rejected that culture he was no longer himself.

Lastly, the body had to be kept under control and made to respond appropriately to the demands of each new set of events. This control of the body involved mastering a particular body language. There was a range of emotional and moral behaviours corresponding to any given circumstance. The selected behaviour was codified and might take the form of a ritual. Misfortune could be expressed, with no fear of scandal or indecency, by weeping, wailing, whining and screwing up one's face in pain. Misfortune might even take the ritualized form of mourning, with clothes torn to ribbons and hair dishevelled. The most extreme reaction was to suspend one's body *cultus* and to sink into physical squalor: this demonstrated a refusal to live.

PASSION, EMOTION AND FEELING

Reading Latin texts often gives us the impression that the Romans went through life as cool and collected as statues; after all, they were forever condemning passion. But passion should not be confused with feeling. Feelings were deemed legitimate. Romans were roused to action by violent feelings of indignation, love, pity, sorrow, thirst for vengeance and ambition. Far from being coldly calculating, the Romans could in fact be very sentimental. Passion, however, was another matter: a force beyond men's control liable to enslave them; an animal hunger that could eat a man's heart out and draw him to his death. Passion was an emotion or, as the Latin term exactly defines it, 'a movement of the soul', a reaction to an outside shock. Passion exerted a debilitating effect by loosening the soul's hold over the body and giving the body free rein to obey its true animal nature, which for men spelled death. Sorrow could take the form of an overwhelming and lethal passion, but it might also be a feeling, a controlled movement of the soul, that could find expression in the ritual of mourning and thus be overcome. Feelings were emotions that the Roman body language could control. This is precisely why feelings could be expressed with violence.

Romans wept, cried out, raged and were easily moved to pity for themselves or others. They were prone to rapidly changing, simple

but strong feelings. Like anyone who lives for honour, they were
quick to take offence and utterly disarmed by admiration. If an enemy
or a gladiator in the arena displayed courage, generosity, devotion or
a capacity for self-sacrifice, his life might well be spared. Yet the
Romans could be cruel to cowards and to anyone they thought might
seek to betray them. They liked to feel the thrill of emotion both in
real life and at the theatre. They would be tempted to gamble, take
risks and commit all manner of excesses just to see how close to the
brink they could venture without toppling over.

BODY AND SOUL, MORALITY AND HYGIENE

One cannot talk about the Roman body without also discussing the
Roman soul. The Romans did not think of their bodies as isolated
entities, autonomous animal flesh whose functions were matters of
merely physiological interest. The soul exerted an influence on the
body, could make it ill or could make it better; in its turn, the body
influenced the soul, corrupting it or providing a corrective. So there
was a morality for the body and a hygiene for the soul.

   In their eyes a sick body was often the result of a corrupt soul.
Greed induced pallor and effeminacy; avarice made a man hard, dry
and constipated; debauchery made people's bodies and breath stink.
Satirical poets lavished a wealth of details on the nauseating spectacle
of spiritual corruption: 'As God is my witness, where is the difference
between the smell of Aemilius' mouth and that of his arse? The
cleanliness of one equals the filth of the other. And his arse is
probably the cleaner and the more pleasant of the two: there he's
without teeth, while the teeth in his mouth are half a yard long, stuck
in his gums like an old wagon, behind which is the cleft cunt of a she-
mule, pissing in summer heat.'[178]

   Vice was a rot that could penetrate a man's bones and kill him.
Sulla's old age was a long drawn-out process of decomposition. His
flesh was eaten from within by gangrene, because of his life of
debauchery:

> He consorted with actresses, harpists and theatrical people, drinking
> with them on couches all day long. These were the men who had most
> influence with him now: Roscius the comedian, Sorex the archmime
> and Metrobius, the impersonator of women, of whom, though past his
> prime, he continued up to the last to be passionately fond, and made no
> denial of it. By this mode of life he aggravated a disease that was
> insignificant when it began, so that for a long time he did not know

that his bowels were ulcerated. This disease corrupted his whole flesh too, converting it into worms, so that although many people were employed day and night in removing them, what they took away was as nothing compared with the increase upon him. All his clothing, baths, hand-basins and food were infected with that flux of corruption, so violent was its discharge. He immersed himself in water many times a day to cleanse and scour his person, but it was of no use. The change gained upon him rapidly, and the swarm of vermin defied all purification.

Body and soul were interacting. The mild illness that Sulla had contracted only became serious because of the dissolute life he led. It was this that made Sulla's body an easy prey to gangrene. Parasites had invaded his body just as the infamous female impersonators and male singers that he shamelessly paraded had invaded his life. The washing that was intended to disinfect and purify him was to no avail because the plague that gnawed at Sulla's innards came from a stain within his own soul.

Like the illness itself, Sulla's death was a physical and moral accident:

On learning that the magistrate there, Granius, refused to pay a debt that he owed the public treasury, in expectation of his [Sulla's] death, he summoned him to his room, stationed his servants about him, and ordered them to strangle Granius. However, owing to the strain he put upon his voice and body, he ruptured his abscess and lost a great quantity of blood. In consequence of this, Sulla's strength failed, and, after a night of wretchedness, he died.[179]

Sulla's death was triggered by the effects of violent tyrannical rage on a body already in a state of putrefaction. Worn out by the gangrene that was feeding on him, Sulla was unable to withstand the physical effects of violent anger. His body collapsed and dissolved, and he died.

Unless it was properly controlled and sanitized as feeling, passion could destroy a man. Another version of Sulla's end makes no mention of his gangrene and attributes his death solely to a fit of anger:

What shall I say of Sulla? Although, overwhelmed by this passion [anger], he spilled rivers of enemy blood, did he not end up by spilling his own? Burning with indignation at the sight of Granius, the first magistrate of Puteoli, pussyfooting about in his attempts to force the colony's elected representatives to hand over the money they had promised towards the rebuilding of the Capitol, Sulla got so worked up and his booming voice so shook his chest that he vomited up a flood of both threats and actual blood, and thereupon died.[180]

The Romans considered such excessive and dangerous passions to be an indication of *impotentia*, impotence, or the loss of power over oneself. The body became a victim to passions whose violence it could not withstand and that tore it apart. This could happen, for example, if a train of unforeseen events made it impossible for a Roman to recover himself after a flood of emotion had broken over him.

You could even die of joy, if it surprised you in the midst of sorrow and mourning:

> At the time when the army of the Roman people had been cut to pieces at Cannae, an aged mother was overwhelmed with grief and sorrow by a message announcing the death of her son. The report was false, however, and when not long afterwards the young man returned from that battle to the city, the aged mother, upon suddenly seeing her son, was overpowered by the shock of such unlooked-for joy, gave up the ghost and died.[181]

Self-control was not just a moral duty, it was a matter of life and death. Sensual passions threatened to dissolve the body, violent passions to tear it apart. Passions had therefore to be turned into feelings, sanitized and civilized through social rituals, fitted into a pace of living and a code of behaviour that enabled men to survive life's vicissitudes.

Whereas passions corrupted the body, feelings might often come to its rescue. The heroism of Romans in battle not only brought them glory, it protected their bodies against death. The ability to withstand pain and fear was the Roman soldier's main strength. History is littered with bloody accounts of Romans who remained sublimely impassive while the enemy cut them to shreds. The Romans liked to fantasize about death, appalling injuries and torture; civilians would grow drunk on grim stories of pain and blood. Violence was everywhere, always under control but always on display. It was the bravery of the body that counted. Courage waded through muddy fields of battle and grew strong on sweat, tears, the blood of rotting corpses and the murky water quaffed by legionaries from rivers in which the bulging corpses of horses floated belly uppermost.

Destiny often reduced the most celebrated of Roman heroes to mincemeat, whereupon Latin historians took great pleasure in recounting the brave men's ordeals in the most minute and grisly of details. This is how we come to know the precise way in which Atilius Regulus was tortured by the Carthaginians for the greater glory of Rome.

The enemies of Regulus, having captured him in an ambush, sent him back to Rome to negotiate his freedom in exchange for a number of Carthaginian noblemen in Roman hands. Although he was well aware of the fate that awaited him, Regulus advised the senate to reject the Carthaginian offer. He returned to Carthage where his strength of spirit was tested to the utmost. 'The Carthaginians cut off Atilius Regulus' eyelids and then enclosed him in a machine bristling with spikes, thus causing him to die as much by insomnia as by ceaseless pain.'[182]

To endure pain voluntarily was one way of outstripping the enemy and subduing them without engaging in battle. By inflicting on oneself the wounds that might be expected to result from battle, one could demonstrate indifference to injury and thereby prove that no blow the enemy could strike would ever force one to retreat. It the enemy did not feel equally courageous, they would give in. War was a competition of pain: those who could suffer the most would win. Sometimes war was reduced to a clash between two men. Both Mucius Scaevola, during the heroic wars against the Etruscans, and later Pompey, at the end of the republic, engaged in this kind of combat.

Indignant at the relentless way in which Porsenna, king of the Etruscans, had for a long time been waging war upon us, Mucius Scaevola crept secretly into the enemy camp, a dagger at his belt. Porsenna was in the act of offering a sacrifice. Mucius Scaevola approached to slay him before the altar, but was surprised and prevented from carrying out his plan. Rather than lie about the purpose of his presence in the camp, Mucius made an extraordinary display of impassivity, showing that he was beyond the reach of any pain that torture might inflict. For as if he were angry with his right hand for its inability to do its duty and kill the king, he placed it on the altar fire and, completely impassive, left it there to smoulder . . . Forgetting the danger he had been in, Porsenna's resentment turned to admiration. 'Go back,' he said, 'to your own people. I spare you your life, though you were seeking to take mine.'[183]

History then recounts that Porsenna, frightened by the courage of the young Romans, decided against war.

Several centuries later, Pompey copied Scaevola's feat.

Taken prisoner, owing to treachery during a mission to Illyria, Pompey was threatened with torture unless he revealed to King Gentius the plans of the Roman senate. Pompey thereupon placed his finger in the flame of a lamp and held it there while it burnt. Such impassivity made the king realize that it was pointless to torture Pompey and made him long to become the friend of the Roman people.[184]

These accounts reveal a whole conception of war and of the role of the body in war. War was an ordeal, a test of the soldier's mastery over physical pain and fear. If you withstood pain indefinitely and even courted it to show that it held no terror for you, you were invincible, your city could never fall into enemy hands, you were a free man forever. Mastery over one's body was therefore essential to anyone wishing to retain his freedom. The Roman soldier's body was that of a free citizen.

As long as one's spirit held out, one's body could withstand anything. A soldier need have no fear of death. In his courage lay his country's and often his own salvation. The Etruscan or Illyrian enemy would rather back down than put Roman courage to the test. Pompey and Mucius Scaevola would have been killed had they not inflicted torture on themselves.

Resistance to pain and indifference to injury were often what saved a man from death on the battlefield. The coward would die from a wound in his back while the brave man would face the onslaught. Arrows would rain down on his shield, his armour, his chest, wounding him but then falling away, as if blunted by the hardness of his flesh. Horatius Cocles prevented the Etruscans from taking the only bridge over the Tiber that could give them access to Rome. Singlehandedly, he confronted the massed enemy. Then, once the bridge had been cut off behind him, he dived into the river and swam across under a hail of arrows that made him bristle like a porcupine, arriving safe and sound on the Roman shore.

Insensitivity to pain came from physical and spiritual toughness. Roman soldiers would carry on fighting, indifferent to wounds, dripping with their own or with enemy blood. Their victories were as much over themselves as over the enemy. Courage made them virtually invulnerable. Such moral strength was entailed in the physical feats they performed that Roman soldiers can best be compared with those warriors of such traditional societies as Bali or Australia, whose bodies could, under certain circumstances, become as impervious as wood; on such bodies even deep wounds would heal over in a matter of hours. Some civilizations drugged their warriors to dull their sensitivity, but for the Romans courage itself acted as a drug. The thrill of victory would exert an astonishing curative effect on their wounds, leaving behind on the citizen's breast the glorious tokens of battle, like so many military medals.

Wounded soldiers would fight on regardless, remain on the battlefield and re-enlist for the next campaign. Lucius Sicinius Dentatus, who had fought in 120 battles, had not a single scar on his back but forty-five on his front.[185] Catiline's great-grandfather, a hero in the Punic Wars, was horribly mutilated during his first two campaigns. He not only lost his right hand but twenty-three different wounds also deprived him of the normal use of his remaining hand and his feet. Shrugging this off, he had made for him a replacement iron hand and continued to serve in the army. He even managed to escape from one of Hannibal's prisons, after twenty months in chains.

Even to the Romans, there was something monstrous about such excruciating heroism: mutilated bodies had no place in a city at peace. However glorious a sight a war invalid might present, he was no longer a perfect citizen. Catiline was in such a piteous state that when he was elected praetor, there was a move to prevent him from officiating at sacrifices.[186] The glorious body of the combatant was not that of the citizen returning to civilian life. To sacrifice to the city gods you had to be intact. After all, citizens had to be priests as well as soldiers.

DAILY BODY RHYTHMS

The Roman citizen's body was a product of culture rather than of nature and obeyed a civic rather than a biological rhythm. Depending on the time and place, it could be hard or soft, braced for action or languid in repose.

During the morning, the time set aside for *negotium*, a man's body would be tense with effort, *labor*, and for most of life's business he would remain standing. He would work in the fields, speak in the senate or forum, meet with his clients or pursue his own or the state's business. While his body was not made of the same iron as that of the heroic soldier, it was none the less the body of a fighter, tough and patient. Rising at dawn, he would face impassively the winter cold, wind and rain or the summer's sun and dust.

The soul too had to be phlegmatic. Politicians had to listen impassively to the insults their opponents would hurl at them and to all manner of allegations about their political past, their private life and their childhood. They might stand accused of prostituting their youth, ruining their father, swindling women or bribing electors; they might be called traitor, adulterer, drunkard or assassin.

The Roman also had to demonstrate *industria*. He had to invent, build, sell, deliver a speech – even in the midst of chaos and clamour. The city buzzed with people rushing to and fro, bodies and souls in agitation. The Roman soul was stirred by all the emotions and feelings attendant on business life. A trader might agonize over his ships laden with wine and the storms that might sink them; a candidate for election might count over and over all the election pledges he had received; a banker might wait with bated breath for an account to be paid; a peasant might live in fear of hail. Hope, fear and regret afflicted the Roman as much as physical agitation.

Yet the Romans attached no importance whatever to the skills and precision involved in craftwork. An artist was respected provided that he took care over his work, but no particular moral value was attached to artistic achievement: civilians were not trained to be skilful or quick workers. Indeed, manual activities that strained the body out of its natural shape were deemed degrading. Whereas ploughing, for example, was a noble activity demanding strength and endurance, harrowing was a servile chore that kept you bent double; like weaving, it was fit only for women.

Throughout the morning the Roman had no respite from work. If he stopped to eat, it would be a quick cold snack, for example bread and figs, taken standing up. The only purpose of such breaks was to revive his strength without slackening his effort or concentration. He kept his body hard, tensed, oblivious to pleasure or weariness. His soul, like his body, was braced and solemn. All morning, Romans would stand by, ready to deliver or to receive blows.

This active life took place outdoors. To the stress of action was added the non-stop attention that a Roman had to pay to his appearance. Anyone who took part in politics, whether as patron or as client, was on display. The image that he projected when at work would become his public image as citizen, magistrate or senator.

The evening was the time for leisure, *otium*, a time when the Roman could relax and let his body go. It was also a time to rest the soul and forget the worries of the day. Just as the banquet wine helped the soul to put politics on one side and savour repose, Rome had inserted the bathing ritual between the exertions of the morning and the pleasures of the evening, to ease the transition from *negotium* to *otium*.

Rest and leisure helped restore balance to a life of work, just as festival extravagance offset everyday austerity, and life in the country made up for life in the city. Men who could never relax, who systematically refused any kind of pleasure or gentleness, who could never indulge either themselves or others, were disquieting. Their extreme rigour indicated a lack of *humanitas*, a lack of human feeling and culture.[187]

The evening's relaxation was organized around the meal, the *cena*, which varied in its sumptuousness according to the calendar and the wealth of the household. The men would relax, stretching out on couches to laugh, joke, drink and converse. They were not morally obliged to present anything but an indulgent and benevolent face to the world. As their body unwound, their soul too could rest. It no longer had to draw the body tight, protecting it behind iron cladding. The emotions could at last have free rein.

As night closed in, the time of leisure and bodily relaxation came to an end. Sleep acted as a transition, preparing men for the renewed stresses of the early morning. A bout of insomnia or a banquet that continued too late into the night could be very damaging to one's health. Sleep afforded the soul a measure of tranquillity and allowed the body to regather its strength. Those plagued by a bad conscience, whose souls were troubled by remorse, regret, worry or longing, or who dwelt too much on the past or the future, would not get much sleep. Eventually they would fall ill as surely as those who woke up every time there was a noise in the street. They would grow exhausted and their bodies would disintegrate.

SEASONAL BODY RHYTHMS

The seasons of the year also imposed different rhythms on the Roman body. The months of spring and early summer were considered to be the morning of the year. In March began the season of war and work, soldiering and labouring. Winter was a time of peace. Just as the bath and the banquet came between the exertions of the morning and nightly repose, so the great games in the autumn, bringing the soldiers flooding back into the city, provided a transition between war and peace. At the games, men's bodies could grow languid, soften up and become sensitive once again to pleasure. On the circus or theatre terraces, Romans sat and joked, all serious thoughts banished.

But bodies that had grown soft and slack were vulnerable – the sitting position, halfway between standing and lying down – was a posture of semi-relaxation. In the open air, with no roof to protect them, bodies might fall prey to miasmas carried in the air. Architects had to take special precautions when they designed theatres:

> A site as healthy as possible is to be chosen for the exhibition of plays on the festivals of the immortal gods . . . for at the play citizens together with their wives and children remain seated; their bodies, motionless with pleasure, have their pores opened. On these the breath of the wind falls, and if it comes from marshy districts or other infected quarters, it will pour harmful spirits into the system.[188]

Autumn, the season of the great games, was generally considered to be a perilous time of year. After all, it could hardly be mere coincidence that the worst time of year for fevers and illness was the autumn, when everyone was at their most physically relaxed.

BODY POSTURE

Whether sitting, standing or lying down – according to place and circumstances – Roman bodies had to observe, as in other civilizations, ceremonial etiquette that comprised not only religious and ritual elements but also considerations of common courtesy. What marked Rome out from other Mediterranean countries was the preference for sitting as against squatting or crouching. Chairs, benches, stools and armchairs, usually made of wood, sometimes adorned with strips of leather, were important articles of Roman furniture. If called upon to wait for a long period, one adopted not a reclining or recumbent position but rather a sitting position on a raised chair. Inside houses, during the daytime, people mainly sat. Seats were not fixtures in each room; they had to be fetched according to need. They were only used in circumstances of intimacy and presupposed a degree of social proximity and the ability to relax together. When someone was first admitted to a house, he would remain standing in the *atrium*, talking with the master of the house, who would also stand. But once accepted into the household, and invited, for example, to discuss some matter with the head of the house, he might be shown into one of the rooms adjoining the *atrium*, used normally as a library, or records office. A slave would then bring him a chair. The sedentary position symbolized full admission to a particular place. To offer a seat to a visitor was therefore to throw one's house open to him, however temporarily.

The beds used for sleeping on, consisting of a wooden frame and a straw mattress covered with two woollen blankets, were permanently installed in the bedrooms. Women, children and slaves lay down only to sleep. Free adult men, on the other hand, stretched out on couches during banquets. It was almost as if the extreme exertions that free men performed in the mornings had to be offset by assuming this extremely relaxed supine position in the evening. Reception beds were only used at banquets when not only the master of the house but also all the male guests lay down to eat. It would have been thought most impolite for a Roman to receive seated guests lying down, unless he happened to be ill.

Body positions also played a role in public life and the symbolism of power. The curule chair, a sort of armchair without a back, the prerogative of higher magistrates, enabled them to sit through assemblies while the people remained standing. The magistrates would rise only to speak, as a sign of respect for the people. In the presence of a magistrate, all Romans, even those who were former magistrates, had to stand and remain silent. Even a magistrate's own father was not exempt from this. Fabius Maximus, one of the heroes of the war against Hannibal, arrived one day on horseback to see his son, who was a consul, and found him surrounded by soldiers standing in respect. The young man was deeply offended and at once dispatched a lictor to command his father to dismount. Fabius thereupon congratulated his son for insisting that consular dignity be accorded its rightful respect.[189]

An anecdote dating from the end of the fourth century BC reveals how a Roman could play on the different meanings of the seated position in private and in public. Gnaeus Flavius was a curule aedile. Being a scribe and the son of a freedman, Gnaeus owed his advancement to the support of Appius Claudius, the censor in 312 BC. The patricians, however, continued to look down their noses at this new man in their midst. 'But one day Flavius went to the house of a colleague of his who was sick. There were numerous young members of the nobility in the sick man's bedroom. No one stood up or offered Flavius a seat. Flavius laughed at this and gave orders for his curule chair to be fetched. This he then placed on the threshold of the house so that no one could leave without seeing him seated on it.'[190]

The patricians had insulted Flavius by not inviting him to sit down with them, thereby making it clear that he was not welcome. By making him stand, they treated him like a slave, a client bringing a message or a domestic servant. Denied a private seat, Flavius sent for his seat of public office, the curule chair, which entitled him the honour of remaining seated while the others had to stand before him.

As an aedile, Flavius also enjoyed the privilege of being accompanied by *apparitores* to go before him in the street and to take up a position outside any house he chose to visit. Indeed on this occasion it was one of these *apparitores* who fetched his curule chair and set it down outside the front door of the patrician's house. The young patricians would have to file past him as he sat on the chair that symbolized his power. To the symbolism of private household politesse, Flavius had responded with the symbolism of public privilege.

THE BODY IN PAIN

The Romans had nothing that resembled modern medical practice, but they did have doctors. Roman medicine, making no distinction between the origins of illnesses, none the less had treatments for all physical and even all spiritual ailments. The Romans did, however, make a clearcut distinction between injuries received in battle and other sorts of disorders, and between illnesses affecting individuals and illnesses that affected entire communities to which sick individuals, families or towns night belong.

For a long time war wounds were considered the only fit objects of a doctor's attention. They were noble and, besides, they healed remarkably quickly and thoroughly, leaving behind on Roman chests handsome and honourable scars (see p. 247). This was why the Roman state invited Archagathos, a Greek doctor who specialized in army surgery, to set up practice in Rome in 219 BC.[191] He was granted Roman citizenship and given a surgery at the Acilius crossroads. Initially very popular, his aggressive methods soon turned people against him. He cauterized wounds and was so eager to slice and cut into flesh that he was soon nicknamed 'the executioner'. But the Roman tradition of doctors who specialized in wounds occasioned by violence somehow survived. When Caesar was stabbed by senators in Pompey's curia, a doctor, Antistius, was sent for immediately to examine Caesar's wounds and to see if any of them were fatal.[192]

While medicine was essentially reserved for soldiers, the head of the family would usually treat day-to-day illnesses and disorders. Most stomach troubles were attributed to overeating and cured by starvation, purging and vomiting.[193] Tyrants were known to suffer from nightmares.[194] Diseases of the body, at least in adult free men, were generally viewed as indications of diseases of the soul. Sick people were therefore always suspected of having committed some transgression or at least of being morally weak. Illness, while it was not deemed a punishment as such, was thought to be the inevitable effect of a slackening of the soul that rendered the body less tense and therefore more vulnerable.

CATO'S MEDICINE

Cato was an implacable enemy of doctors, all of whom were guilty, in his eyes, of deliberately poisoning Roman youth. Cato was of the opinion that doctors – all Greeks in his time – harboured a deep hatred of the 'barbarian' peoples who had conquered Greece and therefore longed to wreak ruinous revenge on them. Indeed, doctors only insisted on being paid so that people would wrongly assume it was greed that motivated them. At the same time, he thought it scandalous to demand money to help a fellow human. Cato himself practised traditional medicine and looked after his entire household with advice culled from a huge book about medical treatments that had long been in his family. He even forbade his son Marcus to consult a doctor.[195]

Cato treated sciatica with juniper wood wine,[196] and always kept a pomegranate extract at the ready to combat colic and worms.[197] But in Cato's view, the universal remedy, the true panacea, was cabbage.[198] Eating cabbage aided digestion and facilitated urination. Eaten before a banquet, it would allow one to eat and drink as much as one wished without fearing the consequences. From cabbage Cato also made a powerful diuretic, an emetic and a cure for colic. Carefully washed and crushed, and then applied as a poultice that was changed twice daily, the leaves of cabbage could cure ulcers, heal open sores and dispel tumours. It was also a good treatment for infected wounds, ridding them of pus, and it made boils burst. Eating cabbage could soothe away aches in the head, eyes and joints, and see off stabbing pains in the heart and lungs. Fried in hot fat and taken on an empty stomach, cabbage was an effective treatment for insomnia. Dried and ground to a powder and then taken like snuff, cabbage could detach nose polyps. Drops of tepid cabbage juice applied to the ears could even cure deafness.

Medical treatments were often ineffective unless accompanied by an incantation. But sometimes the words could do the job on their own: 'There are fixed charms that can fashion you anew, if with cleansing rites you read the booklet thrice.'[199]

Cato has also passed on to us an astonishing procedure for healing dislocations and bone fractures:

Any kind of dislocation may be cured by the following charm. Take a green reed four or five feet long and split it down the middle, and let two men hold the two pieces to either side of your hips. Begin to chant: 'motas uaeta daries dardaries astataries dissunapiter' and continue, advancing the ends until they meet. Brandish a knife over them, and when the ends of the reeds are actually touching, grasp them, and cut right and left. If the pieces are applied to the dislocation or the fracture, it will heal. And none the less chant every day, and, in the case of a dislocation, in this manner, if you wish: 'haut haut haut istasis tarsis ardannabou dannaustra.'[200]

Sciatica could be treated very effectively with music: 'Many men have believed and put their belief on record, that when gouty pains in the hips are most severe, they are relieved if a flute-player plays soothing measures . . . So very close is the connection between men's bodies and their minds, and therefore between physical and mental ailments and their remedies.'[201]

PREVENTIVE MEDICINE AND RELIGION

To deal with most kinds of illness, however, the Romans relied not on Greek medicine or traditional remedies but on a form of religious insurance policy. Each community would place its trust in a protective deity, generally Mars, supposed to keep its members safe from ills. Every year, estate-owners celebrated the Ambarvalia festival that was thought to protect their fields and animals and the people who lived on the estate.[202] The estate-owner would sacrifice a calf, a lamb and a sucking pig to Mars, after leading the animals three times round the estate perimeter. He would then ask Mars to keep his estate free from 'sickness, seen and unseen, barrenness and destruction, ruin and unseasonable influence; and that thou permit my harvests, my grain, my vineyards, and my plantations to flourish and to come to good issue, preserve in health my shepherds and my flocks, and give good health and strength to me, my house and my household.' Estates were divided into three parts: cultivated fields; herds and those who looked after them, since herdsmen were deemed to be as savage as the animals they tended; and the people who inhabited the house.

Similarly, Rome, using the college of the Arval Brethren as intermediary, asked Mars to protect the city from any illnesses or scourges that might otherwise attack its people.[203] So whenever illness did strike, it was because prevention had failed.

On occasion, despite such rituals, Rome was visited by a plague or other divine scourge. Plagues, however, were not regarded as epidemics that afflicted individuals; the illness could not be separated from the sterility that afflicted the soil and from concomitant social disorders. It was the whole city that appeared to be falling apart. An individual was physically subject to plague because his body was not merely a private entity: citizens possessed a public body, the *populus*, and it was this that had become afflicted.

If plague struck, the only remedy was collective atonement through supplication, *lectisternia* and games offered to the gods (see p. 186). A grave mistake must have been committed that had upset the divine order of the world and this would now have to be repaired through expiatory rituals in order to restore harmony between the city and the world. Once this was done, the people would get better automatically.

Sometimes, the most difficult thing for religious and political authorities was to gauge where illness ceased and where plague began. At the beginning of the second century BC, when there was an outbreak of plague, for the first three years people talked only of contagious disease. Then the praetor died, soon followed by one of the consuls and then a spate of distinguished men from different walks of life, until so many were dying that everyone began to talk in terms of plague. The *pontifex maximus* was given the task of discovering adequate expiations to assuage the gods' anger. The senate ordered the decemvirs to consult the Sibylline books. Meanwhile the surviving consul dedicated statues to Aesculapius, the Greek god of medicine, to Apollo, the Greek god of plague, and to the goddess of life. Public prayers were said continually for two days at Rome and throughout the whole of Italy. These prayers were attended by everyone over twelve years of age, wearing wreaths on their heads and carrying laurel branches in their hands.[204]

ROMAN HEALTH

There is no way of knowing whether the Romans were subject to many illnesses, nor what these may have been. Those who were ill carried on as if everything was perfectly normal. Polybius refers to an embassy consisting of a man suffering from a severe attack of gout, a madman and a man who 'in consequence of a tile falling on his head had received so many serious wounds that it is a wonder he escaped with his life.'[205]

The Romans seem to have been mainly subject to eye infections, which they treated with ointments, stomach aches, skin diseases and summer and autumn fevers.[206] The city was also full of insomniacs, to whom Horace recommended the following cure: 'Let those who need sound sleep oil themselves and swim across the Tiber three times; then, as night comes on, let them steep themselves in wine.'[207]

By the end of the republic, doctors had taken over the city. They hung about the streets and looked after hard-up customers who would only trust them if they spoke Greek. Every nobleman possessed his own personal slave doctor. There was little, however, to distinguish doctors from philosophers, given that they generally prescribed physical exercise and measures designed to keep their patients in good health and therefore free of any need of their treatment. Medicine sought to be preventive rather than curative.

CATO'S PHYSICAL AND ETHICAL REGIME

Cato owed his political career and his prestige in part to his dietary regime and lifestyle, which enabled him to preserve intact his hardness of body and soul until the end of his life.

> It was natural, therefore, that men should admire Cato, when they saw that, whereas other men were broken down by toil and enervated by pleasure, he was victor of both, and this too, not only while he was still young and ambitious, but even in his hoary age, after consulship and triumph. Then, like some victorious athlete, he persisted in the regimen of his training, and kept his mind unaltered to the last.[208]

> In his economy, in his endurance of toil and danger, he was of almost iron-like body and mind, and not even old age, which weakens everything, could vitiate the keenness of his mind.[209]

This hardness of body and soul was essential to anyone who, like Cato, had wished to get ahead but was a 'new man', without any noble ancestors. Even in his old age, Cato managed to retain this strength, thanks to a way of living that had less to do with biology than economy. Cato managed to retain the vigour of his youth because he spent hardly any money: spending, after all, entailed relaxation. 'He tells us that he never wore clothing worth more than a thousand asses; that even when he was praetor or consul he drank the same wine as his slaves; that as for fish and meats, he would buy thirty asses' worth for his dinner from the public stalls, and he only did this for the city's sake, that he might not live on bread alone, but strengthen his body for military service.'[210]

The list of Cato's economies is endless: he took to extremes the idea that economy is the cornerstone of morality. Cato the Elder was an exemplary figure of a Roman consumed by the desire for civic honour. What made this possible was the fact that morality affected every single aspect of Roman life. Yet, despite his hardness, Cato was not considered an exemplary Roman. He went too far. He worked too hard at being a citizen, at the expense of the man of pleasure, the spectator of the games, the joyful guest and the religious man. Yet the duty of every nobleman was after all to take the value that he had chosen to embody to such an extreme as to earn him an *imago* and a surname. Cato was magnificently successful inasmuch as he became known to posterity as Cato the Censor. During his life his name was changed from Marcus Porcius Priscus to Marcus Porcius Cato – that is, 'the skilful' – and then after his death to Marcus Porcius Censor.

15

Clothing, finery and bathing

The Romans had two reasons for wearing clothes: to maintain a sense of common decency and to display social distinctions. Protection from the cold or heat was not essential; indeed, it was often deemed a personal weakness. The Romans felt duty bound never to be completely naked. In public, on the street or theatre terraces, each person's rank, wealth and age was revealed in the clothes they wore.

There were two kinds of clothing in Rome: outdoor (or 'over') garments for public wear and display; and indoor (or 'under') garments. These two categories of clothing followed different designs. Outdoor clothes were draped round the body, and indoor clothes, or those worn underneath, were stitched together, pulled on to the body and held in place by a belt.

THE TOGA

In the city, at least in the morning, citizens wore togas outside their own homes. The toga was a kind of citizen's uniform. It consisted of a huge length of unbleached wool, which covered the body from shoulders to feet. Initially rectangular, it was later cut in a semi-circle so that it would hang better. Considerable art was involved in donning the toga. The straight edge was placed on the left shoulder from behind, with one-third of it falling in front of the wearer and supported by the left arm. The toga was then drawn across the back, brought under the right arm, and thrown again over the left shoulder.

The right arm was thus free but the left arm remained hidden beneath the fabric. The front of the garment was arranged in a series of folds, forming a pocket called a *sinus*. A citizen officiating as priest would cover his otherwise bare head with the part of his toga that hung down his back. Togas developed in response to changes in fashion. At the end of the republic it was thought elegant to wear a very broad toga, up to six metres in diameter, made of a very fine fabric. It was impossible to don such a garment on one's own, and specialized slaves were therefore entrusted each morning with the artistic arrangement of the toga on their master's shoulders. The simplest togas were woven at home by the citizen's wife, and their size and shape in this case depended on the loom used.

The toga, as the term's etymology suggests (it shares a common root with the Latin word for roof) served to cover a man, to veil him, to make him decent in public life. The Romans complained that this kind of gown was peculiarly uncomfortable and impractical. It was cold in winter, because it did not wrap up the body properly, but was hot in summer because of its weight. Nor did it protect the citizen against rain, wind or sun. In addition, it imposed severe restrictions on body movement. Only the right hand was free, since the left hand had to hold on to the left tail of the toga. It was almost impossible to fight or run in a toga. Yet it was these practical drawbacks that were the toga's *raison d'être*. The toga was first and foremost a garment of peace, only worn within the city, in stark contrast with the weaponry worn by soldiers. (At Rome, a soldier who lost his sword and shield was said to be 'naked'.) The slow movements and the measured gestures that the toga induced befitted a peaceful citizen living in the heart of the city, protected from external attacks by the army and from internal violence by the law. He could walk calmly about the streets: nothing threatened him. A man who wore armour, clearly visible beneath his toga, demonstrated that civil peace was no longer guaranteed, that the republic was in danger.

The toga veiled the body and hid from sight any peculiarities. Romans did not flaunt their physical beauty like ancient Greek city-dwellers. In public only a Roman's hands and head could be seen. Only his right hand was free: it was this hand that undertook commitments, or pledged his faith. A free man's face was the only part of his body considered worthy of examination. Personality was disclosed in a man's eyes, eyebrows and nose and his soul could be read in the expression that his face wore. A Roman's public body consisted of three essentials: a toga a head and a hand.

WHITE, PURPLE AND GOLD

Because the toga was an important part of the citizen's visible body, it was used to indicate civic rank and distinction, symbolized by variations in colour.

The toga worn by the average adult citizen was plain and unadorned, the colour of natural wool, often brownish among the poor. Only election candidates wore pure white, chalk-bleached, togas. Indeed this was how candidates let people in the forum know that they were standing for election as magistrates. The dazzling white of their togas would stand out from the sea of beige and brown. The augurs' togas were saffron-coloured. The toga worn by superior magistrates and children was edged with a broad band of purple and known as the *toga praetexta*. The purple border was woven into the toga using a thread of wool dyed purple.

'Purple' was no one specific colour: it could cover anything from light pink to dark mauve. Besides, the Romans were not sensitive to subtle chromatic shadings. They distinguished between light, *clarus*, generally mistranslated as white, the colour of life, cleanliness and civilization; and dark, the colour of death, dirt, mourning and savagery.

Yet purple was colour itself, in that it was the result of artificial dyeing and was produced by a complex technique involving a lot of boiling and stewing. It was what replaced a fabric's natural shade. Purple was produced from seashells such as mussels and whelks, which were quite common in the Mediterranean, although the best ones came from Phoenicia. The important thing about purple was that, whatever its precise colour, it marked out whoever wore it. It had no magical effect, yet it announced clearly that any attack on the person wearing it, be he magistrate or free-born child, was strictly forbidden.

Like gold, purple signified glamour and wealth and was an emblem of power. Apart from the *toga praetexta*, worn by magistrates and senators, censors wore all-purple togas and triumphant generals purple togas edged with gold. Men in purple stood out in a crowd and attracted attention. Roman glory was expressed in words that literally meant brilliant, *clarus*, and luminous, *illustris*. Purple was a flash of glory.

Senators and knights wore golden rings on their ring fingers to show that they belonged to wealthy society. Mounted on these rings there was often an engraved seal that could be used for signing and sealing letters. At Rome the only two things that visually identified a man were his face and his seal. His public body, hidden beneath his toga, was anonymous and silent. Even his feet were hidden in closed shoes all year round.

INTIMATE CLOTHING

The toga was in a class of its own. The purpose of every other article of clothing was to maintain decency and to protect the vulnerable bodies of children, the elderly and the infirm from heat and cold. These garments differed according to the sophistication or austerity of the wearer. The same clothing would be worn under the toga or indoors, under the roof of a private house or outdoors on an afternoon. Outdoors, a Greek-style cloak might be draped casually over the shoulders or, for greater comfort, a Gallic hooded cloak.

Again for the sake of comfort, when they travelled Romans rigged themselves out in all kinds of cloaks, caps, gaiters and even trousers, garments which they took over from peoples they had conquered. Trousers, however, had to be well hidden from view.

Whether in the city or in the countryside, the strictest men were 'naked' under their togas. The adjective 'naked' meant that they wore no tunic but only a kind of loincloth held by a belt. Decent men kept their belts tight. A loose belt or, worse, no belt at all was evidence of a debauched life and over-indulgence in banqueting and love-making. Cato the Younger, who practised conspicuous austerity, went around naked under his toga and even in the afternoon, when the time came to take off one's toga, he wore neither tunic nor shoes. This was thought very strange in first-century BC Rome. His belt was no doubt kept very tight. The Romans depicted the rough farm workers of the distant past, such as Cincinnatus, naked as they ploughed their land in the sun.

Usually, however, beneath their togas and at home, the Romans would wear one or more tunics, sometimes several, one on top of the other. Tunics were pieces of cloth folded in two and sewn up the sides, with holes for the head and arms. For men tunics were only to cover the chest and belly. Long tunics were for women and Orientals only.

For a man to wear a tunic that came down his arms as far as his wrists, and almost to his fingers, was considered unbecoming in Rome and in all Latium. Our countrymen thought that a long and full-flowing garment was not unbecoming for women, to hide their arms and legs from sight. But Roman men at first wore the toga alone without a tunic; later, they had close, short tunics with short sleeves that just covered their shoulders. Habituated to this older fashion, Publius Africanus reproached Publius Sulpicius Gallus, an effeminate man, because he wore tunics with sleeves that came down his arms and covered his hands.[211]

At one time it was fashionable to wear a tunic with fringed sleeves, like that worn by Julius Caesar. This was a way of having sleeves while appearing not to have them.

Belts were generally attached to tunics, when these were worn. This made it possible to gather up the tunic to thigh level and free the legs. Decency dictated that men should be as little covered as possible, without risking obscenity. Women, on the other hand, were expected to remain relatively well covered up. 'Maltinus walks with his garments trailing low; another, a man of fashion, wears them tucked up indecently as far as his waist.'[212]

Senators were alone in wearing special tunics that served as their official dress. These were light-coloured tunics called *laticlaviae*, which had woven into them two broad vertical strips of purple. Depending on how the belt was arranged, these bands could be either visible or invisible.

At banquets sophistication and unbridled freedom were the order of the day. Diners came in tunics and sandals. People's bodies were relaxed, their clothing soft and loose. But there were as many kinds of attire as their were types of food on offer: the banquet was the place for fantasy and exoticism. The Romans liked to wear strange foreign clothing and had a taste for fancy dress. Transparent dresses, damask jackets, embroidered scarves imported from Asia Minor, Egypt and Libya: anything went because nothing mattered. Some people even turned up covered with jewellery, rings and primitive necklaces.

The only transgression was to play around with official dress, to mix business and pleasure, public and private life. Cicero reported indignantly that Verres, the praetor of Sicily, once wore his *toga praetexta*, his official garb, with a long tunic and sandals: an inappropriate combination.

PHYSICAL CULTURE

Clothing could not be neatly separated from the general *cultus*, or culture of the body. It was also connected with bathing and hairdressing. Mourning, the temporary rejection of physical culture, entailed not only wearing ripped clothing, but also neglecting one's body, and letting beard and hair become dirty and untrimmed. A man who was elegant, on the other hand, would be described as *lautus*, or well washed. This bodily culture, in its more sophisticated ramifications, was part of city life, a kind of elegance known as *urbanitas*. After all, the city was the place for superfluity, for added extras. Refinements of the body were closely related to the values of the banquet and to pleasure. Rustics, when seen shambling round the city, looked incongruous and ridiculous. 'He might awake a smile because his hair is cut in country style, his toga sits ill, and his loose shoe will hardly stay on his foot.'[213]

Refinement meant smelling sweet, waging war on bad breath and body odour. 'Phew! You smell of garlic! Ugh, you lump of native filth, you clod-hopper, he-goat, pig-sty, mixture of mire and manure!'[214] This was how one habitual, perfume-drenched banqueter reacted to the arrival of a peasant.

Excess could take two forms. One might stink of stale sweat, because one had neglected to wash, or reek of perfume through continually sucking on scented lozenges in an attempt to conceal an inward rot. There were two parts of the body where the smells of urbanity or rusticity might appear. The mouths of refined men smelled of perfume or decay. The armpits of uncultivated men smelled of stale sweat.

BATHING

Roman baths served two purposes: they provided a point of transition between the efforts of the morning and the pleasures of the evening, between tension and relaxation. They also provided a daily opportunity for Romans to look after their body *cultus*. This is why Rome associated culture with softness and why excessive culture was deemed corrupting.

In general, it was for reasons of ritual that Romans washed frequently. Before performing any religious action they had to purify themselves. At the gate of every sanctuary stood a tub of water and often a very simple bath-house. A wash before entering the sanctuary was essential: it purified the person and marked the passage from the profane to the sacred world.

So even in very ancient times and even in the depths of the country, Romans, including women and slaves, would wash every day and have a thorough bath on every feast day, if not more often. At Rome itself baths were taken daily. Not only did private houses have baths, there were public baths whose admission fee was a mere one-quarter *as*. Many even quite small estates also had baths – as did Scipio's villa in Campania.

Good baths would operate in two ways: heat and steam would warm up the body in order to relax it, and water would clean the body in order to purify and civilize it.

There were three ways of warming up one's body: by going into a steam-room; by playing ball; or by sunbathing. In Rome what we now call sport was tied in with bathing. It was not physical training as such: only professional athletes and boxers built up their muscles by lifting weights. But everyone played ball, whatever their age: no strength was demanded and the only aim was to work up a good sweat. Sunbathing performed the same function. Before taking their early afternoon bath, Romans would sunbathe under a portico or on a south-facing terrace, thus gaining a fashionable tan. Since sunburn was associated with soldiers and people who lived in the countryside, a healthy tan gave the face a virile austerity that was liked by both aristocratic senators and former soldiers. A pallid complexion, on the other hand, seemed to bespeak the kind of man who spent his life indoors, banqueting and courting women, and who was therefore effeminate.

Young men of good family and of military age would train on the field of Mars, running, throwing the javelin and fencing in the warm sunshine. Then they would jump into the Tiber, even in winter. Bathers, on the other hand, would take things more gently. After sunbathing and playing ball, they would pass from the steam-room to the tepid room before going on to the cold room where, using a scraper, they would remove the dirt that their pores had ejected along with the sweat. Then they would jump into the swimming-pool. Finally, the most sophisticated of the men would douse themselves in perfume and order a massage.

Most of what we know about Roman baths derives from the immense imperial *thermae*. Yet thermal baths, albeit somewhat smaller, existed under the republic also. Scattered throughout most Roman towns, and even in Rome itself, these bath-houses comprised steam-rooms, sports areas, solaria, swimming-pools, changing-rooms and massage-rooms. The architect Vitruvius, a contemporary of Augustus, gave a complete description of such establishments in his treatise *On Architecture*. The building itself would be made of stone or wood, the interior walls lined with ceramic tiles, and the floor would be terracotta-flagged. The ceilings of the steam-rooms were closed off by a bronze dome that could be raised or lowered to control the temperature.

Scipio Aemilianus' own baths in his villa in Campania, dating from the end of the third century BC, were more rudimentary. There was nothing but a single narrow room with a vaulted ceiling and slits for windows. The water, which was neither very clean nor very hot, was contained in a simple basin. The walls were plain roughcast.[215]

BEARDS AND HAIR

Keeping beard and hair properly trimmed was the very essence of the *cultus* of the body. Although the Romans pictured their distant ancestors as long-haired, long-bearded and shaggy shepherds, the excavations of Latium and Rome have uncovered so many razors that one can no longer see such imaginings as anything more than a Roman fantasy about their origins. But because shepherds in charge of huge herds had unkempt heads of hair, the Romans projected on to the past the savagery of such men living at the edges of civilization.

There were many barbers and hairdressers at Rome. They exercised their profession outside their shops, and cut, shaved, curled and even dyed hair. People who kept slaves would have a slave hairdresser, just as they had a slave cook and a slave doctor. This does not mean that the Romans shaved every day. Only the fashionable and the elegant kept their faces more or less permanently clean-shaven. Most Romans normally wore several days' growth of beard. Until their facial hair became heavy and dense, young men usually wore a small downy beard as a mark of their youth. But, at least under the republic, the Romans never wore long full beards as did the Greeks, unless they were followers of philosophy, in which case a beard would be used to signal their conversion. Jokes were made about Epicureans whose beards dripped with wine.

Having one's face shaved at Rome was anything but enjoyable. Barbers worked with water only, knowing nothing of soap, and were not all equally skilful. The more delicate kind of man had the bristles on his chin plucked out one by one with tweezers, which was no less painful. Sophisticated Romans strove to banish facial hair as far as they could, since it smacked of the countryside. There was, however, something decidedly suspect about such practices. They seemed to betray an excessive sensuality: 'For one who daily perfumes himself and dresses before a mirror, whose eyebrows are trimmed, who walks abroad with beard plucked out and thighs made smooth, who at banquets, though a young man, has reclined in a long-sleeved tunic . . . does anyone doubt that he does what wantons commonly do?'[216]

All Romans wore their hair cropped short. Only young slaves much beloved of their masters kept their hair long, thereby earning the description 'long-haired children'. Hair was a typically feminine means of seduction and any man with a long mane of hair would be straightway suspected of engaging in prostitution. Similarly, a fugitive slave who had been recaptured was recognizable by his shaven scalp. Romans poked fun at bald men since baldness suggested lechery. Julius Caesar, himself bald, was overjoyed to win the privilege of wearing the crown of the *triumphator* permanently. At Rome haircutting was an art, ancient scissors being much less easy to use than our modern ones. Clumsy hairdressers often made their customers look ridiculous by cutting their hair into jagged steps. Young people sometimes had their hair curled with irons to give them regular ringlets on their foreheads. Hair was also the place to apply perfume, which in ancient times was oil-based. At banquets, men's hair was therefore shiny and sweet-smelling.

THE LANGUAGE OF DRESSING-UP

Too much body culture either turned city men soft or civilized them, depending on your point of view. Urbanity was ambiguous, as was rusticity. Less sophisticated men from the country had more savage and 'natural' bodies, with body hair and odours that brought them nearer to people in mourning. But taken too far, this feature made a man merely sordid and repugnant. Ill-tempered and foul-mannered, excessively rustic men lacked *humanitas*, amiability and culture. Rusticity was a fault *vis-à-vis* whoever it upset. But a mild degree of rusticity betokened a man whom civilization had failed to corrupt and who had retained a hard and resistant body: a man of his word.

Rusticity and urbanity were not unchanging features of a man's character: the Romans played on both, as if it were a language. The way that Romans arranged their appearance for display in the squares of Rome in the morning was a manner of addressing their fellow citizens. 'Let not their hair, sleek with liquid nard, deceive you, nor the tongue of the belt tucked into the creases it makes; let not the toga of finest texture play you false, nor the many rings on their fingers.'[217]

This kind of man was a sophisticate, a *cultissimus*, as much of a seducer as Julius Caesar, who affected to scratch his head with only one finger in order to avoid dishevelling his impeccably styled hair – or what remained of it. Yet this did not prevent him from being the most indefatigable of cavalrymen, utterly indifferent to what he ate or drank or where he slept when he was in the field. What his sophisticated manners announced was his support for the values of the city, embodying a promise to the Roman people of sumptuous triumphs, grandiose feasts and due compensation for the terrible military campaigns they had to endure. Luxury followed in the train of large-souled generals determined to lead to the edge of the world armies that would then return laden with perfumes from Araby, amber from Britanny and Asian gold, driving before them elephants and giraffes. If Caesar followed sartorial fashions and edged his wide toga with a band of light purple, and if he kept his belt casually loose, it was because he sought to become a fashionable politician and the darling of the people.

Cato the Younger was as different from Caesar as chalk from cheese. Cato affected an old-fashioned rusticity as a way of proclaiming his political opinions. What he wanted was a return to traditions, a brake on luxury, and citizens who did not stray too far from their villages. 'In general, Cato thought he ought to take a course directly opposed to the life and practices of the time, feeling that these were bad and in need of great change. For instance, when he saw that a purple which was excessively red and vivid was much in vogue, he himself would wear the dark shade. Again, he would often go out into the streets after breakfast without shoes or tunic.'[218] None of which prevented him, according to gossip, from loving both wine and money.

But most Romans went about their business in the morning clean and looking reasonably civilized:

> Keep yourself pleasingly clean, and let your skin be tanned by physical training in the field of Mars. Make sure your toga fits well and is spotless. The tongue of your shoe should not be wrinkled, nor should the fastenings be rusty, and your foot should not slip about in too large a shoe. Don't go about with a shaggy mane of badly cut hair; let your hair and beard be dressed by a skilled hand. Let your nails be clean and short, and make sure that any hairs growing in your nostrils are kept well trimmed. Your breath should not be sour and unpleasing, and your body should not stink like that of a he-goat.[219]

Cleanliness was an uphill struggle against stains, hairs, dirty fingernails and unseemly odours, but it was also a sign of good health. Men who were clean had sweet-smelling breath, uncorrupted by a life of debauchery, and they would do physical training on the field of Mars. Civilized men, after all, were also soldiers.

Food, banqueting and the pleasures of the evening

FEEDING OR DINING?

At Rome the evening meal, the *cena*, was one of the high points of the day. It involved more than simply eating one's daily bread; rather, it was a social ritual essential to the cohesion of the community. It was always an eminently cultural event, whether it was an ordinary *cena* for the family or a grand *convivium*, or banquet, with many guests: friends, relatives and clients.

The perfect dinner involved a wide variety of techniques of production, preservation and preparation of foodstuffs and stimulated weighty treatises on agronomy, home economics and gastronomy. Since dinner was also of vital importance to physical and spiritual wellbeing, doctors issued advice on the former and moralists held forth on the latter. Both sets of experts told diners what they could or should eat and what was forbidden. Each doctor promoted his own pet diet. Moralists, for their part, roundly and uniformly condemned luxury, avarice and gluttony, *gula*, and denounced those who threw banquets merely as an excuse to show off their wealth and boost their egos. Satirists tirelessly lampooned the innumerable perversions of diners and banqueters. They pilloried the gluttons who gobbled away their fortunes, the relentless gourmets who, sated with exotic dishes, sought to revive their jaded palates with all kinds of culinary perversions, and the drinkers who prolonged their bouts until daybreak, entertained by dancing mime artists.

Dinners were of sufficient social importance to arouse the active interest of the state. Censors debarred obese cavalrymen from the army and heaped disgrace on anyone who allowed gluttony to be his downfall. They drew up lists of foods prohibited on days other than festivals and fixed a maximum annual sum that could be spent on bacon or salt meat. But to no avail: dinners became more and more costly. Sumptuary laws were enacted and re-enacted but remained largely ineffective. Caesar went so far as to send special supervisory brigades to the markets to seize dainties exposed for sale in violation of the law, and his soldiers went into houses to check what was being served up in people's dining-rooms.[220]

Yet it would be quite mistaken to imagine that Romans were all incorrigibly greedy. Quite the reverse. Generally, Romans were remarkably frugal. They distinguished as clearly between feeding and dining as between human food and livestock fodder. In the Roman view, animals only ate to satisfy a natural need, whereas men asserted their human nature by eating. This was why men could not feed off wild products, roots or acorns, without turning into brutish beasts. It was also why human food varied according to place, time and personality. Soldiers did not eat like civilians, women like men, or children like old people. You did not eat in the morning in the same way as in the evening.

There were two opposing conceptions of food. According to one view, its only purpose was to restore strength and to comfort the body by satisfying hunger. Those who took this view generally stood up to eat food that was both frugal and cold. Soldiers would make do with an evening meal of biscuits washed down with water, travellers would eat bread and figs and Romans in the city, unwilling to wait until the evening to eat,[221] would gnaw at dry bread, boiled vegetables left over from the day before or an onion. The second conception was embodied by the *cena*. The food itself was of better quality, though not necessarily sumptuous, and was cooked and eaten warm. There was furniture, a table and couches, and company, members of one's family or guests. The purpose of the *cena* was to strengthen links between all those who gathered to share the same meal.

FRUGAL FOOD

The frugal food eaten by the soldier or peasant who went off to the field at daybreak, or by the citizen returning home exhausted at midday from the forum, was also highly elaborate, consisting of bread or gruel. Restorative food was made from products that were 'strong' and 'hard'. By this Romans meant that to make them edible such foods had to be subjected to a series of operations designed to soften them, by breaking them down and cooking them in water. This was the only way one's stomach could digest them.

Digestion turned food into vitalizing juices, by cooking it one last time in the stomach. Stomachs were perfectly capable of digesting stronger and more restorative types of food, though they could not deal with food that was both uncooked and hard. If you ate food that was uncooked, *crudus*, you would yourself become 'crude'. The same term for raw or uncooked (*crudus*) was also used to describe someone suffering from indigestion: if you could not digest (that is, 'cook') your food, you became in your turn 'crude' and savage.

To civilize hard foodstuffs and render them digestible, the Romans would use one of three techniques: physically breaking the food down; cooking it in water; or allowing the natural process of putrefaction to take its course.

'Strong' and frugal types of food were cooked to produce two basic foodstuffs: bread and gruel. Bread was baked in an oven under a crock covered with embers; gruel was cooked in a large pot.

The Romans made two kinds of bread: kneaded and leavened. Whether one kneaded dough or added leaven to it, the aim was the same: to soften the wheat. For although the wheat might already have been ground or crushed, if the resulting dough were cooked without either leaven or kneading, the resulting bread would be as hard as stone. Kneading was a violent manner of subduing and smashing the dough – the Roman use of such terms to describe kneading shows that it was a matter of taming savagery or civilizing a rawness ('crudeness') by softening it.[222] As for leaven, it was a kind of deliberately manufactured putrefaction which, mixed into the dough, infected it with its natural softness. Leaven was either dough that had been left to ferment or a mixture of sour grapejuice and flour.[223]

Such bread could be enriched, especially for labourers and for workers, during seasons of particularly hard work. The bread was produced in the same way – a ball of dough placed under a crock to bake – but cheese or honey would be placed in the middle of the ball. The following is a recipe for *libum*: 'Bray two pounds of cheese thoroughly in a mortar; when it is thoroughly macerated, add one pound of wheat flour, or, if you wish the loaf to be more dainty, a half pound of fine flour, and mix thoroughly with the cheese. Add one egg, and work the whole well. Put out a loaf, place on leaves, and bake slowly on a warm hearth under a crock.'[224]

Gruel, on the other hand, was the result of wheat broken down by lengthy boiling in water. The Romans deemed boiling to be more violent than steaming, which in its turn was more violent than roasting or grilling. The fundamental difference was that boiling entailed the addition of water to food, and water had marked softening properties. Roasting and grilling, on the other hand, removed water from food.

Once again, farm labourers were entitled to enriched gruels, like the Punic version prepared in this recipe: 'Soak a pound of spelt in water until it is quite soft. Pour it into a clean bowl, add three pounds of fresh cheese, half a pound of honey, and one egg and mix the whole thoroughly; turn into a new pot.'[225]

Neither oil nor bacon were used to produce such frugal fare. Later in the day, when the frugality of the morning had been abandoned, oil might be used for frying cakes made with honey or cheese.

The Roman's usual diet, provided the individual was adult and healthy, was not very varied. Even bread and gruel were not essential, except for men from whom intense effort was expected. Otherwise, a few vegetables would suffice. Grown in his own garden, in soil that was permanently tended and that formed part of civilized space, such vegetables were a perfectly 'cultivated' type of food, even if they were only par-cooked on a very low flame. Eating vegetables would not make you savage.[226]

THE DINNER RITUAL

Roman citizens required very little food to sustain life, yet they had also to demonstrate their sociability by eating less frugally. In times of peace, an opportunity for this was provided by the *cena*, in both city and countryside.

This dinner, the Roman's only real meal, took place in the dining-room or *triclinium* (see p. 98) and brought together every free member of the family and sometimes guests too. One dined with others of the same social origins: free-born Romans did not dine with former slaves. Adult men would stretch out on couches, leaning on their left elbows, and would eat with their right hand. Women and children sat on chairs around a central table (see figure 5). Dining-rooms usually contained three couches, each of which could hold three people lying down. Private dinners always assembled a small number of guests, unlike public feasts when thousands of banqueters would gather in the streets to eat together.[227]

Plates, dishes and bowls were often made of terracotta but might be made of silver or gold. There were also wine jugs and large bowls used for mixing wine and water, for wine was not drunk neat but rather diluted with (sometimes warm and salty) water, one part wine to two parts water – or the reverse, depending on the guests' preference. Spoons were the only items of cutlery used and servants only handed these round when they were needed. All forms of food, especially meats, must therefore have been cooked until they fell apart. Individual portions were often divided out well in advance.

Each evening, by sharing with others the pleasures of the dining-table, Romans plunged into a human community combining family, friends and religious observance. Only the unfortunate bachelor, on those evenings when he was neither invited out nor himself expecting any dinner guests, was forced to make do with frugal food: a *cena* could not, after all, be celebrated on one's own. Thus Horace, after spending the afternoon at Rome, returned home to a meagre dish 'of leeks and peas and fritters', washed down with a cup of wine.[228]

The most basic *cena* consisted of nothing but vegetables sprinkled with olive oil. Horace was always happy to escape from such austerity: he would not turn down even a last-minute invitation.

> If it falls out that you have not been asked out anywhere to supper, you praise your quiet dish of herbs, and, as though going out was a form of torture, you call yourself lucky, and hug yourself, because you do not have to go and carouse. However, let but Maecenas bid you at a late hour come to him as a guest, just at lamp-lighting time, and its: 'Won't someone bring me oil this instant? Does nobody hear me?' You scream and bawl at your servants, and then rush off.[229]

In the evening, the time set aside for socializing, solitude was harder to bear than frugality. Romans liked to feel that they belonged to a small social circle and they were keen to receive dinner invitations, especially if they had no family of their own. Dinners were what forged bonds between groups of people. Every kind of community held regular banquets. The heads of the aristocracy invited each other to a banquet each year, at the games of the Great Mother.[230] The priests' colleges banqueted together each time they met to officiate or to welcome a new member.

Macrobius describes the menu of a feast given by Metellus, *pontifex maximus* in the middle of the first century BC, for the reception of Lentulus, the new *flamen* of Mars, in his official residence near the temple of Vesta. Three dining-areas were arranged.

Plate 10 *Handling Roman oil or wine jars, Trier, first century* AD
Reproduced by kind permission of the Ancient Art and Architecture Collection (Ronald Sheridan)

Two of these contained ivory couches and were for the men: pontiffs, the chief priest (*rex sacrorum*), the *flamens* and the augurs. The third dining-room was for women: four Vestal Virgins, the wife of the new *flamen* who had now acquired the title *flaminica*, and the mother-in-law of Metellus. The banquet was sumptuous. There was an abundance of shellfish, sea urchins and oysters, fattened fowls cooked in pastry, venison, wild boar, hare and sow's udders. Instead of bread there was a sort of bready cake, or brioche.[231]

The close socializing that dining together promoted could, however, become dangerous, for the friendship of the diners was founded not on mutual esteem but on complicity in pleasure. Furthermore, banquets brought men and women together in a disquieting atmosphere of potential nocturnal free-for-all. The society of the initiates of the Bacchanalia (see p. 156) had been similarly united by a convivial sense of community. There was always the danger that banquets might provide a forum for the creation of an anti-city, a society dedicated to pleasure and crime. This was a further reason for the state to take an interest in private dinners, in particular by restricting the number of guests.

BANQUET FOOD

For the dinner to function as a social ritual, it had to include different, better and superfluous – indeed wasteful – kinds of food. The dishes served at *cena* should give the diners a joyful party feeling. The everyday *cena* was itself something of a feast, even among poor peasants: on ordinary days, a ham bone would be used to enrich a vegetable soup, or bean puree would be made more attractive by adding a drop of freshly pressed oil or a lump of bacon. Diners would eat their bread with a simple mixture of dry cheese, oil, garlic, salt and herbs. If the master of the house wanted to provide a better spread, in honour perhaps of a close friend, he might add a *gustatio*, a tasty hors-d'œuvre, such as a boiled egg, olives or a salad of mallows.

If a neighbour or foreign guest was invited to dinner or there was a marriage, birthday or public feast to celebrate, the mother of the family would fetch bacon, walnuts and dry figs from the cellar, open a jar of candied fruits and uncork an amphora of vintage wine. She would also fetch a chicken from the farmyard and a kid and a lamb from the herd.

The bigger the feast the greater the expenditure. This was why meat – either preserved or freshly killed – was considered the right food for feast days. Wine put everyone in a good mood and a sweet-tasting dessert was pure pleasure, when hunger had already been well satisfied.

Feasts were just more elaborate versions of everyday meals. As suggested by the classic definition ('from egg to apple'), banquets comprised three parts, two of which existed for the mere pleasure of eating.

The meal would begin with the *gustatio*, or 'taster'. Honeyed wine was served with tasty titbits intended to whet the appetite. The term *gustatio* derived from sacrificial ritual. The idea was to take a morsel of food into one's mouth without really getting down to serious eating. Then came the meal proper, the main courses. The most frequent dishes were wild boar, turbot, plump chickens and sow's udders. Last of all arrived the dessert, what the Romans called the 'second table'. By this time the guests would be fully sated and could only eat things that were utterly delectable or so light as to be almost non-existent. Apples and other fruit came into the delectable category, and were therefore served as dessert, as were shellfish, oysters and snails. As the meal progressed, the wine would flow ever faster. Occasionally the master of the house, somewhat in the Greek manner, would mark a ritual break between the *cena* and the *commissatio* (the Roman equivalent of the Greek *symposium*) at which guests limited themselves to drinking and talking only.

The hierarchy of dinners that were more or less sumptuous depending on the importance of the feasts celebrated brought into existence a further hierarchy, apparent in sumptuary laws and satirical texts, between the various types of food served at banquets. At the bottom of the ladder were such products of the earth as cereals, pulses, vegetables, fresh or preserved fruit, olives, oil and wine, if it was Italian.

Next came the meat of animals kept and bred for slaughter. Up one rung from this was game that farmers caught or killed in woodland areas: hares, boars and birds. Game was deemed more luxurious than reared meat because 'softer'. (Until the end of the republic, hunting was neither a sport nor an art but merely a servile job of work whose only purpose was to supply banquets with game. Only such noble youths as the sons of Aemilius Paullus, aping Hellenic princes, or Pompey when in Africa, practised hunting as an aristocratic sport.) The meat of wild animals was always much softer than its domesticated equivalent and once killed it tended to go off more rapidly. This was the reason wild boar, the banquet meat *par excellence*, always smelt slightly rotten.

Rivalling game for luxury were animals fattened up with flour or figs: fowl, chickens and geese, and pigs too. These extremely fatty and soft meats were considered to be particularly good. Sow's udder and vulva, whether or not the animal had been deliberately fattened, were therefore considered special delicacies.

The height of luxury was fattened game. For game in fact often came from nature parks where the animals were reared in the semi-wild. Keepers oversaw their reproduction and fed them during winter. Romans thus contrived to combine the delicacy of fattened animals with the natural softness of game. Lastly, they would remove the animals from the parks and cram them before they slaughtered them.[232]

Next came luxury food: fish and eels.[233] Caught in the sea or the Tiber – the best bass was to be found between Rome's two bridges, where they fed off rubbish – fish and shellfish fetched high prices at market. Down on their farms, Roman nobles had their own fishponds, *piscinae*, where they fattened up large lampreys, bream and eels that they had caught in the sea. Cato the Younger sold a well-stocked fishpond he had inherited for 40,000 sestertii. Lucius Crassus, the great orator and former censor, a contemporary of Cicero, put on mourning when a lamprey died in a fishpond at his house.[234]

The pinnacle of luxury was food that was disquietingly soft and liable to rapid putrefaction: shellfish and oysters. Indeed there was debate as to whether oysters could be classed as living animals at all. Oysters were farmed in special beds and fattened up in the Lucrine lake or in the gulf of Naples.

It was the very softness of banquet foods that marked them out as delicacies and justified their cost: in every respect they were the opposite of the hard foodstuffs produced by arable farming. Because of the softness verging on putrefaction of banquet delicacies, they were infinitely moreish. Unlike more 'filling' food, they required no further cooking when they reached the stomach. Yet this semi-rotten matter threatened to infect the diner's belly with its corrupting influence.

The high price of meats and other delicacies made their consumption all the more luxurious. *Pecunia–pecus*, the money–animal nexus that defined wealth in Rome (see p. 48), also informed the notion of luxury food. One could no longer tell whether such foods were expensive because they were soft and delicious or soft and delicious because expensive. Be that as it may, expenditure was the root of all luxury. Sumptuary laws and satirists tirelessly repeated that luxury consisted in purchasing the ingredients for one's dinner rather than having them delivered from one's farm in the country.

Rome was a natural market city and the city was the only place to shop: even fish became typical city food. As the centre of luxury and social life, Rome had both a cattle market and a fish market where prices were so high that some shoppers took their bankers along with them. Cato the Elder was scandalized to see that a bullock cost less than a barrel of salt fish and less even than a fresh fish.[235] In the Velabrum, between the forum and the Tiber, there was even a special confectionery market. Foods of every kind and from every corner of the known world flowed into Rome, enabling its inhabitants to throw ever more sumptuous and costly banquets.

FASHION AND THE CULINARY ARTS

Cooks too were expensive and exotic and contributed to the luxury of meals as much as the high cost of the food they prepared. The *cena* demanded elaborate and sophisticated cuisine: it was the task of culinary technique to civilize types of food that were inherently less civilized or indeed – as in the case of game – literally wild. Even butcher's meat was felt to be rather uncivilized: food fit for barbarians. So the culinary trick was to bring these soft products into the realm of culture, without destroying them through overcooking. This is why cooks made such use of condiments and sauces. 'It is not everyone that may lightly claim skill in the dining art, without first mastering the subtle theory of flavours. Nor is it enough to sweep up fish from the expensive stall, not knowing which are better with sauce, and which, if broiled, will tempt the tired guest to raise himself once more upon his elbow.'[236]

Slave cooks gradually gained ground in Rome. They were generally referred to as *pistor*, baker, indicating their starting skills. As bakers, they had been involved in the most technically sophisticated and 'cultivated' aspect of food preparation. From bread-making they moved on to the equally sophisticated field of banquet cuisine. By the second century BC, such artists were exorbitantly expensive.

The basic principles of Roman cookery were as follows. First, natural products had to be softened, while ensuring they did not disintegrate altogether. If an ingredient was too damp, it would be grilled; if too dry, boiled. Everything else would be steamed in closed terracotta pots. Oil or *garum* was added if the result was not already sufficiently oily. Oil was always a little acrid and care was taken to ensure that only just enough olives were pressed at any one time to meet immediate requirements, for oil quickly went rancid. *Garum*, also considered an oily product and able to stand in for oil, was derived from rotting fish guts mixed with salt and aromatic herbs. The Romans got through a great deal of *garum*, which it is now thought must have been rather like the fermented fish sauce used in South-East Asian cooking.

To whet the appetite and ease digestion strong, sharp flavours and spices were added, especially onions, leeks, sorrel, salt, pepper and cumin. The cook would then have to make the natural products unrecognizable. This would be achieved either by producing specific dishes such as stews, sausages or pâtés, or by deliberately misleading the diners. Shellfish shapes were made of vegetables and pork fashioned to look like fish – especially useful for getting round sumptuary laws. Sometimes, instead, cooks left the appearance of products unchanged but transformed their taste: 'As main course, we ate fowl, oysters, and some fish which had a flavour very different from any we had previously known. The reason for this became clear at once when I was handed the livers of a plaice and a turbot, a dish I had never tasted before.'[237]

The Romans loved to play tricks on their dinner guests by presenting them with delicacies that at first sight looked disgusting. Fish innards were generally discarded in Rome,[238] yet in the above case they had been turned into a delicate dish – though one wonders how.

Roman cooks excelled in the kinds of cooking that totally transformed their raw materials and they were particularly expert in producing stuffings. One famous recipe was known as 'Trojan pig', because it was full of other creatures stuffed inside it, just as the famous Trojan horse had been full of armed men.[239]

Theatricality was an important aspect of Roman cuisine,[240] and the Romans often derived as much pleasure from looking at a dish as they did from eating it. Sometimes such theatricality took the form of a dramatic text or running commentary on the dish. In the first century BC, many Roman citizens grew interested in cookery. Guests were therefore quite likely to be amateur cooks themselves, and their host might well set before them dishes made following his own personal recipes. This, for example, is how Maecenas was presented with a lamprey at one dinner party at which he was a guest:

> Then a lamprey is brought in, outstretched on a platter, with shrimps swimming all around it. Upon this the master discourses: 'This,' said

he, 'was caught before spawning; if taken later, its flesh would have
been poorer. The ingredients of the sauce are these: oil from Venafrum
of the first pressing, roe from the juices of the Spanish mackerel, wine
five years old, but produced this side of the sea, poured in while it is on
the boil – after boiling, Chian suits better than anything else – white
pepper and vinegar made from the fermenting of Lesbian vintage. I was
the first to suggest adding some green leaves of rocket and bitter
elecampane to the sauce; Curtillus uses unwashed sea-urchins to season
the dish, which is better than using brine.'[241]

This passion for cooking spurred citizens on to invent new recipes,
alter old ones and introduce new and previously unknown kinds of
food. Dinner-parties followed fashions. Hosts copied and vied with
one another so that what passed for luxury food was continually
changing. A century earlier than Horace, Publius Gallus launched the
vogue for sturgeon, which at that time created a scandal.[242] By
Horace's day, however, everyone had grown tired of sturgeon and
now preferred turbot and stork. These poor creatures, after centuries
of undisturbed peace and quiet, were quickly decimated.

When fashion took over, flavour was soon forgotten. Cooks
struggled to render edible all kinds of outlandish items whose high
price reflected their rarity and oddity, not their flavour. 'Should
someone decree that roasted gulls are delicacies, our Roman youth,
quick to learn ill ways, will obey', was Horace's wry comment. In the
first century BC, the two sons of Quintus Arrius used to breakfast on
nightingales purchased at vast cost. Aesopus' son was the first person
tempted to dispatch one million sesterces in a single gulp. To do this,
he unhooked from the ear of Caecilia Metella, one of his aristocratic
girlfriends, a huge pearl that he then dissolved in cup of vinegar.[243]
Cleopatra went one better and swallowed a pearl worth ten million
sesterces; she had bet Antony that she could prepare him a banquet
more costly than even he could imagine.[244] Eating precious stones
was an ostentatious celebration of the limits of the culinary arts.
There was nothing harder, less edible or more, as it were, frugal than
stones: they were harder than acorns, harder than wood. Yet, thanks
to culinary skill and the use of an ingredient stored in every kitchen,
stones became not just soft, but liquid.

These, however, were excesses that roused satirists to indignation:
they were not the norm. Ordinary citizens who were enthusiastic
cooks applied themselves to their art with greater moderation. The
only purpose of culinary sophistication was to ensure that the social
ritual of the *cena* went off perfectly, that one's guests were happy and

that one avoided looking like a bad host. To take pleasure in eating well, without being ill the next day, without any discomfort during the meal due to the wine or the food served; to maintain one's good mood; and to enjoy chatting with one's friends: this was the ideal banquet.

The following is a condensed account of the teachings of a professor of a gastronomy club.[245] For there were schools of gastronomy just as there were schools of rhetoric. There were even head teachers who wrote lengthy tomes on the subject, like Varro, the satirist, who published a treatise on elegance in banquets and viands, entitled *On Edibles*.[246]

Rule number one: there is no such thing as good cooking without good ingredients. It is essential to know where the best products come from, to distinguish between the delicate-tasting wild boar reared on acorns in the forests of Umbria and wild boar from the marshes, which tastes quite awful. The best oysters come from Circeii, the best sea-urchins from Cape Misenum. Cabbages grown on dry soil are less bland; fruit from Tivoli looks delicious but fruit from Picenum is tastier. Rule number two: you must know the various flavours wrapped up in each product and understand how best to prepare it. You also need to know how to make the various different kinds of sauce, the basic ingredients of which are olive oil, full-bodied wine and fish brine. There are a variety of tricks for improving food: chicken can be made more tender by soaking it in wine from the Falernian territory diluted with a little water; wine that is too sharp will improve if left out under a clear night sky; Falernian wine can be purified by dropping the yolk of pigeon's egg into it – the yolk will draw all impurities down to the bottom of the amphora. Rule number three: you must respect the natural rhythm of the meal by bringing in the various dishes and wines at the right moment. Falernian wine, for example, is not to be served at the beginning of a meal, because it is too strong to drink on an empty stomach. Salad should not be brought forth at the same time as wine, which is mainly drunk towards the end of the meal. By that stage, guests will prefer spicy but simple food, such as sausage and ham. But it is more sophisticated to serve mantis prawns and African snails. Rule number four: make sure everything is well-presented and that both the dining-room and the dinner-service are spotless. The mosaic floor should be strewn with sawdust and then swept, and cushions should be cleaned. Waiters must have clean hands. Rule number five: you must know how to cure mild ailments with simple recipes. Mussels, ordinary shellfish and sorrel, cooked in wine from Chios, make an effective laxative. To avoid summer fevers, mulberries picked before the sun is too high in the sky should be eaten between meals.

CREATING THE RIGHT ATMOSPHERE

Guests would arrive for dinner relaxed by their baths and ready to enjoy that part of the day dedicated to unwinding and the *cena*. The *cena* combined all that was best about this part of the day: pleasure, relaxation, socializing for socializing's sake. It brought people together to share good food, because this sharing took place in a good-humoured context of abundance and freedom from constraints.

At dinner-parties, good humour – for which the Romans had a special term, *hilaritas* – was not an optional extra: it was a must. On stepping into the dining-room, guests had to leave their cares behind and bring no worries about politics or wars to the table.[247] If you failed to show your host a carefree face, it suggested that the delights on offer were insufficient to put you in a good mood. Hosts too had to look relaxed, for otherwise it might be thought that they resented the cost and sacrifice entailed by such displays of friendship. They had to keep smiling even when their guests seemed determined to drink their cellars dry.[248]

This compulsory good humour was the first rule of banqueting, and regulated conversations and the etiquette of drinking and speaking. Diners should prevent sauces from dribbling down their chins, for fear of disgusting their neighbours; they should take care not to sink into brutish or aggressive inebriation; they should indulge neither in tedious chatter nor grotesque dances or singing. Before arriving, they should be sure to banish all unpleasant odours from their person. 'Tactlessness at table is a thing I tax my memory to avoid. I take my fair share of talking, and my share of silence too. I'm none of your spitting, hawking, sniffling fellows, either, not I . . . I never make free with another guest's girl at a party, or appropriate the titbits, or grab the loving cup out of turn, or start a quarrel at a party. Not I. Never.'[249]

The art of conversation was a vital ingredient of good humour and was practised as much among country people as it was in the city: farmers took special care to avoid any rumour-mongering, which could soon lead to quarrels.

Horace describes the end of a 'divine' banquet held in his part of the country. After eating plentifully of greens 'well larded with fat bacon', Horace and his friends drank as much or as little as they wanted, each according to his mood. 'And so begins a chat, not about other men's homes and estates, nor whether Lepos dances well or ill; but we discuss matters which concern us more, and of which it is harmful to be in ignorance – whether wealth or virtue makes men happy, whether self-interest or uprightness leads us to friendship, what is the nature of the good and what is its highest form.'[250] Such philosophical considerations then gave way to old wives' tales, and before long one of the guests was telling the fable of the town mouse and the country mouse.

A successful dinner was a collective achievement, the work of both guests and host. It was up to the host to provide the food, the wine and the dining-room. If he was rich, the walls would be covered with frescoes, the floor with mosaics, the couches provided with cushions and purple rugs, the tables made of ivory or inlaid. He would have cooks, long-haired slaves to serve at table, and carved candelabra to illuminate the feasting late into the night. He might also lay on entertainment: musicians playing the lyre or the flute and singers celebrating love, wine and banqueting. There might also be theatre actors who would dance a monologue or improvise comic dialogues.[251] Guests would contribute scintillating conversation or would dance and sing. Even the most aristocratic of Romans loved dancing. Appius Claudius the censor, the consul Gabinius, Licinius Crassus who died in Parthia and Caelius Rufus, a young friend of Cicero, were all famous dancers.

'It is up to the diners', ran a proverb, 'to improve their wine.' Both food and drink were concentrates of sweetness and gentleness. But the dinner would be a mere ritual of collective consumption and the food and drink would soon grow wearisome if the group of diners failed to retain its good humour. It was company that mattered: individual egos were placed on temporary hold. But this 'indulgence' of both oneself and others presupposed a physical and spiritual relaxation that threatened to lead excessive diners into the ways of physical and moral corruption. And so only the hardest and most austere of men were equal to the greatest feasts, for example soldiers back from the wars. This was why it was thought unwise to attend too many sumptuous dinners. Too much banqueting quickly undermined one's ability to enjoy them. With heavy head, bloated stomach and flabby frames the banquet-fly scowled like a caricature dyspeptic. He would be best advised to go to the country for a spell of digging and wood-collecting or to the Campus Martius for a run, followed by a dip in the freezing Tiber. That would restore his appetite and improve his humour!

GAMES OF LOVE AND BANQUETING

Pleasantly relaxed by the wine, the bodies of the diners were ready for pleasure and drawn towards love. Banquet love affairs were outpourings of sensuality of little consequence that took place in the absence of any women or children of the family. Instead there would be dancing-girls, pretty flautists, curly-haired young men and more or less mercenary freedmen and freedwomen, who would flit from one banqueter to the next.

Nothing serious was allowed to develop during a banquet. The *cena* provided the opportunity for different sorts of games, or *ludi* (see p. 207). Banquet love affairs were part of the games, even if actual sexual relations might take place once the banquet was over. Diners who took part in such playacting would assume Greek nicknames and dress up in exotic tunics: Clodia, for example, renamed Lesbia, received many an ardent love poem from Catullus. In the first century BC, nobles only invited poets to their banquets on the Palatine in order to steal their lines for use in such games. Poets had become mere court jesters. Catullus, Propertius, Tibullus and Horace accordingly took to translating and adapting Greek lyrics so that aristocratic banqueters could live out their dreams of an erotic Greece. This was taken further by painters who would cover walls with scenes of bucolic bliss and amorous shepherds. Love's folly was a fine game for such as Quintus Lutatius Catulus, the austere conqueror of the Germans, who wrote gushing epigrams to a young man by the name of Roscius, whose beauty Catulus compared favourably to that of the sun: 'I stopped still. Dawn was breaking. I greeted it. Suddenly, to my left, Roscius arose. Gods of the sky, spare me if I declare that a mere mortal seemed to me more beautiful than a god.' By the next morning everything was forgotten – except the poets' clever couplets, which, like discarded masks, could be snatched up and used again at a future banquet.

Banqueters had to be careful not to mix business with pleasure, by turning up at a banquet in triumphal garb, for example, or by exerting their authority during a *cena*. This mistake was made by Lucius Quinctius Flamininus when he was governor of Gaul, and it led to his expulsion from the senate and permanent disgrace.[252] He had brought his lover with him from Rome, a well-known gigolo called Philippus the Carthaginian. Always one for a joke, Philippus coquettishly complained that Flamininus had dragged him away from Rome the day before a gladiatorial combat and that he would never get over missing it. This had become a constant source of banter between the two men. But one day, during a banquet given by Flamininus, when the wine had gone to their heads, Flamininus was informed that a Gallic noble had given himself up to the Romans and that he wished to speak to the consul. The Gaul was ushered in and began to talk through an interpreter. Flamininus then turned to his young lover and said: 'Do you wish, since you missed the gladiatorial show, to see this Gaul die?' Not taking the offer seriously, Philippus nodded his assent. Flamininus then seized a sword and threw himself upon the Gaul, wounding him. The bewildered Gaul tried to escape, but the consul caught up with him and finished him off.

Catullus also moved from dinner-party flirtation to more serious business. Having amused himself for some time with Clodia, he asked for her hand in marriage, after the death of her husband, the consul Metellus.

THE KISS

Public opinion tolerated these banqueting love affairs just so long as they remained within the strict bounds of the *cena*. But owing to the Romans' profound puritanism and their horror of explicit sexuality, it did not take much to rouse the forum chatterboxes to torrents of obscenity. These banquet love affairs were like kisses. For the purpose of banqueting, bodies were reduced to mouths. There was the *gula*, the mouth that ate and tasted, and the *os*, the mouth that spoke. Then there was the mouth that kissed. The erotic banquet kiss, the *basium*, was completely different from the *osculum*, the innocent kiss that members of the same family would give each other on the mouth.

This *basium*, or erotic form of kissing, may have been just a slight brushing of the lips, a tiny gesture towards a wider sensuality that took a mainly verbal form and never really materialized.

> You ask how many of your kisses, Lesbia, will satisfy me. As many as there are grains of sand in the Libyan desert, between the oracle of sultry Jove and the sacred tomb of old Battus; or as many as are the stars, when night is silent, that see the stolen loves of men. So many kisses, Lesbia, would be enough for your mad Catullus; kisses so numerous that curious eyes cannot count them nor an evil tongue bewitch.[253]

But these kisses also made the mouth of those, of either sex, who practised fellatio, stink: 'You read of those thousand kisses and you deduced an effeminacy was there. You were wrong.'[254]

If their playfulness made banquet love affairs light-hearted and poetic, what was involved above all was word-play. The art of the banquet and lyric poetry did not pave the way to actual eroticism. Romans got their sex over with quickly – to linger would be embarrassing and obscene. Hence the appalling descriptions of over-willing lads and rutting women: 'What a sweat and what a rank smell rise all over her flabby flesh, when a penis is primed, and she fumbles to ease her insatiable frenzy, and then her makeup runs, her complexion of moist chalk and crocodile dung, and then as she reaches the peak of her spasm, she tears at the mattress and sheets.'[255]

Conclusion

Roman citizens lived within a web of both one-to-one and collective relations. Family, clientele, kinship, professional life, military comradeship, religious ties, the senate, the people's assembly, the college of magistrates: each social sphere gave the citizen a place, provided him with protection and passed judgement on him.

Such relations, however, were never experienced as external constraints. A citizen did not surrender his freedom to an overarching state. If social relations necessarily entailed certain limitations, they also provided the only context within which a free – that is, civilized – man could fulfil himself.

This was why the Romans dedicated so much time and energy to the various relations that linked them to their city. There was no distinction between a Roman's identity as a man and as a citizen. It would be absurd to think of a man's day-to-day private existence as his 'real' self and to contrast this with a public life, frozen by social ritual. The moral dramas of political life that inspired so much Latin literature were no sham façade hiding from view a more concrete and humdrum Rome. Public life and its dramas constituted the authentic life of the Romans. It was here that they experienced the intoxication of power, the joy of being acknowledged and admired. Public life was the only sphere in which the Romans really lived, breathed and died.

It was a life spent mostly out of doors. Roman citizens devoured space. They travelled the length and breadth of Italy, the provinces and Latium, whether as soldiers, magistrates or free men entrusted with their patron's business. When at Rome, they made various calls, lingered in the forum after court hearings, strolled through the streets, accompanied their patrons, joined acquaintances at the baths and dined with old friends on feast days. Even if he lived in the country, citizen would come up to Rome regularly for the market, would attend electoral assemblies, vote on bills and go to games or gladiatorial combats.

A distinction must, of course, be made between the political class and the rest of the city, between those who held the levers of real power and those who could never aspire to *honores*. Yet there was only one model of humanity: citizenship. Citizens lived only through communication with other members of their city, through the multiple communities to which they belonged and which defined them. Citizenship was a particular form of humanity; the Roman city brought into existence a kind of individual designed for freedom, glory and effort. In short, the Roman republic was a civilization founded on honour.

Much more than a political revolution separated the republic from the empire. For the Roman citizen to become a mere subject, the entire fabric of social relations had to be overturned, for it was the republican city that had informed the way in which each citizen experienced space, time, others and himself. In the passage from republic to empire, Rome underwent a cultural sea change. Under the empire, the Roman, even if he spoke Latin, lived at Rome and styled himself a citizen, was a new kind of man. Words might sound the same, but their meanings mutated. 'Roman' armies, manned by Germans, Greeks, Bulgarians, were now permanently stationed thousands of miles from the Campus Martius, on distant frontiers drowned in freezing mists or swept by sandstorms. Romans no longer came to Rome to be entered in the census: they lived out their lives in Spain, Gaul, Egypt, Libya; they were neither soldiers nor citizens. Now a mere spectator of the omnipotence of the *princeps*, the Roman would go to the circus or the theatre to catch a glimpse of things he could only dream of – courage, glory, freedom. Rome sprawled out over ground formerly protected by religious restrictions. Values became confused and inverted. On the Campus Martius, dedicated in ancient times to war, there arose an altar to peace. Roman gardens, once miracles of fertility, were turned into arid parks whose evergreen trees were sculpted like stones. Time was halted, its rhythm of peace and war, spelling out the seasons, was suspended, as was the round of consular elections, the alternation of effort and leisure. Romans now had to forget the ambitions they had once cherished in times of freedom. In exchange, they could, if they so desired, enjoy permanent leisure.

That is the way it had to be, for otherwise the *princeps* would have assumed all the appearance of a tyrant, the opposite of the ideal citizen, a figure regularly and violently exorcised throughout the whole history of the republic. Under the empire, the only way to live as a free citizen was to die, or to convert to the philosophy of Stoicism.

Notes

Unless otherwise indicated, the translations are edited versions of those given in the Loeb Classical Library editions.

1   Plutarch, *Cato the Younger*, 70–2.
2   Livy, *History of Rome*, 1.43.
3   Horace, *Epistles*, I.16.40ff.
4   Lucretius, *De rerum natura*, II.11–13.
5   Plutarch, *Cato the Elder*, 15.
6   Plutarch, *Camillus*, 12.
7   Plutarch, *Cato the Younger*, 25.
8   Cicero, *For Murena*, 71–2.
9   Dionysius of Halicarnassus, 2.9–11.
10 Polybius, *Universal History*, VI.12.1–9.
11 Livy, *History of Rome*, XXXIX.42.
12 Plutarch, *Lucullus*, 38ff.
13 M.I. Finley, *The Ancient Economy*, 2nd edn, The Hogarth Press, London, 1973, 49.
14 Horace, *Satires*, II.3.168ff.
15 Ibid., II.2.115ff.
16 Horace, *Epistles*, I.7.46ff.
17 Livy, *History of Rome*, XLII.32ff.
18 Ibid., XLII.33ff.
19 Ibid., III.26ff.
20 Plutarch, *Tiberius and Gaius Gracchus*, 9.
21 Aulus Gellius, *Attic Nights*, IV.12ff.
22 Horace, *Satires*, II.6.1ff.
23 Pliny the Elder, *Historia Naturalis*, XVIII.11 and XXXIII.13; Cicero, *The Republic*, II.9.16; Varro, *On Agriculture*, II.1.9.

24   Cicero, *De Officiis*, II.89.
25   Plutarch, *Aemilius Paullus*, 31–5.
26   Valerius Maximus, *Works*, Belles Lettres, Paris, V.1.
27   Plutarch, *Crassus*, 2.
28   Plutarch, *Cato the Elder*, 21.
29   Valerius Maximus, *Works*, VI.7.4.
30   Ibid., VI.8.6.
31   Livy, *History of Rome*, XXII. 57.12ff.
32   Ibid., XXIV.14–16.
33   Valerius Maximus, *Works*, VI.8.5.
34   Ibid., VI.8.1.
35   Cicero, *Letters to his Friends*, XVI.21.
36   Cicero, *Letters to Atticus*, VII.2.8.
37   Livy, *History of Rome*, I.12.10; I.13.5.
38   Ibid., VII.6.1–6.
39   Polybius, *Universal History*, I.1.
40   C. Nicolet, *L'Inventaire du monde*, Fayard, Paris, 1988.
41   Livy, *History of Rome*, XLI.28.10.
42   Varro, *On Agriculture*, I.2.1.
43   Horace, *Satires*, II.7.28–9.
44   Ibid., I.5.
45   Ovid, *Fasti*, II.643–79.
46   Valerius Maximus, *Works*, I.5.2.
47   Ibid., I.5.3.
48   Ibid., I.5.6.
49   Livy, *History of Rome*, V.35ff.
50   Aulus Gellius, *Attic Nights*, IX.4.
51   J. Maurin, in *Ktema*, 1984.
52   Vitruvius, *On Architecture*, VI.5.
53   Cato, *On Agriculture*, 5.
54   Ibid., 134, 139, 140, 150.
55   Ibid., 143.
56   Plutarch, *Aemilius Paullus*, 5.
57   Livy, *History of Rome*, V.46.
58   Suetonius, *Augustus*, 12.
59   Plutarch, *Cato the Elder*, 17.
60   Ibid., 24.
61   Plutarch, *Pompey*, 2.
62   Plutarch, *Aemilius Paullus*, 5.
63   Valerius Maximus, *Works*, VI.3.
64   Cicero, *Philippics*, II.77ff.
65   Plutarch, *Cato the Elder*, 8.
66   Livy, *History of Rome*, VIII.18.
67   Ibid., XL.37.
68   Michel Foucault, *History of Sexuality*, II and III, tr. R. Hurley, Penguin,
     Harmondsworth, 1986, 1988.

69 Plutarch, *Pompey*, 48.
70 Plutarch, *Camillus*, 11.
71 Livy, *History of Rome*, XLII.28.
72 Cicero, *Letters to his Friends*, IV.5; IV.6.
73 Horace, *Epistles*, I.1.22.
74 Plutarch, *Tiberius and Gaius Gracchus*, 1.
75 Ibid., 40.
76 Plutarch, *Coriolanus*, XXXIIIff.
77 Livy, *History of Rome*, XL.37.
78 Cato, *On Agriculture*, Preface.
79 Virgil, *Aeneid*, VII.606–15.
80 Livy, *History of Rome*, XXXVI.3.
81 Polybius, *Universal History*, VI.37.1–4.
82 Plutarch, *Fabius Maximus*, 22.
83 Livy, *History of Rome*, XXXIX.31.
84 Plutarch, *Fabius Maximus*, 20.
85 Livy, *History of Rome*, VIII.36.
86 *Les Problèmes de la guerre à Rome*, ed. J.P. Brisson, Mouton, Paris, 1969, Introduction.
87 Livy, *History of Rome*, VIII.6.
88 Ibid., IX.6.
89 Ibid., IX.7.
90 Suetonius, *Caesar*, 68.
91 Livy, *History of Rome*, VIII.7.
92 Cicero, *On Agrarian Law*, II.35.96.
93 Livy, *History of Rome*, V.55.
94 Horace, *Epistles*, II.2.72–5.
95 Livy, *History of Rome*, V.55.4.
96 Cicero, *Letters to Atticus*, XIII.33.
97 Livy, *History of Rome*, XXVI.34.7.
98 Cicero, *Invention*, II.50.
99 Terence, *Adelphoe*, Penguin, Harmondsworth, 1965, 573ff.
100 Plutarch, *Publicola*, 10.
101 Livy, *History of Rome*, VIII.19.
102 Plutarch, *Publicola*, 20.
103 Propertius, *Elegies*, II.32.15.
104 Livy, *History of Rome*, XXXIX.16.
105 Ibid., XXXIX.13.
106 Ibid., XXXIX.9–13.
107 Horace, *Satires*, I.9.
108 Ibid., II.2.55ff.
109 Catullus, *Works*, 29.
110 Suetonius, *Caesar*, 49.
111 Ibid., 22.
112 Livy, *History of Rome*, II.23.
113 Plutarch, *Fabius Maximus*, 17.

114 Livy, *History of Rome*, V.7.
115 Ibid., III.44–8.
116 Ibid., III.47–52.
117 Ibid., III.57–8. On the workings of the legal system at Rome, see J.M. David, 'Du comitium à la roche Tarpéienne', in *Du châtiment dans la cité*, Colloque de l'Ecole Française de Rome, 1984, 131–76; Y. Thomas, 'Se venger au forum', in *Vengeance, pouvoirs et idéologie dans quelques civilisations de l'antiquité*, Cujas, Paris, 1984, 65–100.
118 Livy, *History of Rome*, VI.16–18.
119 Ibid., VIII.7; IX.24.
120 Plutarch, *Camillus*, 36.
121 Livy, *History of Rome*, VI.20.
122 Horace, *Odes*, III.30.
123 Livy, *History of Rome*, I.18.
124 Valerius Maximus, *Works*, I.1.3.
125 Ibid., I.4.3.
126 Livy, *History of Rome*, V.55.
127 Valerius Maximus, *Works*, I.5.4.
128 Terence, *Phormio*, Penguin, Harmondsworth, 1965, 705–10.
129 Plautus, *Curculio*, 483–4.
130 Livy, *History of Rome*, VII.2–3.
131 Pliny the Elder, *Historia Naturalis*, VII.213–14.
132 Horace, *Odes*, II.13.1ff.
133 Plutarch, *Camillus*, 19.
134 Ovid, *Fasti*, III.523–40.
135 Ibid., IV.721–82.
136 Cato, *On Agriculture*, 134.
137 Horace, *Satires*, II.7.1–5.
138 Cicero, *For Caelius*, 26.
139 Dionysius of Halicarnassus, VII.72–3.
140 Juvenal, *Satires*, X.36ff.
141 Virgil, *Aeneid*, V.144–55.
142 Livy, *History of Rome*, XXXIX.22; XL.40; XLII.10 and XLII.28; Plutarch, *Fabius Maximus*, 4; Suetonius, *Caesar*, 39.
143 Suetonius, *Caesar*, 10.
144 Livy, *History of Rome*, XLII.28.
145 Horace, *Odes*, III.8.
146 Ibid., IV.11.
147 Ibid., III.28.
148 Ibid., III.13.
149 Ibid., III.23.
150 Ibid., III.18.
151 Ibid., III.22.
152 Ibid., I.36.
153 Plutarch, *Caesar*, 61.

154 Y. Thomas, in *Histoire de la famille*, I, Armand Colin, Paris, 1985, 196ff.
155 Aline Rousselle, in *Histoire de la famille*, I, 237ff.
156 Plutarch, *Cato the Elder*, 20.
157 Ovid, *Fasti*, IV.131ff.
158 Aulus Gellius, *Attic Nights*, IV.19.
159 Plutarch, *Camillus*, 10.
160 Plutarch, *Cato the Elder*, 20.
161 Plutarch, *Aemilius Paullus*, 5.
162 Horace, *Satires*, I.6.81ff.
163 Aulus Gellius, *Attic Nights*, X.24; Polybius, *Universal History*, II.20.
164 Valerius Maximus, *Works*, V.4.4.
165 Cicero, *Philippics*, II.44–5.
166 Valerius Maximus, *Works*, V.4.4.
167 Plutarch, *Cato the Elder*, 20.
168 Aulus Gellius, *Attic Nights*, X.28.
169 Cicero, *Old Age*, 68.
170 Plutarch, *Camillus*, 40ff.
171 Cicero, *Old Age*, 34.
172 Livy, *History of Rome*, XXXIX.40.
173 Valerius Maximus, *Works*, VIII.13; Pliny the Elder, *Historia Naturalis*, VII.156–9.
174 Cicero, *Old Age*, 51ff.
175 Ibid., 36.
176 Ibid., 44–6.
177 Cicero, *De Officiis*, I.126–7.
178 Catullus, *Works*, 97.
179 Plutarch, *Sulla*, 36–7.
180 Valerius Maximus, *Works*, IX.8.
181 Aulus Gellius, *Attic Nights*, III.15.4.
182 Valerius Maximus, *Works*, IX.2.5; Cicero, *De Officiis*, III.99–101.
183 Valerius Maximus, *Works*, III.3.1.
184 Ibid., III.3.2.
185 Aulus Gellius, *Attic Nights*, II.11.
186 Pliny the Elder, *Historia Naturalis*, VII.101–6.
187 Plutarch, *Cato the Elder*, 5.
188 Vitruvius, *On Architecture*, V.3.
189 Plutarch, *Fabius Maximus*, 24.
190 Valerius Maximus, *Works*, II.5.2.
191 Pliny the Elder, *Historia Naturalis*, XXIX.12.
192 Suetonius, *Caesar*, 82.
193 Horace, *Satires*, II.7.15.
194 Suetonius, *Caesar*, 45.
195 Pliny the Elder, *Historia Naturalis*, XXIX.4–16.
196 Cato, *On Agriculture*, 123.
197 Ibid., 126.

198 Ibid., 157.
199 Horace, *Epistles*, I.1.36–7.
200 Cato, *On Agriculture*, 160.
201 Aulus Gellius, *Attic Nights*, IV.13.
202 Cato, *On Agriculture*, 141.
203 G. Dumézil, *La Religion romaine archaïque*, Payot, Paris, 1966, 230ff.
204 Livy, *History of Rome*, XL.37.
205 Polybius, *Universal History*, XXXVI.14.2.
206 Horace, *Epistles*, I.1.29–31.
207 Horace, *Satires*, II.1.7.
208 Plutarch, *Cato the Elder*, 4.
209 Livy, *History of Rome*, XXXIX.40.2.
210 Plutarch, *Cato the Elder*, 4.
211 Aulus Gellius, *Attic Nights*, VI.12.
212 Horace, *Satires*, I.2.25–6.
213 Ibid., I.3.30ff.
214 Plautus, *Mostellaria*, 39–41.
215 Seneca, *Letters*, 86.4–13.
216 Aulus Gellius, *Attic Nights*, VI.12.
217 Ovid, *The Art of Love*, III.433ff.
218 Plutarch, *Cato the Younger*, 6.
219 Ovid, *The Art of Love*, I.510ff.
220 Suetonius, *Caesar*, 43.
221 Horace, *Satires*, I.6.127–8.
222 Cato, *On Agriculture*, 74.
223 Pliny the Elder, *Historia Naturalis*, XVIII.102.
224 Cato, *On Agriculture*, 75.
225 Ibid., 85.
226 Plutarch, *Cato the Elder*, 2; Cicero, *Old Age*, 55.
227 Suetonius, *Caesar*, 38.
228 Horace, *Satires*, I.6.115.
229 Ibid., II.7.29–35.
230 Aulus Gellius, *Attic Nights*, II.24.3.
231 Macrobius, *The Saturnalia*, tr. P. Vaughan Davies, Columbia University Press, New York and London, 1969, III.13.10.
232 Macrobius, quoting Varro, *Saturnalia*, III.13.14–15.
233 Macrobius, quoting Varro, *Saturnalia*, III.15 and 16.
234 Macrobius, *Saturnalia*, III.15.
235 Plutarch, *Cato the Elder*, 8; Polybius, *Universal History*, XXXI.25.5.
236 Horace, *Satires*, II.4.35–8.
237 Ibid., II.8.26ff.
238 Petronius, *Satyricon*, 33.
239 Macrobius, quoting a republican writer, *Saturnalia*, III.13.13.
240 Horace, *Satires*, II.2.23.
241 Ibid., II.8.42ff.
242 Ibid., II.2.45.

243 Ibid., II.3.239ff.
244 Macrobius, *Saturnalia*, III.17.14.
245 Horace, *Satires*, II.4.
246 Aulus Gellius, *Attic Nights*, VI.16.
247 Horace, *Odes*, III.8.
248 Horace, *Satires*, II.8.35.
249 Plautus, *The Boastful Soldier*, 644ff.
250 Horace, *Satires*, II.6.65ff.
251 Ibid., I.5.50ff.
252 Livy, *History of Rome*, XXXIX.42.
253 Catullus, *Works*, 7.
254 Ibid., 16.
255 Horace, *Epodes*, in *The Odes and Epodes of Horace: A Modern Verse Translation*, tr. J. P. Clancy, Phoenix Books, Chicago, 1960, X.117ff.

Selected bibliography

Everything we know about how the Romans lived from day to day is contained in ancient Roman texts. Most of these are available in the Loeb Classical Library edition.

The following provide first-hand accounts of the republican period: Livy, *History of Rome*; Cicero, *Works*; Sallust, *Works*; Horace, *Satires, Epistles, Odes* and *Epodes*; Cato, *On Agriculture*; Varro, *On Agriculture*; Ovid, *The Art of Love* and *Fasti*; Polybius, *Universal History*.

Written during the imperial period, the following works provide second-hand accounts of republican times: Valerius Maximus, *Works*, available in the French Belles Lettres edition, but not in English; Aulus Gellius, *Attic Nights*; Macrobius, *The Saturnalia*, available in an edition published by Columbia University Press, 1969, though not in the Loeb collection; Suetonius, *Lives of the Caesars*; Plutarch, *Lives*; Pliny, *Historia Naturalis*.

The essays in G. Wissowa (ed.), *Pauly's Real-Encyclopädie der Klassischen Altertumswissenschaft*, Stuttgart, 1893–1978, are also useful, above all for the references they contain.

The following are also recommended:

On the history and institutions of the republic:
C. Nicolet, *Rome et la conquête du monde méditerranéen*, I, Presses Universitaires de France, Paris, 1977.

On Roman topography:
P. Grimal, *Les Jardins romains*, Presses Universitaires de France, Paris, 1969.
J.P. Néraudau, *Urbanisme et métamorphose de la Rome antique*, Belles Lettres, Paris, 1983.

On political life:
C. Nicolet, *The World of the Citizen in Republican Rome*, tr. P.S. Falla, London, 1980.

On the Roman family and conception of time:
M. Bettini, *Antropologia e cultura romana: Parentela, tempo, immagine dell'anima*, Nuova Italia Scientifica, Rome, 1986.

On religion and the Roman calendar:
G. Dumézil, *Archaic Roman Religion*, Chicago and London, 1970.
J. Scheid, *Religion et piété à Rome*, La Découverte, Paris, 1985.

On circus games and the theatre:
F. Dupont, *L'Acteur-roi*, Belles Lettres, Paris, 1985.

Important dates

312	Construction of the Via Appia from Rome to Capua.
298–290	Third Samnite War. Victory of Curius Dentatus.
281–272	War against Pyrrhus, king of Epirus (kingdom to the north of Greece) and conquest of southern Italy.
269	Earliest Roman minting of coins.
264	Introduction of gladiatorial combats.
264–241	First Punic War.
264–256	War in Sicily.
256–254	War in Africa.
256	Regulus captured by the Carthaginians.
254–241	War in Sicily. Roman victory.
241	Construction of Via Aurelia from Rome to Pisa.
240	Earliest staging of Latin comedies and tragedies.
238	Carthage yields Corsica and Sardinia to Rome. The two islands become, in 227, Rome's second colony.
229–219	Conquest of Illyria.
227	Sicily becomes Rome's first colony.
225–222	War against Po valley Gauls. Victory at Clastidium. Milan taken.
220	Construction of Via Flaminia from Rome to Rimini.
219–201	Second Punic War.
219–218	Hannibal takes Saguntum (Spain), crosses the Ebro river, marches over the Pyrenees, through southern Gaul, over the Alps and down into Cisalpine Gaul. After rallying the Gauls, he then marches on Rome.
217	Roman defeat at Lake Trasimene.
216	Roman defeat at Cannae.
212	Romans capture Syracuse. Archimedes dies.
202	Victory of Scipio Africanus over Hannibal at Zama.
200–197	First Macedonian War against Philip V. Victory of Flamininus.
197	Spain becomes a Roman province.
192–188	Asian War against Antiochus III, king of Syria.
187	Construction of Via Aemilia.
186	Bacchanalia outlawed.
185–184	Cato the Elder's censorship.
184	Construction of Basilica Porcia.
173	Construction of Basilica Aemilia.
171–168	Second Macedonian War against Perseus. Victory of Aemilius Paullus at Pydna.
170	Construction of the Basilica Sempronia, later replaced by the Basilica Julia.
149–146	Third Punic War.
148	Macedonia becomes a Roman province.
146	Carthage captured and razed to the ground by Scipio Aemilianus Africanus. Africa becomes a Roman province. Greece becomes a Roman province. Secular games held.

133	Tiberius Sempronius Gracchus elected tribune of the *plebs*. He introduces an agrarian law to parcel out the *ager publicus* (public land). He is then assassinated by Publius Cornelius Scipio Nasica, a relative of his mother.
123–122	Gaius Sempronius Gracchus becomes tribune of the *plebs* twice, but is then assassinated.
125–117	Creation of Roman province of Gallia Narbonensis.
122	Foundation of Aquae Sextiae (Aix-en-Provence).
113	Creation of Roman province of Asia.
112–106	War in Africa against Jugurtha.
107	Jugurtha defeated by Marius.
106	Jugurtha captured by Sulla, after being betrayed.
113–101	War against Cimbri and Teutones who had invaded Gaul.
102	Victory of Marius against the Teutones at Aquae Sextiae. Victory of Marius against the Cimbri at Campi Raudii, near Vercellae in Italy.
91–88	Rebellion by Italy's allies who obtain Roman citizenship.
88–82	Wars against Mithridates. Civil wars at Rome.
87	Marius seizes power. Proscriptions.
86	Death of Marius.
82–79	Sulla's dictatorship. Proscriptions.
78	Sulla abdicates and dies.
74–67	War against Mithridates and Armenia.
73–71	Slave revolt. Spartacus repeatedly defeated.
67–63	War in Syria. Pompey creates Roman province of Syria.
63	Seizure of Jerusalem by Pompey. Cicero's consulship. Cicero defeats Catiline's conspiracy.
60	First triumvirate: Caesar, Pompey and Crassus.
58–51	Caesar conquers the whole of Transalpine Gaul.
55	First stone theatre in Rome, built by Pompey on the Campus Martius.
54	Basilica Julia.
54–53	Expedition against the Parthians. Death of Crassus.
49	Caesar crosses the Rubicon.
49–48	Civil War.
48	Victory of Caesar over Pompey at Pharsalus.
48–44	Caesar's dictatorship.
46	Death of Cato the Younger at Utica. Introduction of Julian calendar.
44	Caesar assassinated on Ides of March.
43	Second triumvirate: Octavian, Antony and Lepidus.
31	Victory of Octavian at Actium over Antony and Cleopatra.
30	Seizure of Alexandria. Egypt becomes a Roman province.
27	Octavian establishes monarchical power and assumes the name Augustus.

Index

wars (*cont.*):
  victory processions 50–3
  wounds received in 246–7, 252
water supply 152–3
water towers 153
wealth
  and freedmen 67
  and sacrifice 47–9
weddings 109
widows 118–19, 119–21
wine 273, 276
wine production 101
winter 178, 179, 190, 249
winter solstice 197
wives 108–16
  convictions for poisoning 116
  family funeral masks 23
  of farmers 101, 102, 215
  infertile 109–10, 115, 118–19
  loyalty of 115
  pregnant 111, 114

women
  bathing 263–4
  children of freedwomen 112
  clothing 261, 262
  at dinner 99, 272, 275
  freedwomen 181
  in the house 94, 99
  marriage and kinship 104–5
  names 5
  as soulless bodies 10
  status of 57
  and superstitions 184
  without children 109–10,
    118–19
work 56–7
writing 223–4, 225–6

years 192–3
young noblemen 13–15
youth 219